Managing and Marketing Health Services

Managing and Marketing Health Services

Angus Laing, Moira Fischbacher, Gillian Hogg and Anne Smith

THOMSON

Australia • Canada • Mexico • Singapore • Spain • United Kingdom • United States

C ontents

Preface

Consumption is the sole end and purpose of production; and the interest of the producer ought to be attended to only so far as it may be necessary for promoting that of the consumer.

(Adam Smith) *The Wealth of Nations,* Book 4, Chapter 8

Background and purpose of this book

The organisation and management of health care services is a central theme within public policy across the post-industrial world as governments wrestle with the challenges arising from the intersection of demographic and socio-economic changes and technological development. Policy makers, together with health care managers and professionals, are continually confronted at strategic and operational levels by the need to balance increasing user expectations and demands with the available resources. Given the highly politicised nature of health care in many post-industrial nations, there is a constant pressure for reorganisation of health care systems in pursuit of a 'utopian', accessible, high quality, cost-effective health care system. As a result, there is a constant demand on the part of managers and professionals for the development of effective, robust managerial frameworks to support their efforts in managing within this complex environment.

Reflecting these pressures, the organisation and management of health care systems has attracted increasing attention from academics from a range of disciplinary backgrounds. The product of such attention has been a plethora of books and journals addressing the organisation and management of health care services, at both strategic and operational levels, from public policy, economic, sociological and managerial perspectives. Within the managerially anchored literature the predominant focus has been on issues of organisational change, professional managerial relationships and organisational design. Although reflecting the centrality of such themes in the organisation and management of health care, in part this focus reflects the dominance of organisational behaviourists within the health care field. Such a focus and background inevitably leaves significant gaps in the literature, with key issues relating to service delivery processes having received only limited attention.

The collective experience of the authors in the delivery of a range of post-experience and postgraduate health management programmes highlighted the absence of health management texts which specifically addressed the process of health care service delivery. Although there is a rich literature on generic service delivery management, the applicability of such literature to the health care setting is limited due to the particular nature of health care services and markets. In seeking to address this deficiency, the book deliberately eschews the organisational behaviour perspective, utilising instead strategic and marketing management perspectives as the conceptual lenses through which to view the organisation and management of health care services. In adopting such perspectives as the conceptual framework within which to critically examine the management of health care services, this book does not aim to provide an introduction to either strategic or marketing management per se. Rather it introduces a number of key concepts relating to service design, inter-organisational relationships and consumer behaviour which provide lenses through which to explore the challenges confronting managers and professionals in the delivery of health care.

Adopting such a perspective, the book seeks to provide a critical overview of the key challenges facing health care policy makers, managers and professionals in managing the design and delivery of health care services. The book is likely to be of interest to readers from a number of different academic, professional and managerial backgrounds. Its policy underpinnings and theoretical material provide a robust platform for using the book as part of an honours or Masters degree in, for example, health policy or health management where there is a focus on organising and delivering services from an integrated perspective. It may also be attractive to readers wishing to dip in and out according to their areas of interest since each chapter, although related to the others, is self-contained and specialised. The holistic perspective – drawing together inputs and perspectives from management, clinicians and patients – also means that the book would be well suited as a focus for multidisciplinary discussion or study.

Central themes

The chapters draw on the collective research experience of the authors in the health management research field. This research experience encompasses issues of service design, inter-organisational relationships, service user behaviour, and service quality. Although the authors have published extensively in management and health care journals, such publications provide only fragmentary snapshots of the broader managerial agenda confronting health care managers and professionals. Critically the underlying links between these individual themes, and their collective impact on the delivery of health care services, are commonly neglected. The research collectively addresses four elements of what can be understood as a service cycle comprising: service design, service structure, service consumption and service evaluation (see Figure 0.1). Each of these four elements is embedded within the actions and perspectives of key players within the health care context i.e. patients, policy makers, professionals and organisations.

In drawing these research strands together, the aim of this book is to provide a structured overview of the key strategic and operational challenges facing health care professionals in managing service design and delivery within modern health care systems. In this regard the primary rationale behind the structure of the book is to enable managers and professionals to look beyond that specific part of the health care system within which they operate and to develop a more integrated, holistic perspective on the delivery of health care services. In providing such an overview the book can be subdivided into four main thematic sections:

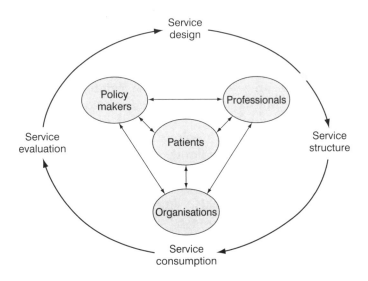

Figure 0.1 **The service cycle for health care**

1. The service design process;
2. The management of inter-organisational relationships;
3. Understanding health care consumers; and
4. Evaluating service quality.

Given the central impact of government policy on the operation of modern health care systems, any such analysis of the delivery of health care services has to be set within the context of government policy. There are, however, dangers in linking this analysis too closely to prevailing health policy, both in terms of the critical depth of the analysis and its ongoing relevance beyond the duration of the prevailing policy regime. Consequently, when addressing the policy context within which health care services are delivered, the focus has been on identifying of underlying policy themes which are likely to have an enduring impact on the management of health care services. In this regard the core policy themes which underpin the book are first, governance and accountability, second competition versus collaboration, and third patient empowerment.

Structure

Turning to the main thematic sections, the starting point of the book is the process of service design. It is evident from the review of underlying policy themes that a number of the specific components of these themes, notably the increasing emphasis on improving clinical and service quality, the development of inter-organisational partnerships, and the increasing involvement of consumers, directly impinge on the process of designing health care services. The concept of service design and the nature of the design process, as well as the significance and role of design within the health service context, are examined in light of these developments. It is argued that the complexity of the service design challenge confronting health care professionals is considerable. This reflects the fact that service design within health care encompasses not only clinical, occupational, and intra/inter-organisational considerations, but may also involve complex parallel processes of commissioning new facilities and decommissioning old facilities. The consequent scale of the design activities necessitates a detailed understanding of the range of organisational and professional stakeholders involved, and the respective interests of such stakeholders. Thus the ability to integrate the expertise located among different professional groups and across different organisations, as well as integrating consumer views on the format of service provision, is central to managing the design process. These issues of inter-organisational relationships and consumer involvement are explored in subsequent sections. In addressing the specific design issues Chapter 2 starts with an examination of the strategic significance of service design, the context and content of service design and the overall design process. Integrating health care and broader management literature, the chapter concludes by introducing a strategic approach to service design within the NHS.

Following on from the analysis of service design, Chapters 3 and 4 provide an in-depth examination of the nature of inter-organisational relationships and hence the structuring of service provsion within the NHS. Reflecting both the underlying policy tension between competitive and collaborative approaches to service organisation, and the centrality of inter-organisational relationships to the service design process, Chapter 3 examines the conceptual basis for alternative approaches to the organisation of inter-organisational relationships. Specifically drawing on managerial, sociological and economic perspectives, the chapter examines the evolving dynamics of inter-organisational relationships in the NHS. Central to this is the examination of market and network-based models of organisational governance, and the dynamics of relationships under such macro level governance frameworks. Examining such inter-organisational relationships within the context of predominantly competitive (market) and collaborative (network) policy regimes, the chapter considers the importance of broader organisational, professional and social networks in shaping the structure of service delivery within the NHS. Utilising this base, the chapter concludes by examining the relevance of conceptualisations of inter-organisational relationships derived from public and private sector contexts in understanding the delivery of health care services. This provides the conceptual basis for a detailed examination of the operational dynamics of inter-organisational relationships within the NHS in Chapter 4.

In developing an understanding of the structuring of health service delivery in health care the primary focus of Chapter 4 is on the specific nature and format of the relationships which have emerged under different policy frameworks in the NHS. Central to this is an in-depth examination of the building blocks of these relationships, that is both the formal exchanges occurring between the constituent organisations and the informal ties which exist between professionals in these organisations. Adapting an analytical framework derived from business–business markets, the chapter explores the changing nature and dynamics of inter-organisational relationships across the primary–secondary care divide, as well as within the primary care sector. In this regard the shift in emphasis from conflict to cooperation between primary and secondary care, and from isolation to integration within primary care, will be critically examined. From this analysis of inter-organisational dynamics, the chapter concludes with an examination of the changing role of patients, and other service users, in the management of such relationships. This provides the organisational context within which the patient's perspective on the design and delivery of health care services is examined in the subsequent section.

One of the underpinning themes of recent government policy towards the public sector has been the idea that service users should be viewed as consumers, enjoying the same rights in respect of health care as they possess with regard to private sector organisations. For the NHS, which has traditionally emphasised the responsibilities rather than the rights of patients, this emphasis on patients as consumers requires a refocusing of services to put the patient rather than the system at the heart of the organisation. Against this backdrop understanding the nature of patients as consumers and evolving patterns of consumer behaviour is consequently imperative. In this regard Chapter 5 begins with an examination of the evolving conceptualisation of consumer behaviour in professional service settings such as health care. Drawing on this conceptual base the chapter considers first, patterns of consumer behaviour in the selection of health care providers and second the nature of the service encounter and the pattern of consumer–professional interaction. Following on from this analysis of the dynamics of consumer behaviour in health care, Chapter 6 considers some of the main influences on health care consumers which effect consumption patterns and the changing nature of these influences. In particular it examines the evolving consumer–professional informational asymmetries and the implications of such changes for the design and delivery of health care services. Central to this is an examination of the role of emerging information sources on the formation of consumer expectations prior to consumption, and evaluation subsequent to utilisation. Such analysis of patterns of consumer behaviour in health care underpins the final section of the book, which considers the evaluation of service quality and consumer satisfaction.

It is evident from the review of underlying policy themes that enhancing service quality and meeting the expectations of service users lies at the heart of modern health policy. The emphasis on patients as consumers has placed concepts of consumer-defined quality and service satisfaction at the core of the health care agenda. For health care managers and professionals consumer satisfaction is one of the critical measures of the effectiveness of service design and delivery processes. Within this context Chapter 7 provides a detailed analysis of the problems and issues inherent in the measurement of service quality and consumer service satisfaction. Central to this is defining the concept of service satisfaction and its relationship with other service quality constructs. Anchored within this context the chapter critically examines the core dimensions of consumer service satisfaction and addresses the issue of what health care managers and professionals ought to be addressing in assessing service satisfaction. The actual assessment of consumer service satisfaction constitutes the second core theme within Chapter 7. Specifically the chapter examines the use of a range of approaches to measuring consumer satisfaction and service quality together with a critical review of the major problems encountered in assessing service satisfaction.

Taken together, these four thematic areas provide an overview of the main issues confronting managers and professionals in the delivery of health care, from initial service design through to consumer evaluation of service consumption. At the core of this overall process of service delivery, as encapsulated in the service cycle, is the management of a complex set of relationships. Indeed the management of health care services is ultimately concerned with the management of a number of key interactions and relationships. In this regard the complex network of relationships involved in the delivery of health care services, and the changing pattern of interaction between patients and professionals, are central to the delivery of modern health care. Together they constitute unifying strands linking the four core thematic areas around which the book is organised.

1 Health care policy themes

Introduction

This book deals with issues of service design and delivery which the authors believe are fundamental to the effective and efficient delivery of health services. These issues both transcend and pervade the health policies and practice that prevail under any particular government. For this reason, the discussions within each chapter have been written in a manner that demonstrates their relevance to current policies without locating them in any particular policy or organisational framework, as this might render them more transient.

To ignore the policy context would, however, be folly and would neglect the fact that the issues tackled in the book have not only become increasingly important in the eyes of politicians, health service managers, clinicians and academics, but have been at the heart of enduring policy themes during the last 30 years, surviving changes in both political and organisational leadership.

This chapter outlines three key themes that have developed during this time, and which underpin the overall message of this book. The discussion draws on the historical context where appropriate, whilst also presenting the themes in the context of current policy in the UK.

Enduring policy themes

Founded by the Labour Party in 1948, the underpinning ethos of the NHS was a free service for all at the point of delivery, and one that met the needs of the UK population from the cradle to the grave. These ideals, which reflected those of the party in government at the time, have remained largely intact, not least because they are rigorously upheld both by health service professionals and the general population. How those ideals should be met, however, has been the subject of discussion and debate from the outset and concerns not only the appropriate organisational structures and mechanisms for governing service delivery, but also the balance of interests and power between key stakeholders.

The growth and development of the NHS has been influenced substantially both by Conservative and Labour party policies as each party has been in government at various junctures during the lifetime of the NHS. These governmental interventions reflect not only political ideology, but also contemporary perspectives from academia and organisational and clinical practice both domestically and internationally. The development of the NHS in the UK – now evolved into separate systems for Scotland, and for England and Wales – thus provides a rich case study when exploring a range of subjects from policy to practice. As a case study, however, it is also complex. Isolating the effects of individual policies and initiatives is fraught in the NHS context, where change can be both continuous and revolutionary and where the parallel initiatives emanating from governmental and service level players create a complex dynamic of influences and requirements that become difficult to identify and capture.

On the one hand, the range of policies, frameworks, initiatives and measures that prevail at any one time in the health service presents a substantial agenda; an agenda about which many in the service become confused, overwhelmed, disengaged and disenchanted. On the other hand, when standing back to survey the forest rather than the individual trees, one can see consistent themes that pervade the NHS agenda despite changes to the party that governs it.

There are undoubtedly a number of ways in which the NHS agendas could be classified, but for the purposes of this book, three underpinning themes have been identified and are developed in turn in the remainder of the chapter.

1. *Governance and accountability* The current pre-eminence of quality and clinical governance in the health service can be seen to be founded upon the development of evidence-based practice (which has focused mainly on clinical performance), and on the assessment of organisational performance. These agendas have now come together under the framework and arrangements for measuring NHS performance, which has generated not only changes to clinical and organisational practice, but has lead to the creation of new local and national structures and processes designed to deliver improved clinical quality throughout the NHS.

2. *Competition or collaboration* Since its inception, governments have sought to find ways of organising the NHS so that the optimum efficiency and effectiveness of resource allocation can be achieved. In so

doing, they have tried to identify what they believe to be an appropriate combination of competition and collaboration across the health and related public service providers. Whether the NHS organisation at any one time is more akin to a 'market' or 'hierarchy' does not negate the fact that service delivery needs to be understood as being enacted within a complex network of providers, and that management in a network situation requires an understanding of the factors at work, and a tailored perspective and approach.

3. *Patient-focused services* Consistent with other service industries, health services have become the subject of increasing consumer expectations. As a result, service providers have turned attention to considering how best to organise the service delivery process, and have drawn on concepts such as business process re-engineering to help reorient their services so that they are designed around the needs of the patient rather than the 'production function' (i.e. service delivery). Moreover, greater emphasis has been placed on the need not only to understand but also to involve patients in the design, delivery and evaluation of services.

Governance and accountability

The Labour government's publication in 1997 of *The New NHS: Modern and Dependable* (Department of Health, 1997) and its Scottish equivalent *Designed to Care* (Scottish Executive Health Department) introduced the concept of clinical governance, which it defined as:

> A framework through which NHS organizations are accountable for continuously improving the quality of their services and safeguarding high standards of care by creating an environment in which excellence in clinical care will flourish. (Scottish Executive Health Department, 1998)

In so doing, the Government brought issues of quality, performance and accountability to the forefront of the minds of clinicians, managers and politicians in the health service, and accompanied this with the creation of a range of external and internal bodies and procedures that would support the development and implementation of quality standards. Whilst essentially a new concept, clinical governance to some extent brings together, and further develops, two themes in policy and practice that have been developing over the last 20 years: the improvement of organisational performance, and the creation of an ethos of evidence based practice.

Improving organisational performance

Improving organisational performance became a focus of attention not long after the NHS was created. Politicians quickly recognised that there was no fixed pool of ill health that once treated would be eradicated. Rather, the demands upon NHS resources were increasing (Teeling Smith, 1984; Vaizey, 1984; Enthoven, 1985). Anxious to contain the levels of public money devoted to the NHS, the Government sought to devise improved organisational structures and procedures that would better allocate and deploy scarce resources. In response, they introduced various administrative, structural and managerial reforms, each seeking to drive out inefficiencies believed to be inherent in the NHS system (Klein, 1989).

Attention to the way in which scarce resources were used in the NHS was particularly focused during the 1980s following a review of the NHS conducted by the then Chairman of Sainsbury's, Sir Ron Griffiths. The report contained strongly critical views of how the system operated, the spirit of which is often captured in his comment that 'if Florence Nightingale were carrying her lamp through the corridors of the NHS today she would almost certainly be searching for the people in charge' (cited in Klein, 1989: 208). As a direct consequence of the review, a general management structure was implemented to increase the degree of responsibility for decision making throughout all levels of the service, and to develop a system of performance management. This policy measure was not only to affect structural change 'but more ambitiously it was to change roles, "ways of doing things", [and] create[d] a new cadre of "leaders" who could energise decision making and even produce "a new culture"'. (Pettigrew *et al.*, 1994: 31–2). A Government level Supervisory Board and Management Board (known as the National Health Service Management Executive (NHSME) was installed to enhance the coordination and central leadership of the NHS, and was coupled with performance indicators and management budgets for clinicians (1985 and 1989) and a shift in the mode of management from (clinical) consensus management to (managerial) hierarchical control (Klein, 1989).

Although managerial reform concentrated – but did not unite – the minds of politicians, clinicians and managers on improving performance, the demands on NHS resources continued to burgeon. It was clear by the late 1980s and early 1990s that more needed to be done to find ways of improving the efficiency of the service. The then Conservative Government designed the internal market reforms of the 1990s to tackle this very issue (Department of Health, 1989). Here the emphasis was on using competitive forces to drive efficiencies into the system as purchasers – Health Authorities and certain GP practices – sought out lower prices and shorter waiting times. Purchasers were expected to 'move money to where the work is best done' (Department of Health, 1989: 37) with the incentive that they could make savings in their own budgets by seeking out lower prices. (For further discussion see 'Competition and collaboration' below).

Improving clinical performance: evidence-based practice

Although much of the policy emphasis during the 1980s concentrated on improving organisational performance, at the same time, the need for evidence-based clinical practice also gained credence (Walshe and Rundall, 2001). As Davies and Nutley (1999b) point out:

> Until recent years, health care has been characterized not by uncertainty about efficacy but by an often unwarranted certainty of therapeutic success ... more recently, the presence of uncertainty has been made explicit and health care workers ... have striven to become more 'evidence-based'.

Greater use of evidence was reflected initially by an augmented role for clinical audit, 'a systematic, critical analysis of the quality of medical care, including the procedures used for diagnosis and treatment, the use of resources, and the resulting outcome for the patient' (Department of Health, 1989: 39). Systems to ensure participation of clinical staff, professional bodies and health service managers were established along with review procedures and accountability structures, the overall objective of which was to improve quality as well as efficiency and effectiveness in resource utilisation (Department of Health, 1989).

The profile of evidence-based decisions has since continued to grow. The approach of the Labour government in raising evidence to a central position in the policy decision-making process (Davies *et al.*, 1999a) is such that now even 'greater reliance [is] placed on scientific evidence and less on ideology or expert opinion' (Lohr *et al.*, 1998), and the implications for health services are substantial:

> We must root out inefficient and ineffective clinical procedures, subject new drugs and therapies to painstaking analysis in terms of their clinical and cost-effectiveness, eliminate inefficiencies that result from bureaucracy and address the differences in the availability of health care which re-enforce inequalities.
>
> (Scottish Executive Health Department, 1997)

In the UK, two main approaches underpin evidence-based practice: evidence-based medicine (EBM) (Rosenberg and Donald, 1995; Sackett *et al.*, 1997) and clinical practice guidelines (Forrest *et al.*, 1996). (See also Lohr *et al.*, 1998; Davies and Nutley, 1999b). Both draw on input from clinical research, clinical epidemiology, health economics and health services research (Perleth *et al.*, 2001), in order to identify and encourage best practice and patient-centred treatments that improve the standards of care delivered.

EBM is defined by Sackett *et al.* (1996) as 'the conscientious, explicit, and judicious use of current best evidence in making decisions about the care of individual patients ... [by] ... integrating individual clinical expertise with the best available external clinical evidence from system-atic research'. It is a 'bottom-up' approach in which the clinician and patient make a joint decision on the approach that best suits the patient, i.e. there is an explicit role for the patient in the decision-making process. Clinical practice guidelines, however, are statements developed in a systematic, 'top down' manner and designed to guide practitioners and patients during decisions about approaches to specific clinical circumstances (Lohr *et al.*, 1998). Guidelines are also systematically developed from the research literature and are designed to propose the correct management of particular diseases or patient groups. They are often incorporated into Integrated Care Pathways (ICPs)[1] (Campbell *et al.*, 1998) that are used to guide clinical decision making by setting out expected patient journeys, expected clinical outcomes and care management. One advantage of this approach is that the implementation of guidelines can be readily audited.

Whilst of increasing interest, the development use of EBM and clinical guidelines is not unproblematic. Difficulties remain in the methodologies used for each approach (Davies and Nutley, 1999b), and there are questions over their effectiveness (Lohr *et al.*, 1998). However, the momentum of the evidence-based movement seems unlikely to relent, and as Davies and Nutley (1999b) write:

> We can expect accelerating activity in attempts to meet these evidence needs, at least in part because as knowledge solidifies it often serves to sharpen our view on the complexity of the situation and the extent of our ignorance.

Health technology assessment, which Perleth *et al.* (2001) consider a third activity for improving effectiveness and efficiency, has also been adopted in the UK. This involves evaluating the cost-effectiveness of health care innovations, including drugs, and advising service providers accordingly on future innovation adoption.

Improving service quality and measuring performance

The present emphasis on clinical governance, clinical and organisational performance is one aspect of a new 'spirit of service quality' (Navaratnam and Harris, 1995) which has emerged throughout public services, and which has brought together the two streams of clinical and organisational performance, combining them in an integrated notion of 'quality'. In its wake, there has been a range of measures to ensure that the desired level of accountability for quality is realised. Davies *et al.* (2001) recently captured the scale of these changes:

> In the New Year of 2001 the Government announced yet another initiative to tackle perceived quality failings in the National Health Service. The establishment of the National Clinical Assessment Authority provides 'a new approach to the problem of poorly performing doctors' (Department of Health, 2001). This is just the latest in a whole raft of initiatives since 1997. Since that time we have seen white paper after discussion document, and the establishment of a bewildering array of agencies and schemes: the National Institute for Clinical Excellence (NICE), the Commission for Health Improvement (CHI), the Performance Assessment Framework (PAF), the Modernization Agency, proposals for reform of the General Medical Council (GMC) and the introduction of revalidation and, now, The National Clinical Assessment Authority (NCAA).

Collectively, these (and other) agencies and performance frameworks[2] represent a comprehensive approach to changing organisational structures and processes to ensure the necessary ongoing improvements in service quality, and are also an attempt to change the culture of the NHS.

Implementing clinical governance as the basis for improving quality is one of the most significant challenges facing the NHS today. In particular, efforts need to be made to ensure that clinical governance does not simply become an instrument focused on improving productivity (Holzer, 1993; Davies *et al.*, 2001; Dixon, 2000). As Dixon (2000) notes:

> Notions of performance should be uncoupled from notions of productivity and coupled instead with notions of quality and development. Though productivity is important, it might easily be a sign of reduced performance ... Too often 'performance' conjures up a traditional narrow image of 'performance

management' – a managerial agenda concerned with managing emergency admissions, waiting lists, and financial balance. 'Quality', however, conjures up clinical governance – largely a clinical professional agenda. Policies to improve non-clinical aspects of performance ... should be reviewed alongside those targeting clinical performance ... as part of the same spectrum.

It is also the case that substantial efforts will need to be made to developing the information required to underpin clinical governance (McColl and Roland, 2000). This includes information relating to what Allen (2000) sets out as four dimensions of accountability:

- Fiscal, which concerns financial probity and thus the ability to trace and adequately explain all expenditure;
- Process, which concerns the use of proper procedures;
- Programme, which concerns the activities undertaken and, in particular, their quality; and
- Priorities, which concerns the relevance or appropriateness of the activities chosen.

Of particular relevance to clinical governance are process and programme governance (Allen, 2000) since they address appropriate procedures for recording care delivery and accountability and reviewing them in light of national and local standards and frameworks, as well as the quality of those activities which may involve annual reports, publicly available audits and the involvement of patients in setting priorities.

The integration of organisational and clinical performance measures are set out in the Government's Performance Assessment Framework (Department of Health, 1998) which identifies six areas of performance (see Box 1.1). Developing the information infrastructures required to support these dimensions of accountability and areas of performance requires substantial resources that have not yet been made available

---

Box 1.1 National performance framework – key areas

- Health improvement
- Fair access
- Effective delivery of appropriate health care
- Efficiency
- Patient/carer experience
- Health outcomes of NHS care

(Baker, 2000). The collation, monitoring and interpretation of information also needs ongoing development. Agencies such as NICE, the Clinical Standards Board (Scotland) and the Health Technology Board (Scotland) were formed only recently and have a long way to go in developing the raft of standards and measures required to fully support clinical accountability and quality improvement. The design of outcome measures and the selection of appropriate benchmarks is complex and underdeveloped (Mannion and Goddard, 2001; Mulligan *et al.*, 2000; Shaw, 2001), particularly in a service where many outcomes are difficult to define (Radin and Coffee, 1993).

The move to improve health services through enhancing quality and increasing responsibility and accountability for quality has been suggested since at least 1979 (Shaw, 2001) and it seems likely that the scrutiny of standards in public services will grow. It is also the case that in addition to improving clinical and organisational performance, services will be measured on the ways in which they meet customer rather than service provider needs, decentralise decisions and encourage participation and teamwork within and between public sector organisations, as we will now discuss.

Competition and collaboration: organising for efficiency and effectiveness

The objective of enhancing both the efficiency and effectiveness of health care provision has been at the core of successive reforms of the NHS from the 1980s onwards. Reflecting ongoing growth in the demands on the NHS as a result of both demographic changes and technological developments, policy makers have been confronted with the need to optimise the return on public investment in health care in order to meet patient expectations (Lapsley, 1994). The complexity of this challenge is exacerbated by the multiplicity of organisations and professional groups involved in the delivery of health care. Encompassing not only NHS organisations but also local authority and voluntary agencies, a central challenge in the delivery of health care is the management of the interaction between the multiple organisations involved in the process of service delivery. Confronted with this challenge, a clear policy dichotomy has emerged between those approaches emphasising the value of market mechanisms and competition, and those focusing on creating network structures and fostering collaboration. This contest between competitive and collaborative approaches to the organisation and management of the NHS at a macro level has been a central feature of the health care policy debate in the United Kingdom since the 1980s.

However, this is not a uniquely British debate. Rather it is a debate which, allowing for adaptations reflecting specific organisational arrangements within individual health care systems, has characterised health policy across post-industrial economies (Ham, 1999).

Within the United Kingdom this debate has been underpinned by the prevailing political view that the established hierarchical and bureaucratic arrangements for the management of the NHS had failed to deliver either high quality or cost-effective health care. Mirroring developing managerial practice in private sector organisations, NHS policy makers have consequently sought alternative structural arrangements, that is governance mechanisms, to enhance the efficiency of resource allocation and the coordination of activity within the NHS. Against this contextual and conceptual backdrop, the late 1980s witnessed the introduction of competitive principles into the NHS via the creation of a quasi-market mechanism, the internal market. Then reflecting the perceived failure of such competitive arrangements, and an ideological shift within government, in the late 1990s this market-based competitive approach was replaced by an emphasis on collaboration through the promotion of network type boundary-spanning structures (Light, 1997). Although portraying these successive reforms as representing a shift from hierarchy to market to network is unduly simplistic (Exworthy *et al.*, 1999), the changing balance between competition and collaboration has been a central feature of health policy in the United Kingdom over the past two decades. In understanding the ongoing policy debate between competition and collaboration within health care, it is valuable to review, albeit briefly, these successive policy regimes.

The introduction of competition and market-based governance into the NHS, what Wistow *et al.* (1996) referred to as 'bringing the market into government', reflected the intellectual hegemony enjoyed by neo-classical micro economic theory in shaping the formulation of public policy during the 1980s (Ferlie, 1992). From such an ideological perspective, markets were seen as synonymous with efficiency, choice and dynamism as a result of the interplay of competitive market forces. By contrast bureaucratic hierarchies were uniformly associated with inefficiency and inertia as a result of both their protected monopoly position and the absence of effective incentives. This reflected in part an underlying belief that the NHS, as with other public sector organisations, contained pockets of inefficiency and consequently needed to be subjected to economic incentives and competitive forces in order to make efficiency savings and contain the level of public spending on health services (Maynard, 1994). These assumptions were clearly reflected in the tenor of policy development preceding the 1989 NHS reforms:

A great deal of discussion centred on the role of competition in improving the quality and efficiency within the NHS. ... If some form of effective competition could be introduced between different parts of the health service, it could introduce the best features of a market system ... .

(Teeling-Smith, 1986)

The central organisational consequence of such views was the de facto fragmentation of the NHS. This saw the NHS shift from being a monolithic internalised professional bureaucracy towards a decentralised cluster of separate organisations operating within the framework of a market structure. Relationships between the constituent parts of the NHS, and indeed external organisations involved in the delivery of health care services, would be managed on the basis of formal contractual arrangements. Equally significant was the emphasis placed, at least initially, on encouraging competitive patterns of market behaviour through the tenor of the regulatory regime and performance indicators that were established. The operational objectives and mechanisms are apparent from the 1989 White Paper, *Working for Patients*.

An NHS Hospital Trust will earn its revenue from the services it provides. The main source of revenue will be from contracts with health authorities for the provision of services to their residents. Other contracts and revenue will come from GP practices with their own NHS budgets ... This form of funding will be a stimulus to better performance. There will be an opportunity to finance improved and expanded services because the money will flow to where the patients are going. Hospitals which prove more popular with GPs and patients will attract a larger share of NHS resources available for hospital services.

(Department of Health, 1989)

Although this quasi-market structure and the associated contractual arrangements remained in place until the election of the Labour government in 1997, the operation of this market evolved substantially. Specifically the early emphasis on competitive patterns of behaviour was increasingly replaced by more collaborative patterns of working. This shift reflected the underlying complexity and interconnected nature of health care services as well as evolving patterns of contracting within the private sector (Laing and Cotton, 1995; Flynn *et al.*, 1996). The emergence of such relational contracting within the context of a notionally competitive quasi-market structure may be viewed as laying the groundwork for the collaborative approach to the management of inter-organisational relationships within the NHS introduced by the subsequent Labour government.

Whereas for the Conservative governments from the 1980s onwards belief in the virtue of markets and competition had been an article of faith, for the subsequent Labour government collaboration and partnership was the central tenet of public sector reform. The invocation of a 'third way based on partnership' (Department of Health, 1997) marked an ideological abandonment of markets and competition as a mechanism to organise and manage the delivery of health care. Although the financial pressures facing policy makers were as acute in the late 1990s as in the late 1980s, and ensured continuing emphasis on efficiency, performance measurement, cost-effectiveness and quality, the mechanisms by which such objectives were to be pursued differed. Rather than seeking to stimulate competition, such objectives were to be achieved via collaboration through the creation of inter-organisational partnerships and network structures. This realignment in policy reflected what Hudson *et al.* (1999) described as the 'self-evident virtue of collaboration' in managing complex social problems. The promotion of collaborative approaches reflected the interconnected nature of health care problems and the need for the development of effective boundary spanning mechanisms in order to ensure seamless service delivery. As with the preceding government's embrace of markets and competition, this policy shift mirrored increasing private sector interest in partnership and networks due to the perceived contribution of such approaches to enhancing organisational learning and innovation as well as their seemingly efficient governance of transactions (Bianchi, 1995; Huxham, 1996).

The operational objectives of such a collaborative partnership agenda within the NHS are readily apparent from both the initial policy documentation and the subsequent political debate. Although relating specifically to primary care, the following extracts provide a clear sense of the emerging direction of NHS policy. In so doing they serve to highlight effectively the distinctions between the respective approaches embraced by Conservative and Labour administrations.

> General medical practitioners and their teams are increasingly aware of the advantages of working together ... practices are forming alliances, creating the foundations for new primary care organisations which will overcome the artificial boundaries.
>
> (Department of Health, 1997)

> What the primary care groups fundamentally do ... is begin to break down barriers between services and indeed professions. There is a unique opportunity here to see the beginnings of the

provision of more integrated care services than has been possible in the past.... What we want to see in the future is all local health services not competing in secret but comparing in public.

(Health Select Committee, 1999)

The creation of boundary spanning structures based on notions of reciprocity, trust and longevity in place of formal, arm's-length contractual arrangements has marked a distinct shift in the organisation and management of the NHS at a macro-level. However, in the same way as the operation of the NHS internal market ultimately evolved to reflect the complex reality of health care delivery, there are emerging suggestions that such collaborative approaches are equally likely to evolve and adapt to the particular circumstances of the NHS (Exworthy *et al.*, 1999). In particular the distinction between collaboration and competition may not be as clearly defined as policy makers would wish to suggest. Kirkpatrick (1999) in reviewing the concept of a 'third way' in the reorganisation of public services in the face of ongoing financial pressures concludes with the observation that:

While the government now places more emphasis on collaboration (as a way of improving service quality), it remains to be seen how far this message will win over the temptation to encourage 'competition' as a mechanism for raising efficiency.

Arguably, health services have always been provided through a complex set of inter-organisational arrangements between health, social and voluntary care organisations (Alter and Hage, 1993). Such relationships are shaped by, and through human agency shape, the institutional and market-based structures and processes within which services are delivered. Consequently, to adequately understand the management of health service delivery it is critical to understand the complex and evolving relationship between competition and collaboration in the organisation of modern health care systems. The changing balance between what are frequently presented as alternative approaches to the organisation and governance of modern health care systems arguably constitutes one of the enduring themes of the health policy debate in post-industrial economies.

Empowering patients: promoting patient focused services

The successive public sector reform initiatives introduced in the United Kingdom from the early 1980s onwards have been characterised by efforts to replicate private sector management practices and culture in public sector settings. Collectively such changes have been encapsulated in the catch all term, 'new public management' (Ferlie *et al.*, 1996). At the core of this evolving new management ethos in the public sector is a change in the relationship between service providers and users. From being a relationship framed in terms of the concept of citizenship with myriad mutual commitments and obligations on the part of the citizen, it is increasingly expressed in consumerist terms with emphasis placed on the primacy of the rights of service users, both individually and collectively (Keaney, 1999). This central emphasis on empowering public sector service users has reflected the perceived need to address the introverted and unresponsive nature of public sector service provision. Although the specific mechanisms employed in addressing this failure have varied across the political spectrum, there has been remarkable unanimity in the underlying critique of public sector service provision.

> In different ways both right and left are suspicious of providers and ... the way in which the public service has developed in the post war period seeing it as monolithic and unresponsive ... professionalism is an excuse for avoiding the pressures of competition and individual choice and the need to be responsive.
>
> (Walsh, 1991: 9–10)

Breaking the unchallenged power of self-interested producers has been seen as critical to the effective reorienting of public sector service provision in fields such as health care. Central to breaking this producer dominance has been the idea that service users should be viewed as consumers, enjoying the same rights in respect of public sector services as individuals enjoy in respect of private sector service organisations. The application of commercially derived marketing concepts has thus been central to the reorientation of public sector service provision. This has been reflected in the panoply of policy initiatives, the most notable and enduring being the Citizen's Charter, which have been introduced by successive governments in order to promote consumerist patterns of behaviour and hence consumer-focused service provision.

The underlying assumption behind such initiatives has been that encouraging consumerist patterns of behaviour among service users, when coupled to the provision of information on performance and service standards, would force public sector service providers to become more responsive in the design and delivery of services (Power, 1997). The implicit policy emphasis on the individual service user, though central to the reorientation of public sector service provision, has been tempered by the need to take account of communal rights and requirements in the design and delivery of services (Wistow *et al.*, 1996). Such policy initiatives must, however, be seen within the context of the broader socio-economic and increasingly technological changes occurring from the 1980s which impacted on the expectations and behaviours of public sector service users. Central to these socio-economic developments has been the increasing emphasis on the rights of the individual and declining emphasis on community and communal values (Abercrombie, 1994). Thus this enduring policy focus is as much a reflection of the changing reality of public expectations and behaviour as of any fundamental shift in ideology.

The successive reforms of the NHS from the 1980s onward are to be viewed in this context, with continuing emphasis being placed on the empowerment of service users. The objective of making the NHS more responsive to service users can consequently be seen as a constant theme underpinning the reforms of the health service introduced over the past two decades. This promotion of a user focus or orientation, albeit within different organisational frameworks, is evident from the proposals contained in the 1989 and 1997 White Papers relating to the NHS, as well as the subsequent policy implementation initiatives and guidelines launched to support the respective reforms. 'We aim to extend patient choice. All proposals in this white paper put the needs of patients first. The patients needs will always be paramount' (Department of Health, 1989). 'Our starting point is that every aspect of the planning and delivery of services should be designed from the perspective of patients' (Department of Health, 1997).

Such stated commitment to the development of user-focused service provision is supported both by the substantial proposals contained in these white papers and the resultant policy implementation initiatives. In promoting such a user orientation there has been an enduring focus on the management of the service delivery process rather than on service performance, that is, clinical outcomes. In particular there has been a consistent emphasis on the importance of tangible aspects of the service delivery process as both indicators of service quality and as measures by which users evaluate service provision. This has clear resonance, with the emerging focus in the literature on health care quality on the patient's experience of care. Perhaps nowhere within the policy documentation is this emphasis more clearly articulated than in *Working for Patients*:

At present the service provided on admission to hospital is sometimes too impersonal and inflexible. This is not what either the Government or those working in the Health Service want to see. It wants a service which considers patients as people. It believes that each hospital should offer:

- Appointments systems which give people individual appointment times that they can rely on. Waits of two to three hours in out-patient clinics are unacceptable.
- Quiet and pleasant waiting and other public areas with proper facilities for parents with children and for counselling worried parents and relatives.
- Clear information leaflets about the facilities available and what patients need to know when they come into hospital.
- Clearer, easier and more sensitive procedures for making suggestions for improvements and, if necessary, complaints.

(Department of Health, 1989)

This emphasis on the processual or experiential aspects of health care service delivery, what Gabbott and Hogg (1994) term the 'care' dimension of health service delivery, has remained the dominant focus in the reforms introduced by the post-1997 Labour government. This is reflected in the ongoing emphasis on the importance of the management of the 'patient pathway' or 'patient journey', that is the user's experience of the service delivery process, to the attainment of user-oriented service provision. In this regard health policy in the United Kingdom can be viewed as drawing heavily on the re-engineering agenda characteristic of the public sector from the early 1990s (Jones and Thwaites, 2000). Central to the re-engineering agenda was the centrality of consumer sovereignty and the concomitant need for increased responsiveness to consumers on the part of the producer (Hammer and Stanton, 1995). Within the NHS such concepts specifically found expression in the idea of patient focused care: ... patient focused care brings elements of process re-engineering and TQM together with multi-skilling and team working to focus service processes around the consumer. (Fischbacher and Francis, 1998: 22).

The attraction of such concepts lay in that the perceived problem with prevailing approaches to the delivery of health care services – that no-one was responsible for the patient and had end to end experience of the service process. This critique was echoed in policy statements emphasising the need to enhance the management of the patient journey through the health care system. Drawing specifically on policy evidence from the NHS in Scotland, it is apparent that this focus on the total patient experience has been central to the reform of the health care system. 'We believe that our modern NHS must care as well as it cures. We will improve the patient's journey – from GP surgery to outpatient clinic, from hospital to home.' (Scottish Executive Health Department, 1999a).

> Modernising the NHS is about reorganising the entire health care system. Making the patient journey as good as it can be. People talk to me about their experience through the system ... Cancellations, changes to appointment, disruption to family life.
>
> (Scottish Executive Health Department, 2000a)

The ultimate objective of such reorientation of the service delivery process has been that both health service organisations and the constituent professionals fundamentally reappraise their approach to service delivery, both individually and collectively.

> This would (a) put the individual at the centre of its policies and practices; (b) recognise and support diversity by striving to meet the widest possible range of needs; (c) seek to achieve the best 'match' between provision and the needs of the individual.
>
> (Scottish Executive Health Department, 1999b)

> This means looking at each service from the patient's point of view, making the best use of the skills of all members of the health care team, adopting a whole system approach and challenging traditional ways of working.
>
> (Scottish Executive Health Department, 2000b)

Although clinical standards, that is service outcomes, have been addressed in the 1997 NHS White Papers, reflecting growing public disquiet with the medical profession as a result of increasing evidence of professional malpractice, the dominant focus has remained on the processual aspects of service delivery. This does not imply that technical quality is insignificant, but rather the continuation of such a focus reflects evidence that consumers' evaluation of complex professional services is largely framed in terms of the process or experiential attributes of service delivery (Taylor and Cronin, 1994).

Central to such service process redesign has been the improvement of communication between health service professionals and service users. Long perceived to be the Achilles heel of the NHS, the focus has been on ensuring that service professionals provide users with the information they require both to facilitate the service delivery process and to contribute to clinical decisions about service provision (Entwhistle *et al.*, 1997). '... clear and sensitive explanations of what is happening – on practical matters such as where to go and who to see, and on clinical matters, such as the nature of illness and its proposed treatment' (Department of Health, 1989).

> Information is crucial in determining people's access to health
> care, and to ensuring that they can contribute as equal partners to
> decisions about their health. ... This is about more than issuing
> leaflets, it is about ensuring that staff at all levels in the NHS
> become more skilled in communicating with the people they serve.
>
> (Scottish Executive Health Department, 2000b)

The importance of such a shift in the culture of information provision
reflects the impact of the informational asymmetries which are a core
characteristic of complex professional services such as health care. Such
improvement in communication and information provision is seen to be
critical to the effective reorientation of service provision, that is in shifting the delivery of health care away from a professionally dominated
paternalistic model to a more egalitarian participative model (Toop,
1998). Alongside such policy initiatives, emerging developments in
information and communication technology are further contributing to
the empowerment of health care consumers, in turn necessitating changing patterns of professional behaviour and consumer-professional interaction (Hogg *et al.*, 2001).

This commitment to the development of user-oriented service provision inevitably has fundamental implications for the way in which
health care services are designed and delivered. As a result, policy implementation initiatives have emphasised the need for sweeping changes to
the way in which services are organised and managed. Such redesign
processes have significant implications for those front-line professionals
involved in the actual delivery of health care services.

> The patient journey involves a huge range of people, from cleaners
> to consultants. It's these people together who are delivering health
> care. And the quality of care will be determined by how effectively
> these people work together as a team. Until now, patients have had
> to fit into the system. That's not good enough. Now it's crucially
> important that people get the care they need as quickly and as
> effectively as possible.
>
> (Scottish Executive Health Department, 2000a)

The increasingly explicit acknowledgement of the need for radical
redesign, and the expressed determination to challenge established
models of service delivery and professional practice marks a clear
continuation of the policy drive towards the development of a user-
oriented health service initiated originally under the aegis of *Working
for Patients*. Consequently, in understanding the management of health

care services in the modern world it is critical to understand the way in which consumers utilise and evaluate complex professional services and the way in which they interact with health care professionals.

References

Abercrombie, N. (1994) 'Authority and Consumer Society' in Keat, R., Whiteley, N. and Abercrombie, N. (eds) *The Authority of the Consumer*, Routledge: London.

Allen, P. (2000) 'Accountability for Clinical Governance: Developing Collective Responsibility for Quality in Primary Care', *BMJ* 321: 608–11.

Alter, C. and Hage, J. (1993) *Organizations Working Together*, SAGE Publications: London.

Baker, M. (2000) *Making Sense of the NHS White Papers*, 2nd edn, Abingdon Medical Press: Radcliffe.

Bianchi, M. (1995) 'Markets and Firms: Transaction Costs Versus Strategic Innovation', *Journal of Economic Behaviour and Organisation* 28: 183–202.

Campbell, H., Hotchkiss, R., Bradshaw, N. and Porteous, M. (1998) 'Integrated Care Pathways', *BMJ* 316: 133–7.

Davies, H. T. O. and Nutley, S. M. (1999a) 'What Works? The Role of Evidence in Public Sector Policy and Practice', *Public Money and Management* January–March, 3–5.

Davies, H. T. O. and Nutley, S. M. (1999b) 'The Rise and Rise of Evidence in Health Care', *Public Money and Management* January–March, 9–16.

Davies, H. T. O., Mannion, R. and Marshall, M. N. (2001) 'Treading a Third way for Quality in Healthcare', *Public Money and Management* April–June, 6–7.

Department of Health (1989) *Working for Patients*, HMSO: London.

Department of Health (1997) *The New NHS: Modern and Dependable*, HMSO: London.

Department of Health (1998) *A First Class Service: Quality in the New NHS*. Department of Health: London.

Dixon, J. (2000) 'Performance and Productivity', *BMJ* 320: 1462–4.

Enthoven, A. C. (1985) *Reflections on the Management of the National Health Service*. Occasional Papers Number 5, Nuffield Provincial Hospitals Trust: London.

Entwhistle, V., Sheldon, T., Sowden, A. and Watt, I. (1997) 'Evidence Informed Patient Choice', *International Journal of Technology Assessment in Health Care* 14(2): 212–25.

Exworthy, M., Powell, M. and Mohan, J. (1999) 'The NHS: Quasi-market, Quasi-hierarchy and Quasi-network?', *Public Money and Management* 19(4): 15–22.

Ferlie, E. (1992) 'The Creation and Evolution of Quasi-Markets in the Public Sector: A Problem for Strategic Management', *Strategic Management Journal* 13: 79–97.

Ferlie, E., Ashburner, L., Fitzgerald, L. and Pettigrew, A. (1996) *The New Public Management in Action*, Oxford University Press: Oxford.

Fischbacher, M. and Francis, A. (1998) 'Managing the Design of Health Care Services' in Davies, H., Tavakoli, M., Malek, M. and Neilson, A. (eds) *Managing Quality: Strategic Issues in Health Care Management*, Ashgate Publishing: Aldershot.

Flynn, R., Williams, G. and Pickard, S. (1996) *Markets and Networks: Contracting in Community Health Services*, Open University Press: Buckingham.

Gabbott, M. and Hogg, G. (1994) 'Competing for Patients: Understanding Consumer Evaluation of Primary Care', *Journal of Management in Medicine* 8(1): 12–18.

Hammer, M. and Stanton, S. (1995) *The Re-engineering Revolution*, Harper-Collins: New York.

Health Select Committee (1999) *Primary Care Groups*, 2nd Report, HMSO: London.

Hogg, G., Laing, A. W. and Winkelman, D. (2001) 'The Internet Empowered Consumer: The Professional Service Encounter in the Age of the Internet', Paper presented at the Academy of Marketing Conference, University of Wales, Cardiff.

Holzer, M. (1997) 'Productivity and Quality Management' in Shafritz, J.M. and Hyde, A.C. (eds.) *Classics of Public Administration*, 4th edn, Harcourt Brace: Fort Worth.

Hudson, B. and Hardy, B. (1999) 'In Pursuit of Inter-Agency Collaboration: What is the Contribution of Research and Theory', *Public Management: International Journal of Research and Theory* 1(2): 235–60.

Huxham, C. *Creating Collaborative Advantage*, Sage: London.

Jones, M. and Thwaites, R. (2000) 'Dedicated Followers of Fashion: BPR and the Public Sector', in Knights, D. and Willmott, H. (eds) *The Reengineering Revolution: Critical Studies of Corporate Change*, Sage: London.

Keaney, M. (1999) 'Are Patients Really Consumers?', *International Journal of Social Economics* 26(5): 695–706.

Kirkpatrick, I. (1999) 'The Worst of Both Worlds? Public Services without Markets or Bureaucracy', *Public Money and Management* 19(4): 7–14.

Klein, R. (1989) *The Politics of the National Health Service*, 2nd edn, Longman: London.

Laing, A. W. and Cotton, S. (1995) 'Towards an Understanding of Health Care Purchasing: The Purchasing Behaviour of GP Fundholders', *Journal of Marketing Management* 11(6): 583–601.

Lapsley, I. (1994) 'Market Mechanisms and the Management of Health Care', *International Journal of Public Sector Management* 7(6): 15–25.

Light, D. (1997) 'From Managed Competition to Managed Co-operation', *Millbank Quarterly* 75: 297–341.

Lohr *et al.* (eds) (1990) *Clinical Practice Guidelines: Directions for a New Program*, National Academy Press: Washington.

Lohr, K. N., Eleazer, K. and Mauskopf, J. (1998) 'Health Policy Issues and Applications for Evidence-based Medicine and Clinical Practice Guidelines', *Health Policy* 46: 1–19.

Mannion, R. and Goddard, M. (2001) 'Impact of Published Clinical Outcomes Data: case study in NHS hospital trusts', *BMJ* 323: 260–3.

Maynard, A. (1994) 'Can Competition Enhance Efficiency in Health Care? Lessons from the Reform of the UK National Health Service', *Social Science and Medicine* 39(10): 1433–45.

McColl, A. and Roland, M. (2000) 'Knowledge and Information for Clinical Governance', *BMJ* 321: 871–4.

Mulligan, J., Appleby, J. and Harrison, A. (2000) 'Measuring the Performance of Health Systems', *BMJ* 321: 191–2.

Perleth, M., Jakubowski, E., and Busse, R. (2001) 'What is 'Best Practice' in Health Care? State of the Art and Perspectives in Improving the Effectiveness and Efficiency of the European Health Care Systems', *Health Policy* 56(3): 235–50.

Pettigrew, A., Ferlie, E. and McKee, L. (1994) *Shaping Strategic Change*. Sage Publications: London.

Power, M. (1997) *The Audit Society: Rituals of Verification*, Oxford University Press: Oxford.

Radin, B. and Coffee, J. (1993) 'A Critique of TQM: Problems of implementation in the public sector', *Public Administration Quarterly* 17(1): 42.

Rosenberg, W. and Donald, A. (1995) 'Evidence-Based Medicine: an Approach to Clinical Problem-solving', *BMJ* 310: 1122–6.

Sackett, D. L., Rosenberg, W. M., Muir-Gray, J. A., Haynes, R. B. and Richardson, W. S. (1996) 'Evidence-based Medicine: What it is and What it Isn't', *BMJ* 312: 71–2.

Sackett, D. L., Richardson, W. S., Rosenberg, W. and Haynes, R. B. (1997) *Evidence-based Medicine: How to Practice and Teach EBM*. Churchill Livingston: London.

Scottish Executive Health Department (1997) *Designed to Care: Renewing the National Health Service in Scotland*, The Scottish Office Department of Health: Edinburgh.

Scottish Executive Health Department (1999a) *Making it Work Together*, HMSO: Edinburgh.

Scottish Executive Health Department (1999b) *Implementing Inclusiveness*, HMSO: Edinburgh.

Scottish Executive Health Department (2000a) *NHS Way Ahead*, HMSO: Edinburgh.

Scottish Executive Health Department (2000b) *Our National Health: A Plan for Action, A Plan for Change*, HSMO: Edinburgh.

Shaw, C. (2001) 'External Assessment of Health Care', *BMJ* 322: 851–4.

Taylor, S. A. and Cronin, J. (1994) 'Modeling Patient Satisfaction and Service Quality', *Journal of Health Care Marketing* 14(1): 34–43.

Teeling Smith, G. (ed.) (1984) *A New NHS Act for 1996?* Office of Health Economics: London.

Teeling-Smith, G. (1986) *The Politician's Dilema*, Office of Health Economics: London.

Vaizey, J. (1984) *National Health*, Martin Robertson & Company Ltd: Oxford.

Walsh, K. (1991) 'Citizens and Consumers: Marketing and Public Sector Management', *Public Money and Management* 11(2): 9–15.

Walshe, K., Rundall, T. G. (2001) 'Evidence-based management: From theory to practice in health care', *Milbank Quarterly* 79(3): 429–60.

Wistow, G., Knapp, M., Hardy, B., Forder, J., Kendall, J. and Manning, R. (1996) *Social Care Markets: Progress and Prospects*, Open University Press: Buckingham.

Notes

[1] ICPs are also referred to as care pathways, critical pathways, anticipated recovery pathways, clinical pathways, care tracks, care maps, clinical algorithms, care protocols, collaborative care plans, patient/user pathways, and expected recovery pathways.

[2] For a useful overview of related NHS white papers for England and Wales see Baker, 2000.

2 Service design

Introduction

It is clear from the preceding chapter that several key themes have consistently underpinned policy developments in recent years. Of those, the need to improve service and organisational performance, the importance of evidence-based practice, the increasing involvement of consumers and the development and management of networks and partnerships in particular, directly impinge on the design and delivery of health services.

This chapter sets out to examine the concept of service design and to consider the significance and role of design in the health service setting in light of these policy themes. It will become readily apparent from the discussion that the design challenge presented to health service organisations is considerable. Designing a service can encompass not only clinical, occupational, intra- and inter-organisational considerations, but may also involve the parallel processes of commissioning new, and decommissioning old, services and buildings. The scale of design activities necessitates recognition of a range of stakeholders, many of whom have considerable interest in the design process and the new service. Managing the design process therefore involves the ability to draw on a range of different skills and expertise that are located among different professional groups and across various organisations.

The strategic significance of design

The strategic significance of design in NHS organisations can be considered from two main points of view. First, as was explored in the previous chapter, health policy has developed in such a way that over recent years, the management and organisation of health services and the standards of care patients should reasonably expect, have been the focus of much government and academic attention. Growing scrutiny of clinical practice has been accompanied in recent years by increasing expectations of clinical and organisational performance and a continual pressure for public accountability (Allen, 2000). The NHS has also experienced greater patient expectations and a rise in consumerism, fuelled by measures such as the Patients' Charter. These pressures and expectations have in turn inevitably contributed to the launch of more explicit Government mandates that obligate conscious, philosophical and methodical attention to service design and delivery (see for example Scottish Executive Health Department, 1997).

Organisational research also highlights the strategic significance of design, where developing new products and services[1] is crucial to sustaining a competitive advantage in the marketplace. New products not only lead to increased sales, but also provide a range of other benefits including opening up new market opportunities; enhancing the profitability of other products; attracting new, and increasing the loyalty of existing, customers; improving company image; and providing a platform for future new products (Storey and Easingwood, 1999). New product innovation is also thought to be a means of corporate renewal (Dougherty, 1992). Moreover, firms seeking external investors increasingly need to be able to demonstrate innovative capability as well as profitability (Cooper, 1999). Design is also of significance because of the resources it requires. Recent calculations suggest that by the 1990s, the costs of R&D within the G5 countries were in excess of $1 billion per day.

Whilst the NHS cannot be considered to experience the competitive pressures for new services developments witnessed in manufacturing, retailing and elsewhere in the service sector, there are pressures to improve service and organisational performance (see Box 2.1). Of particular significance to design is the Government's emphasis on quality. Research suggests that service quality problems may be difficult to resolve because they are built into the services being offered as a result of poor service development/design processes (Edvardsson, 1992; Juran, 1992). In quantitative terms it has been estimated that as many as

---

Box 2.1 **National performance managerial framework**

- Health improvement
- Fair access
- Effective delivery of appropriate health care
- Efficiency
- Patient/carer experience
- Health outcomes of NHS care

(Source: Department of Health, 1997; Scottish Executive Health Department, 1997)

70–90 per cent of service quality problems are built into internal service processes (Crosby, 1989). Clearly then, if service quality is to be prioritised, monitored and evaluated, service providers need to step back and consider the design process in order to ensure that poor quality is not designed into services at an early stage.

Understanding design

The literature on design is eclectic, extensive and interdisciplinary, offering a wealth of material on product design that ranges from the practice and study of medieval guilds, to architecture, graphic and industrial design. Within this literature, one can read of the skills and philosophies of the 'art school' orientation which encompass visualisation, the capabilities of designer as intermediary between the client and the customer, and the ability to crystallise ideas (Dreyfus, 1976) drawing on analytical, judgemental and creative cognitive abilities to recognise, isolate, define and solve problems (Papanek, 1984).

Within the field of engineering, however, there is also an extensive literature on the methods and practice of design. Studies here place an emphasis on systematic, often mathematical/formulaic approaches to managing design activities (Hollins and Hollins, 1991; Pahl *et al.*, 1984; Pugh and Morley, 1988). Such studies form the basis of methods such as blueprinting (Shostack, 1982) that are used to assist the process of product and service design in a range of settings. It is also from the engineering and manufacturing environment that the now widely accepted models of the design process were first developed.

Studies of the design process have not, however, been restricted to the disciplines of art and engineering. Recognition has increasingly been given by academics to the business and management aspects of design, and a considerable body of material is being developed from this disciplinary perspective, whilst also using the concepts and practices described in the art school and engineering literatures. The management literature focuses largely on understanding design from an organisational point of view. This includes studies of organisational structures; innovation; knowledge management; creativity; change management; marketing; strategy; product development; manufacturing; supply chain management and many others. (See, for example, Baker and Hart, 1999; Henry and Walker, 1991; and Tidd *et al.*, 1997 for a summary and synthesis of these aspects).

Within this broad, interdisciplinary literature, however, relatively little material can be found that addresses the service sector generally, and health services in particular. Although studies in services are increasing, the territory remains under-represented when compared with manufacturing, for example. Nevertheless, since much of the literature on NPD, innovation and creativity is generic in nature, there are many guiding principles that can be applied to the (health) service context, whilst at the same time being sensitive to the specific characteristics of the service environment.

For the purposes of this discussion, the management literature is divided into two broad areas. One area focuses on managing the activities that together comprise the design process. These are the activities that take the product/service from the point of inception through to its launch or obsolescence. The other area of literature discusses contextual factors associated with managing design. Included here are organisational and market factors necessary for enabling a design orientation as well as processes and structures required for the design process to be enacted. The discussion here continues by concentrating on the latter area – contextual factors – before turning later in the chapter to discuss in detail the activities involved in design.

Design in context

One of the keys to understanding health services design is recognising the complex range of factors, and actors, which make up the environment within which the design process is enacted (Fischbacher and Francis, 1999). These factors include the role of individuals within the design process as managers of design, champions of the new service and key political stakeholders and players within the organisation. The culture or internal environment shapes and influences the success and/or failure of the service design process according to the organisational structures in place, and the incentives for creative and innovative behaviour. The ability of the organisation to access and draw on external developments in related technology or service areas, as well as relationships with external organisations and the broader society, also feature strongly in determining the success of an organisation's design process. These elements of the design environment are represented in Figure 2.2. Discussion of these elements is supported by a recent health services case study which is presented below and that is developed throughout this section.

Case Study: The Community Hospital

During the early 1990s, a UK Health Authority decided to reconfigure some community services in one of its localities. The HA began by establishing a project group comprising representatives from local stakeholder organisations such as social work, the local council, the police, voluntary agencies and primary and secondary care providers. The focus for the HA's activities was twofold. First, a broad service specification had to be developed to integrate existing primary and secondary care services and the community care strategy, and to decommission those services that would become redundant.

Second, a bidding process needed to be arranged where potential service providers could be invited to bid for the contract to design, build and operate the hospital. Because of the market structures that prevailed at the time, the system offered public and private health service organisations the opportunity to bid. Those who entered the bidding process were a local NHS Acute Trust and a local NHS Community Trust. Their challenge was to develop an innovative approach which met the WHO *Health For All* criteria (equity, efficiency, effectiveness, access, choice, comprehensiveness, appropriateness and flexibility), which was financially robust, and which took a creative approach to managing patient care.

The successful bidders – the Community Trust – then needed to gather the perspectives and knowledge they required. They established a small design team drawing on experts in finance, community care, mental illness and estates project management plus a representative from general practice and an architect. The group had only six weeks to develop their design, which had to include drawings for the building, specifications for the service, and details of the potential workforce.

The design of the community hospital occurred in a public sector environment, where the role of the macro environment was of particular significance as a driver. The stimulus for design came in the first instance from the government's community care policy and in the second, from the Health Board's desire to reconfigure services in the area in a way which fulfilled regulatory requirements. The 'innovating architecture' (see later discussion) was given little explicit consideration within the Trust at the time, rather the pragmatic response to the Health Board's action necessarily took priority. Innovative design, however, was a priority and was crucial to success. '[The winning design was] innovative in two respects, the physical solution ... and ... its integration with the service...they came up with something that hadn't been done previously' (Health Board Project Team Member).

Individuals to be included in the Community Trust's team were carefully selected for their technical expertise (e.g. the dementia specialist and architect) as well as managerial competence (e.g. the project manager in particular). This cross-functional team of diverse interests and knowledge led, in their view, to a range of creative design solutions. A further key individual was a senior Trust Board member whose involvement was 'partly to protect the core group from the rest of the world, so that they could get on with what they were supposed to be doing'

(Project team member). Moreover, this individual was a gatekeeper to the group for non-members. Thus, there was recognition of the need to provide adequate resources, motivated individuals, and sufficient resources in terms of time, staff, and money.

At an (inter-)organisational level, the decision-making process for the Health Board was far from straightforward. Despite all project team members agreeing on the WHO criteria and the need to redevelop services, the two GP representatives had 'essentially irreconcilable views ... the Chief Executives ... had very strong and opposing views.' These players had to be 'taken along, and kept part of the process even if they didn't agree with aspects of it, keeping them on board so that we got their knowledge and skills into it was really quite a challenge' (Health Board Project Chairman). Further complexities were evidenced when members of this group were asked to score the range of service options against the WHO criteria

> Nine out of 11 respondents returned completed forms, five of which were accompanied by written comments explaining the scores given. The remaining two respondents felt that none of the options were appropriate and that written comments would capture the complexities of the arguments for and against the options more adequately than numerical scores. They put forward an alternative option.
>
> (Source: official project documentation)

At a societal level, there were further political tensions during the tendering process. Support groups (e.g. the league of friends from a local elderly support unit), GPs and the public were divided as to the most appropriate location for the new services, such that they each became involved in lobbying by delivering information leaflets and obtaining signatures for petitions in the local shopping centre. Managing public relations became a sensitive priority issue.

Those involved in managing the design therefore needed to simultaneously develop a solution which reconciled diverse interests from a range of stakeholders; to manage the design project in a timely and creative fashion; and to consider implications for broader issues of service integration.

Individual factors

Individuals within organisations are important both as sources of product/service ideas and as managers of the design process. Individuals also represent tangible resources which the organisation can deploy.

Amabile *et al.* (1996) suggest that supervisory encouragement is one aspect of promoting the generation and development of new ideas. Open interactions between supervisors and supervisees, clarity of goals and supportive team work stimulate creativity. Similarly, carefully selected and managed teams where members are diverse and open to

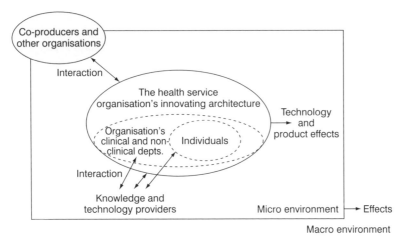

Source: Adapted from Trott, 1998

Figure 2.1 **National performance management framework**

each others' ideas and where there is a climate of constructive criticism and personal motivation are contributors to creativity (Amabile *et al.*, 1996; Monge *et al.*, 1992).

Individuals also possess intangible resources in the form of knowledge, accumulated learning and experience. Organisational and new product development (NPD)/new service development (NSD) success is highly dependent upon the ability of the organisation to tap into and exploit these intangible resources (Cohen and Levinthal, 1990; Nonaka *et al.*, 1996).

Managerial competence within the organisation also plays a key role in relation to the design process and the organisation as a whole. The ability of the 'management team' to work together, to perform as individuals and to draw on one another's experience is a principal determinant of the growth and development of the organisation (Penrose, 1997). Senior managers, for example, play a powerful role in shaping the technological capabilities within firms, often through a series of decisions over time and by engaging in prototyping activities (Pisano, 1996; Leonard-Barton, 1995). Thus, the wisdom with which senior organisational members organise the firm and direct its actions will to a large extent determine the internal organisational conditions within which design is conducted. Individuals both directly and indirectly involved in a particular design project are, therefore, of integral significance to the success or failure of NSD.

The firm's functions – organising design

The organisational structures within which individuals conduct their design activities also have a bearing on the success of new service development. Staff are often organised into departments or directorates according to their professional skills and experience, i.e. a functional structure. Design, however, is a process which transcends functional boundaries, involving input from a range of departments such as design, R&D, engineering, marketing, sales, finance and so forth. Organisations therefore need to create structures which enable multidisciplinary input into new service developments, and which encourage problem-solving processes (Kanter, 1983). This is often addressed through the creation of a matrix structure or process-based teams that bring functional specialists together and integrate their perspectives and focus on, for example, a specific product, or the improvement of organisational processes.

Creating these process-based structures can, however, be difficult in large, mature organisations, where there are strong occupational identities and disciplinary divisions, particularly as these structures and their reward systems often discourage people from extending their role (Dougherty and Hardy, 1996). Moreover, developing effective collaboration also involves considerable time 'up front' where departments simply learn about each other (Dougherty and Hardy, 1996). Although costly, this process of socialisation has two important effects. First, it provides a basis for effective collaboration in design, something which Dougherty and Hardy and others (see for example Francis, 1987) have found to be a defining characteristic of successful innovators. Second, such social interaction is necessary for knowledge creation within the organisation (Dougherty, 1992; Nonaka *et al.*, 1996) as is further discussed below.

The firm's innovating architecture

Individuals within the firm represent one of a number of resources available to organisations. The total set of resources on which a service provider may have to draw, however, will include tangible, intangible and financial resources. As proponents of the resource-based view of the firm point out, however, the resources themselves are not the prime source of value (see for example Wernerfelt, 1984). Rather, what matters is a firm's ability to integrate and deploy those resources: i.e. the firm's capabilities (Prahalad and Hamel, 1990). Creating the appropriate conditions or internal environment for developing capabilities then becomes a key consideration for the service organisation. Thus, not only are the appropriate resources necessary, but so too is the motivation to innovate and the requisite management practices and capabilities (Amabile *et al.*, 1996). It is in this area of improved capabilities – managing and exploiting the synergy between resources – that design can be an important source of corporate renewal (Burgelman, 1983; Verona, 1999).

Motivation to innovate is directly related to the firm's attitude to risk, the values placed on innovation throughout the organisation and the level of support offered to new ideas (Amabile *et al.*, 1996). Evidence from innovative firms (e.g. 3M) indicates that this is supported by the open flow of ideas throughout the organisation, which encourages participation in decision-making and increases the generation of further ideas (Amabile *et al.*, 1996; Tidd *et al.*, 1997). Appropriate organisational structures and an innovative culture need to be supported by incentives and resources for individuals. Product development responsibilities also need to be accompanied by resources in terms of time, money and staff, as well as by clear objectives for product managers that specify product targets and the expected resource inputs. (See the later discussion on design models on pp. 43–4).

Organisational slack

Organisational slack (Nohria and Gulati, 1996) is also crucial. Nohria and Gulati define slack as 'the pool of resources in an organisation that is in excess of the minimum necessary to produce a given level of organisational output'. This includes unused capital expenditure or capacity, which can be used for exploring new opportunities, experimentation and developing improved practice and performance. Given that the NHS operates in a climate which for some time has prioritised efficiency and the reduction of waste, the notion of slack is of particular interest. In summarising much of the research on slack and innovation, Nohria and Gulati (1996) note the arguments in favour of a positive relationship between slack and innovation, and those against slack.

In favour, they cite slack as a catalyst for innovation because it causes controls to be relaxed and funds to be used on projects which, due to their uncertain outcome, might otherwise be refused. This can be a mechanism for reducing goal conflict between political groups within the organisation, and can allow projects of narrower, more marginalised interest and application to be pursued. The contrasting perspective is, however to view slack as waste, and a reflection of 'managerial self-interest, incompetence and sloth' (Nohsia and Gulati, 1996). Slack allows organisational members to pursue their own self-interest, and whilst R&D expenditure may increase, it may not lead to the development of value added products/services. The challenge for the NHS, then, is to find what Nohria and Gulati consider to be an optimal relationship between slack and innovation whereby slack is understood to 'promote experimentation', but where measures are in place to ensure some discipline over the selection and continuation of projects.

Knowledge and learning

A firm's capabilities are largely composed of knowledge, which is sourced by the learning processes in which organisational members are involved (Verona, 1999). Managing knowledge and learning is, therefore, a further component of the architecture for innovation. It is not enough to recognise knowledge as a resource that is available to the organisation. For knowledge to be of use, there needs to be a mechanism for accessing, integrating and continually developing/creating knowledge. 'Organisational knowledge creation, therefore, should be understood as a process that "organisationally" amplifies the knowledge created by individuals and crystallizes it as a part of the knowledge system of the organisation' (Nonaka *et al.*, 1996). This system, according to Nonaka *et al.*, needs to recognise the dynamic relationship between tacit and explicit knowledge, and the role of social interaction in the development of knowledge or 'knowledge conversion'. Social interaction involves four processes: socialisation, externalisation, combination and internalisation (see also Nonaka *et al.*, 1998). Socialisation involves sharing experience that creates tacit knowledge in the form of shared mental models and technical skills. Acquisition can be through observation (as an apprentice observes the master) or through discussion, so long as there is experience. Externalisation is the process whereby tacit knowledge is articulated into explicit concepts and models. This is mostly through written and verbal communication. Combination involves organising explicit knowledge into a system and sharing it through documents, meetings, networks and so forth. Internalisation, the process that completes the circle, involves embodying explicit knowledge into tacit knowledge. Experiences gained through the previous stages become internalised by the individual as part of their tacit knowledge base through experience and learning by doing. Together, the processes of creating tacit, then explicit knowledge transcend the individual, groups and the organisation as a whole (see Figure 2.2).

Politics and power

As we have already touched on in our discussion of slack, there is a political dimension to the design process and more broadly, to innovation. Machiavelli's well known quote from *The Prince* is often cited in this context: 'The innovator makes enemies of all those who prospered

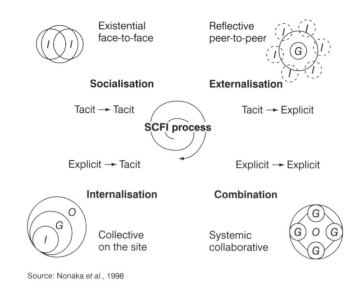

Source: Nonaka *et al.*, 1998

Figure 2.2 **The innovation process**

under the old order, and only lukewarm support is forthcoming from those who would prosper under the new ...' (cited in Frost and Egri, 1990). Any new service inevitably intrudes on previously accepted practice about how services ought to be delivered. This in turn, can offend the proponents or originators of the 'old way' (Frost and Egri, 1990; Stuart, 1998).

As Frost and Egri also point out, however, there are not only the struggles among actors operating from different perspectives, there are also struggles for collaboration between actors. Collaboration between individuals and organisations is often fraught with conflict as well as creativity, which can be particularly difficult when the conditions are complex or uncertain (Jones *et al.*, 1997). Since both the design and the delivery of services necessarily involves collaboration between departments and organisations, the ability to engage in and maintain collaborative relationships and cultures is crucial in the NHS.

Frost and Egri suggest that there are three levels on which power and politics can operate: individual level; organisational level (within and between organisations); and societal level (see also Drazin and Schoonhoven, 1996). The interaction of these levels can be captured in Graziano's (1969: 10) words, 'The *conception* of innovative ideas in mental health depends upon creative humanitarian and scientific forces, while their *implementation* depends, not on science or humanitarianism, but on a broad spectrum of professional or social politics'. Typically, new service innovations will meet with opposition, or facilitation, from well-known political strategies such as networking, coalitions, selective use of objective criteria, bargaining, and management of committees, which delays decision-making or withdraws financial support.

Organisational slack, knowledge and learning, politics and power are clearly core elements of what comprises the innovative architecture of the firm. They are, however, not the only elements. Also of relevance to this discussion is the organisation's ability to interact with other organisations.

Interaction beyond the firm – inter-organisational relations

An organisation's capacity to absorb knowledge through external linkages is a further dimension of the design context (Verona, 1999). As the next two chapters discuss, public and private sector firms are increasingly engaging in partnerships, alliances and joint ventures. There are many reasons for doing so (such as the ability to combine complementary resources, the opportunity to gain knowledge (Hakansson and Johanson, 1993), but often the purpose is specifically to develop new products, or product-related technology. Thus the ability of each organisation in the partnership to develop relationships, to create new cultures and to engage collaboratively in new ways of working, becomes central to their ability to absorb knowledge and to access other resources through these linkages. Also of significance is each firm's own absorptive capacity, i.e. 'the ability of a firm to recognise the value of new, external information, assimilate it, and apply it to commercial ends' (Cohen and Levinthal, 1990) and this, according to Penrose (1997), will be determined to a large extent by the firm's managerial capabilities.

There needs to be clear intent to learn within the firm, and sufficient transparency about the knowledge and organisational arrangements such that knowledge transfer and learning can take place. Developing transparent, effective relationships and managing within a network of organisations is a formidable challenge, not least due to the potential number and range of different players involved (see Figure 2.3).

Macro environment

As the previous section highlights, an organisation does not operate in a vacuum but rather interacts with a range of customers, suppliers and other stakeholders, many of whom are often involved in the co-production and delivery of services (Alford, 2000). All these parties are influenced by broader – or macro-environmental – factors. Public sector organisations are, of course, particularly sensitive to the political environment that shapes both their strategic and operational agendas on a domestic and international level. The case study presented earlier illustrates the direct

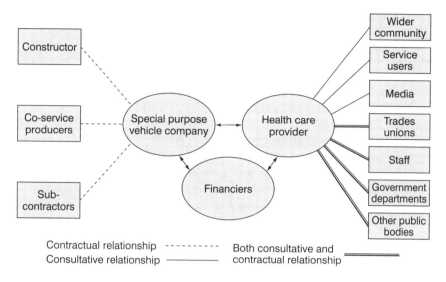

Contractual relationship ---------
Consultative relationship —————

Both consultative and
contractual relationship —————

Adapted from Audit Commission, 1998

Figure 2.3 The SCEI self-transcending process

impact of a change in Government policy upon the need for an organisation to design new types of service provision. Similarly, the Private Finance Initiative (PFI) has radically altered the way in which large capital projects are being commissioned, designed and funded.

It is clear from the discussion so far that the micro and macro context in which NHS services are designed and delivered, have a significant influence at a service level and more broadly at an organisational level. Whilst a comprehensive understanding of this context is crucial, so too is an understanding of what it is that is being designed – the design content and the nature of the service. It is to this matter then that the discussion now turns.

Design content

The case study introduced in the previous section was an example of a large-scale design project encompassing the building, the clinical service and the staffing element of the service. Whilst not all cases of new, or redesigned, services will be of this scale and scope, most will touch on each of the elements. This section of the chapter therefore draws together frameworks that help conceptualise these components.

What's in a service?

Health services comprise tangible elements such as buildings and facilities, staff, patient information, and intangible elements such as the atmosphere, the way in which patients are spoken to, sense of security and trust etc. (Grönroos, 1990). Both these tangible and intangible elements are important to patients and to service providers and are inextricably linked in any patient's (or external monitoring body's) assessment of the quality of the service they receive.

> A service can be defined as a process consisting of a series of more or less intangible activities that normally ... take place in interactions between the customer and service employees and/or physical resources or goods and/or systems of the service provider, which are provided as solutions to customer problems.
>
> (Grönroos, 2000: 46)

Services differ from products in that the customer (patient) is involved in the process of service delivery, they are heterogeneous, involve simultaneous production and consumption, are intangible, cannot be stored and do not involve transfer of ownership. Of these characteristics, one particularly important one is the degree of human involvement in health service delivery, both in terms of input from the service provider and from the consumer. It is this characteristic that often causes variability in service provision. In sectors such as retail and financial services, for example, this potential variability has led organisations to find ways of standardising service provision through automation (e.g. Automated Teller Machines [ATMs]) and/or strict service protocols (e.g. the approach taken by McDonald's).

Many health services rely on automated facilities within clinics, laboratories and primary care settings, and it is likely that the use of new technologies will increase thereby ensuring consistency in diagnosis and, where possible, treatment. However, it remains true that health service delivery is heavily reliant on input from people. Consequently, it is particularly important that staffing roles and the interface between the patient and the service provider are appropriately designed and managed.

One framework that sets out the service elements to be designed in three elements – the concept, process and system – is that developed by Edvardsson and Olsson (1996).

The service concept

The starting point for defining a new service is to consider what primary and secondary needs the provider is attempting to satisfy and what core and supporting service offerings are required to meet those needs (Edvardsson and Olsson, 1996). (See Figure 2.4). Primary needs are those which Edvardsson and Olsson call the 'trigger', i.e. the reason why the customer/patient experiences a certain need. When considering the design of a one-stop pain clinic, for example, the patient's primary need would be pain relief or cessation. In attempting to meet those needs, however, further needs will arise. In this case, these secondary needs might range from requiring information about appointment time/venue and transport, to information about possible treatments. Hence, to relieve pain, certain clinical/therapeutic services will be required (core service), whereas to meet secondary needs, supporting services of administration, diagnostic and laboratory facilities, counselling and so forth may be required.

The identification and definition of these needs may arise out of formal processes such as health authority needs assessment, primary care consultation and/or clinical research. They may also arise from informal processes such as the experience and observation of practitioners working with a specific patient group.

Once identified, decisions need to be made about *how* needs are to be met; i.e. the core and supporting services that are required. This is a particularly challenging aspect of design as views on how services should be delivered may vary between occupational groups and between different health organisations. A recent study (Laing, 2000),

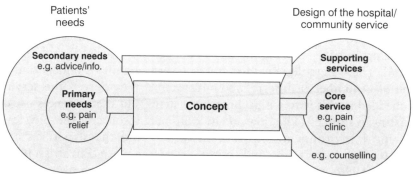

Adapted from Edvardsson and Olsson, 1996

Figure 2.4 **Relationships in a private finance initiative**

Box 2.2 **Conflicting service philosophies**

Service providers differed along spectrums such as:

- Harm reduction vs. abstinence;
- Openness of information between agencies vs. patient confidentiality;
- Customisation of services vs. standardisation; and
- Improving individual motivation vs. individual motivation as a prerequisite.

for example, highlighted the incongruence between organisational philosophies and practice of drug services in a region of Scotland. The health authority seeking to integrate drug services in the area was faced with a number of conflicting stances on how services should be provided (see Box 2.2).

It is also the case that these attitudes towards the appropriate means of service provision will shift over time in light of experience and research. The move from hospital to community-based provision of mental health services is one such example. Such shifts can have a profound impact on the service. This particular change in mental health philosophy, for example, called for services to be relocated, wards and hospitals to be decommissioned, and for new forms of work organisation to be developed for clinical staff (Fischbacher and Francis, 1999). This in turn yielded a direct impact on patients and the communities where new services were located (Dean and Freedman, 1993; Dean *et al.*, 1993).

The service system

Every service is of course embedded in related services, resources and systems, as both the pain clinic and mental health examples demonstrate. Thus, after defining the service concept, it is important that consideration is given to the service system, i.e. 'the resources available to the process for realizing the service concept' (Edvardsson and Olson, 1996). The system designed for any new service must be understood as one of a number of interrelated subsystems. Not only is the service embedded in this way within broader systems, but it also makes use of existing resources. This may include human resources, the physical/technical environment, existing customers and the structures and processes of organisation and control already in place (Edvardsson and Olsson, 1996). (Box 2.3 sets out aspects associated with each of these categories of resource.)

In many health services the supporting services will already be in place. The introduction of a pain clinic, as mentioned earlier for

---

Box 2.3 Resources employed in service delivery

Human resources

- Skills and knowledge (tacit and explicit) of service staff;
- Staff needs (motivation, training, reward);
- Encourage views on the proposed new service.

The customers

- Understanding customer needs, wishes and expectations;
- Appropriate understanding of the level of customer knowledge;
- Fit with the types of equipment and routines the customer uses;
- Ensuring well-designed customer interface (e.g. invoicing process, telephone manner, design and dissemination of information); and
- Clarify role of customer in service delivery – ensuring clarity of role is conveyed to staff and customers.

Physical/technical environment

- Premises, computers, technical systems at the service provider *and* the customer's location;
- Fit with administrative systems and organisational structure; and
- Fit with customer requirements for the new service.

Organisation and control

- Existing and new structures – divisions, line management relationships and professional hierarchies;
- Administrative systems for planning, information, finance, remuneration; and
- Processes for interacting with customers, suppliers and other parties with a service input; and
- Understanding customers and ensuring appropriate management of customer relationships (including customer information).

Based on Edvardsson and Olsson, 1996

---

example, therefore needs to be understood in the context of a number of integrated subsystems such as radiology, laboratory diagnostics, counselling and so forth. Herein lies a tension for the designer(s). Existing systems may constrain the parameters for the new service and reduce the extent to which it can be innovative or reach its full potential. In addition, given the likelihood of services being designed into existing service settings and making use of existing resources, the new service may be regarded as putting a strain on already stretched resources. Both tensions can be the cause of the political and power struggles that were discussed earlier (see also Frost and Egri, 1990; Stuart, 1998).

The service process

Consideration should also be given to the processes underpinning service delivery. This includes the interfaces between departments contributing directly to service delivery, as well as interfaces with customers/patients and suppliers to the health service organisation. Edvardsson and Olsson (1996) argue strongly for a highly detailed consideration of all processes, subprocesses and activities that contribute to the new service in order that the new subsystem can be tailored to existing subsystems with which it is integrated.

This focus on the service process is of considerable value in the context of research cited earlier which found that service quality problems are often difficult to resolve because they had been built (or designed) into the service. Indeed it is on the service process that most academic and practitioner attention has focused. Approaches such as service blueprinting have drawn on methods and techniques in engineering (Shostack, 1982) to map out each stage of the service, identify the time each activity takes and identify potential failure points in the process. This technique then moves to consider how service failures might be recovered. A key concept in this approach is the notion of a tolerance zone, i.e. 'the degree of variation from the blueprint's standards that can be allowed in execution without affecting the consumer's perception of overall quality and timeliness' (Shostack, 1982). Blueprinting can develop the service map to a sophisticated level of detail, identifying where various subsystems interface and indicating which activities are visible to the customer and which take place in the 'back office'.

A more fundamental approach adopted for the redesign of existing services is business process re-engineering (BPR). Introduced in the early 1990s (Hammer, 1990), this approach advocates a fundamental rethink of

---

Box 2.4 Benefits and uses of blueprinting

- Pre-emptive problem solving
- Controlled implementation
- Reduced failure potential
- Systematic thinking about the service
- Reduced time and inefficiency of random service development
- Higher level view of service management
- Provision of a scientific basis (benchmark) against which to make service changes
- Provision of a visual and quantitative description of the service which improves communication of the service concept.

business processes in order to improve organisational performance. Rather than trying to bring about improvements by reducing waste or automating existing processes, BPR involves challenging old assumptions and rules whilst redesigning processes throughout the organisation around outcomes rather than tasks and drawing on cross-functional inputs. As a consequence, it brings about changes to job designs, organisational structures and management systems, amongst others (Hammer, 1990).

This BPR perspective has been translated readily to the health service environment as evidenced in the experiences of Leicester Royal Infirmary (Newman, 1997) and King's Healthcare (Sears, 1994), for example, and the need for the NHS to consider such redesign continues to be recognised (Enthoven, 2000; Smith, 2001). (For further details on BPR activities and related health service design activities see NHS Estates, 1993; Warner, 1997).

Variability and service quality

Although mention has already been made of variability and quality, their significance in the health setting merits some additional consideration here. Blueprints and BPR aim, in part at least, to reducing variability in service processes. There remains, however, an underlying assumption that in any service there will always be some variability from one patient/customer encounter to another. As Shostack (1982) argues:

> Whatever the blueprint for the *potential* service, the *actual* rendering … of the service will almost always deviate in some way … no two haircuts are exactly alike. They may differ in duration, in quality, or in customer satisfaction, even when a specific blueprint has been followed.

More significantly, Shostack goes on to point out that the potential for such deviation increases concomitantly with the complexity of the service. Given the complexity of many health services, we should therefore expect some continued degree of variability. Indeed, variability is in some cases necessary since each patient needs to be given individualised care, and there must be a balance between standardisation and tailored care, according to patient need. It is essential, however, that this variability relates only to *how* a service is delivered and not to the *quality of care delivered*.

When designing the service, attention needs to be given to 'designing in' and monitoring two dimensions of service quality (Grönroos, 2000).

The first quality dimension is that of technical quality i.e. '*what* the customer is left with, when the service production process and its buyer–seller interactions are over' (Grönroos, 2000). This may be recovery from illness, the outcome of an operation, or a diagnosis after a period of illness. Assessing and managing this aspect of quality may, however, be difficult. A less satisfactory outcome than was expected from an operation may be perceived by the patient as a failure of technical quality, and he/she may call into question the technical skills of the surgeon and his/her team. However, it could be the case that there were complications and that the success achieved is commendable given the nature of the complications. Professionals (such as GPs and public health clinicians, for example), may also experience difficulties in measuring technical quality due to a lack of published data on expected outcomes.

Efforts to monitor and control technical quality have been exercised through the introduction of league tables, clinical governance and the creation of bodies such as the National Institute for Clinical Effectiveness (NICE) and the Clinical Standards Board for Scotland and the Health Technology Board (Scotland). The external validation of technical standards within the service, coupled by clearer accountability frameworks and the existing developmental and regulatory roles of professional associations such as the Royal Colleges and the BMA, is expected to ensure that consistency and high standards of technical performance are achieved and maintained.

The second quality dimension is that of functional quality, i.e. '...the way in which the technical quality – the outcome or end result of the process – is transferred...' (Grönroos, 2000: 64). In other words, *how* the patient receives the service. This may include the way in which a patient (and his or her family/carer) is spoken to, the time required to wait in the reception area, the availability of information and the clarity of that information (spoken or written), the ease with which the patient is moved from the ward to the operating theatre, the presence (or absence) of delays during their stay in hospital or visit to the GP surgery and so forth.

Evaluation of functional quality is not so easily done objectively (Grönroos, 2000), however, organisations such as the King's Fund, along with bodies such as the Scottish Health Advisory Service and the Health Councils, are making ongoing efforts to develop audit and benchmarking tools and systems which can more readily measure functional quality. (Aspects of measuring service quality are discussed in more depth in Chapter 7).

The challenge to the service provider therefore is to design services in a way that combines the benefits of a systematic approach to delivery yet which allows for, measures and controls the necessary degree of variability all the time ensuring that the quality of technical and functional quality is not compromised. One 'tool' which can aid this process is discussed below.

Care pathways

One increasingly common approach to managing the health service process is the use of care pathways (Campbell *et al.*, 1998). Care pathways are 'structured multi-disciplinary care plans which detail essential steps in the care of patients with a specific clinical problem'. They set out the 'typical' patient journey, identifying clinical interventions, the input of staff, and expected outcomes at certain points in the pathway. The intention is that they encourage the application of national guidelines in a local context, tailored to local circumstances. Pathways are effectively blueprints for particular conditions that allow a systematic approach to collecting and analysing clinical data that can subsequently be used in clinical audit, demonstrating clinical effectiveness and service redesign (Campbell *et al.*, 1998; Kitchiner and Bundred, 1998 and Thomson *et al.*, 1995). Based on clinical guidelines they are intended to assist clinicians and patients in decisions about patient treatment and to find a balance between national and local practice and between guidance versus command or instruction.

A key tenet of ICPs is that within the pathway there must be scope for variance from the pathway according to individual patient need. An ICP for palliative pain management, for example, may allow for variances due to the patient's inability to tolerate medication, the drug being unavailable, or insufficient diet and fluid intake. The ICP then becomes an important mechanism for combining consistency and best practice with variation according to patient need. Furthermore, since variances must be recorded, the baseline patient data can be readily used for clinical audit and for evaluation and ongoing development of the ICP.

The design process

So far this chapter has discussed the significance of design for service organisations, in particular the NHS, and has explored essential characteristics of the nature of services and the context within which they are designed. What remains then is the question of how the design process can best be managed, what skills it involves and what all this may mean for the NHS.

The 'rational planning' approach to design

Managing the design of a new service involves all the steps and processes needed to take an idea and develop it through to a fully deliverable service. Models of the process typically identify seven key stages (Jenkins *et al.*, 1997; Cooper, 1999) involving: development of a new product strategy; idea generation; screening/evaluation of product concept; full business case and specification; (prototype) development; testing and evaluation; and product launch. This process is often seen as one which yields to, and benefits from, a formalised and structured approach, something Brown and Eisenhardt (1995) refer to as the 'rational plan perspective'. This approach stresses the need to be highly disciplined in the way in which decisions are made, to establish clear milestones along the way, and to ensure that 'stop/go' decisions are made regularly during the process (see, for example, Cooper, 1999; Maffin *et al.*, 1997). The product/service criteria need to be clarified at the outset so that managers can decide whether or not to proceed with the design at each decision 'gate'. Successful NPD/NSD is often attributed to careful planning and efficient execution, coupled with a well-coordinated, cross-functional team that is supported by senior management. Good leadership is also crucial. Product champions have been found to play a key role within this process, as they live with the new product/service idea from conception to launch, control the resources deployed in the product/service development process, and manage the product/service development team.

The benefits of a 'rational planning perspective' have been widely discussed in relationship to both the NPD process and other organisational processes and activities, in particular strategic planning (see for example Ansoff, 1965; Mintzberg, 1990, 1994). Rational planning offers a systematic approach to decision-making, with defined rationale for decision-making, formal recognition of resource requirements, consonance with the organisation's strategic plan and clearly stated objectives and targets that result in a planned approach to implementation.

The 'emergent' approach to design

Whilst the rational planning approach has much to offer, there are limitations to this approach that need to be borne in mind here. As this chapter has already discussed the context within which design takes place is fraught with complexities. Changes in political leadership of the NHS and the ramifications this presents in terms of changing policies, organisational leadership and direction create a climate of constant flux and uncertainty. NHS service providers are organisations in which there are historically embedded cultures, subcultures, practices and routines that can be difficult to challenge. Yet new modes of service delivery may require evolutions in the roles managers and clinicians play and in the development of new philosophies and cultures.

These structures, practices and cultures represent complex systems of behaviour. Shaping behaviours (both those involved in design and those involved in the delivery of new services) becomes an issue not just of manipulating the structures within the organisation, changing people's roles and titles or issuing policy statements on new codes of practice, but rather understanding the fundamental 'internal models, i.e. the unstated models or rules that guide behaviour (Miller *et al.*, 1998; Stacey, 2000).

This type of uncertainty, complexity and fluidity does not lend itself to a planned approach, but more to a crafted and emergent approach (Mintzberg, 1994), where evolving dynamics of the social environment need to be crafted together with the service requirements in a way which is continually informed by the organisational and broader (micro and macro) environments.

Design also needs to be understood and approached as an incremental and adaptive approach to problem solving (Quinn, 1980) in which the stages of the design process are commonly iterative rather than sequential. Managing, or crafting, becomes a process of learning through making sense of, and synthesising (Mintzberg, 1994), information and events in the organisation and its environment (see also Fischbacher and Smith, 2001).

In practice, the challenge to service designers is to find an appropriate balance between a planned and a crafted approach. Studies suggest that non-adoption of a formal approach to new product development is a key contributor to product failure, so there is clearly some role for systematic approaches to design. At the same time, however, flexibility, iteration and emergence are also important. BPR, for example, is based on a systematic methodology yet by virtue of being an approach for business transformation, engages in the complex social and political processes also characteristic of the design context.

Engaging with stakeholders

Regardless of the degree of planning or crafting in the design process, service designers need to find an appropriate mechanism for engaging with a range of different players – stakeholders – as the Community Hospital case study demonstrated. The potential range of stakeholders can be considerable and their input may be required at different stages of the design process (Fischbacher and Francis, 1999) for identifying key service design criteria, ensuring that the service is integrated across all the key areas, and for ownership of, and compliance with, new service delivery requirements (Baker and Hart, 1999; Fischbacher and Francis, 1999; and Dougherty and Hardy, 1996).

A strategic approach to NHS service design

This chapter began by setting out the strategic significance of design, and concludes by setting out a strategic approach to design. Since the process of design transcends a range of layers within the organisation, it must be understood as a matter not only of service level strategy but also of organisational strategy. NHS organisations need to take account of how to create and manage a context that encourages innovation. This includes the development of appropriate structures, incentives and knowledge creation processes, as well as the organisation's approach to managing the resources and developing the capabilities within which design is embedded.

There are already some building blocks in place for this. Trusts often have an R&D function which helps shape and fund its research activities. However, there is often a lack of clarity about how the R&D department contributes to developing a research and development culture. The importance of creating learning organisations also features in the minds of policy makers and practitioners, and is a recognised component of the move towards evidence-based decision-making. The challenge, therefore, is to develop feedback processes which enable the organisation to learn from service development experiences, and to replicate best practice throughout the organisation. The NHS will also need to tackle the issue of allowing organisational slack in terms of staff time, equipment and finance. This is particularly difficult in a resource-stretched service and where annual efficiency targets need to be met yet, if there is no slack, managers will become focused on short-term performance and efficiency at the expense of longer-term investment and development (Nohria and Gulati, 1996).

The need to understand and manage in a network of integrated public, private and voluntary sector provision is well-recognised. When applied in the context of design, this means that health service organisations need to have a design strategy that draws on a network of inputs and designs services which integrate effectively with other players in the network.

References

Alford, J. (2000) 'The Implications of 'Publicness' for Strategic Management Theory' in Johnson, G. and Scholes, K. (eds) *Exploring Public Sector Strategy*, Financial Times/Prentice Hall: Harlow, England.

Allen, P. (2000) 'Accountability for Clinical Governance: Developing Collective Responsibility for Quality in Primary Care', *BMJ* 321: 608–11.

Amabile, T. M., Conti, R., Coon, H., Lazenby, J. and Herron, M. (1996) 'Assessing the Work Environment for Creativity', *Academy of Management Journal* 39(5): 1154–84.

Ansoff, H. I. (1965) *Corporate Strategy*, New York: McGraw-Hill.

Baker, M. and Hart, S. (1999) *Product Strategy and Management*, Prentice Hall: London.

Brown, S. L. and Eisenhardt, K. M. (1995) 'Product Development: Past Research, Present Findings and Future Directions', *Academy of Management Review* 20(2): 343–78.

Burgelman, R. (1983) 'Corporate entrepreneurship and strategic management: Insights from a process study', *Management Science* 29: 1349–63.

Campbell, H., Hotchkiss, R., Bradshaw, N. and Porteous, M. (1998) 'Integrated care pathways', *BMJ* 316: 133–7.

Cohen, W. M. and Levinthal. D. A. (1990) 'Absorptive Capacity: A New Perspective on Learning and Innovation', *Administrative Science Quarterly* 35: 128–52.

Cooper, R. G. (1999) *Product Leadership: Creating and Launching Superior New Products*, Perseus Books: Cambridge MA.

Crosby, P. B. (1989) *Let's Talk Quality*, McGraw-Hill: New York.

Davies, H. T. O., Mannion, R. and Marshall, M. N. (2001) 'Treading a Third Way for Quality in Health Care', *Public Money & Management* April–June, 6–7.

Dean, C. and Freeman, H. (eds) (1993) *Community Mental Health Care: International Perspectives on Making it Happen*, Gaskell and The Centre for Mental Health Services Development: London.

Dean, C., Phillips, J., Gadd, E. M., Joseph, M. and England, S. (1993) 'Comparison of Community Based Service with Hospital Based Service for People with Acute, Severe Psychiatric Illness', *BMJ* 307: 473–6.

Department of Health (2001) 'Assuring the Quality of Medical Practice: Implementing' in *Supporting Doctors, Protecting Patients*, London: Department of Health.

Dougherty, D. (1992) 'A Practice-Centred Model of Organizational Renewal Through Product Innovation', *Strategic Management Journal* 13: 77–92.

Dougherty, D. and Hardy, C. (1996) 'Sustained Product Innovation in Large, Mature Organizations: Overcoming Innovation-to-Organization Problems', *Academy of Management Journal* 39(5): 1120–53.

Drazin, R. and Schoonhoven, C. B. (1996) 'Community, Population, and Organization Effects on Innovation: A Multilevel Perspective', *Academy of Management Journal* 39(5): 1065–83.

Dreyfus, H. (1976) *Designing for People*, New York: Paragraphic Books.

Edvardsson, B. (1992) 'Service Breakdowns: A Study of Critical Incidents in an Airline', *International Journal of Service Industry Management* 3(4): 17–29.

Edvardsson, B. and Olsson, J. (1996) 'Key Concepts for New Service Development', *The Service Industries Journal* 16(2): 140–64.

Enthoven, A. (2000) 'Modernising the NHS', *BMJ* 320: 1329–31.

Fischbacher, M. and Francis, A. (1999) 'Managing the Design of Health Care Services' in Davies, H. T. O., Tavakoli, M., Malek, M. and Neilson, A. (eds) *Managing Quality: Strategic Issues in Health Care Management*, Ashgate Publishing: Aldershot.

Fischbacher, M. and Smith, A. M. (2001) 'Creating a Design Strategy: The Complexity of the New Service Development Process', *International Journal of New Product Development and Innovation Management* 3(1): 59–77.

Francis, D. (1987) *Unblocking Organisational Communication*, Gower: Aldershot.

Frost, P. J. and Egri, C. P. (1990) 'Influence of Political Action on Innovation: Part I', *Leadership and Organizational Development Journal* 11(1): 17–25.

Graziano, A. M. (1969) 'Clinical Innovation and the Mental Health Power Structure: A Social Case History', *American Psycologist* 24(1): 10–18.

Grönroos, C. (1990) *Service Management and Marketing. Managing the Moments of Truth in Service Competition*, Lexington Books: Lexington, MA.

Grönroos, C. (2000) *Service Management and Marketing: a Customer Relationship Management Approach*, John Wiley & Sons Ltd: Chichester.

Hakansson, H., and Johanson, J. (1993) 'The Network as a Governance Structure: Interfirm Cooperation Beyond Markets and Hierarchies', in Grabher, G. (ed.) *The Embedded Firm: On the Socioeconomics of Industrial Networks*, Routledge: London.

Hammer, M. (1990) 'Reengineering Work: Don't Automate, Obliterate', *Harvard Business Review* July–August, 104–12.

Henry, J. and Walker, D. (eds) (1991) *Managing Innovation*, SAGE Publishing: London.

Hollins, G. and Hollins, B. (1991) *Total Design: Managing the Design Process in the Service Sector*, Pitman Publishing: London.

Holzer, M. (1997) 'Productivity and Quality Management' in Shafritz, J. M. and Hyde, A. C. (eds) *Classics of Public Administration*, 4th edn, Fort Worth: Harcourt Brace.

Jenkins, S., Forbes, S., Durrani, T. S. and Banerjee, S. K. (1997) 'Managing the product development process – (Part I: an assessment)', *International Journal of Technology Management* 13(4): 359–78.

Jones, C., Hesterly, W. S., Borgatti, S. P. (1997) 'A General Theory of Network Governance: Exchange Conditions and Social Mechanisms', *Academy of Management Review* 22(4): 911–45.

Juran, J. M. (1992) *Juran on Quality by Design – The New Steps for Planning Quality into Goods and Services*. The Free Press: New York.

Kanter, R.M. (1983) *The Changemasters*, Simon & Schuster: New York.

Kitchiner, D. and Bundred, P. (1998) 'Integrated Care Pathways Increase use of Guidelines', *BMJ* 317: 147.

Laing, A. (2000) 'Eastland Case Study' A Case Study Developed from the Scottish Executive Health Department Multi-Disciplinary Primary Care Leadership Programme, Department of Management Studies, University of Aberdeen.

Leonard-Barton, D. (1995) *Wellsprings of Knowledge: Building and Sustaining the Sources of Innovation*, Harvard Business School Press: Boston.

Maffin, D., Thwaites, A., Alderman, N., Braiden, P. and Hills, B. (1997) 'Managing the Product Development Process: Combining Best Practice with Company and Project Contexts', *Technology Analysis and Strategic Management*, 9(1): 53–74.

Miller W. L., Crabtree, B. F., McDaniel, R. and Stange, K. C. (1998) 'Understanding Change in Primary Care Practice Using Complexity Theory', *The Journal of Family Practice* 46(5): 369–76.

Mintzberg, H. (1990) 'The Design School: Reconsidering the Basic Premises of Strategic Management', *Strategic Management Journal* 11: 171–95.

Mintzberg, H. (1994) 'The Fall and Rise of Strategic Planning', *Harvard Business Review* January–February, 107–14.

Navaratnam, K. K. and Harris, B. (1995) 'Quality Process Analysis: A Technique for Management in the Public Sector', *Managing Service Quality* 5(3): 23.

NHS Estates (1993) *Health Facilities Notes: Design for Patient-focused Care*, London: HMSO Health Facilities Note 01.

Monge, P. R., Cozzens, M. D. and Contractor, N. S. (1992) 'Communication and motivational predictors of the dynamics of organizational innovation', *Organizational Science* (3): 250–74.

Nohria, N. and Gulati, R. (1996) 'Is Slack Good or Bad for Innovation?', *Academy of Management Journal* 39(5): 1245–64.

Nonaka, I., Takeuchi, H., and Umemoto, K. (1996) 'A Theory of Organizational Knowledge Creation', *International Journal of Technology Management* 11(7/8): 833–45.

Nonaka, I., Reinmoeller, P. and Senoo, D. (1998) 'The 'ART' of Knowledge: Systems to Capitalize on Market Knowledge', *European Management Journal* (16)6: 673–84.

Newman, K. (1997) 'Re-engineering for Service Quality: The Case of Leicester Royal Infirmary', *Total Quality Management* 8(5): 255–64.

Papanek, V. (1984) *Design for the Real World: Human Ecology and Social Change*, 2nd edn, Thames and Hudson Ltd: London.

Pahl, G., Beitz, W. and Wallace, K. (1984) *Engineering Design*, Design Council: London.

Penrose, E. (1997) 'The Theory of the Growth of the Firm' (Extract from Edith Penrose, The Theory of the Growth of the Firm (OUP 3rd edn., 1995) in N. J. Foss (ed.) *Resources Firms and Strategies*, 1st edn Oxford Management Readers: Oxford.

Pisano, G. (1996) *The Development Factory. Unlocking the Potential of Process Innovation: Lessons from Pharmaceuticals and Biotechnology*, Harvard Business School Press: Boston.

Prahalad, C. K. and Hamel, G. (1990) 'The Core Competence of the Corporation' *Harvard Business Review* May–June, 79–91.

Pugh, S. and Morley, I. E. (1988) *Total Design: Towards a Theory of Total Design*, University of Strathclyde: Glasgow.

Quinn, J. B. (1980) *Strategies for Change: Logical Incrementalism*, Irwin: Homewood, IL.

Sears, H. (1994) 'Geared up for Re-engineering', *Nursing Management* 1(5): 25–6.

Scottish Executive Health Department (1997) *Designed to Care: Renewing the National Health Service in Scotland*, The Scottish Office Department of Health: Edinburgh.

Shostack, G. L. (1982) 'How to Design a Service', *European Journal of Marketing* 16(1): 140–64.

Shostack, G. L. (1984) 'Designing Services that Deliver', *Harvard Business Review* January–February, 133–9.

Smith, J. (2001) 'Redesigning Health Care', *BMJ* 322: 1257–8.

Stacey, R. D. (2000) *Strategic Management and Organisational Dynamics: The Challenge of Complexity*, 3rd edn, Prentice Hall: Harlow.

Storey, C. and Easingwood, C. J. (1999) 'Types of New Product Performance: Evidence from the Consumer Financial Services Sector', *Journal of Business Research* 46: 193–203.

Stuart, F. I. (1998) 'The Influence of Organizational Culture and Internal Politics on New Service Design and Introduction', *International Journal of Service Industry Management* 9(5): 469–85.

Thomson, R., Lavender, M. and Madhok, R. (1995) 'Fortnightly Review: How to Ensure that Guidelines are Effective', *BMJ* 311: 237–42.

Tidd, J., Bessant, J. and Pavitt, K. (1997) *Integrating Technological, Market and Orgnizational Change*, Wiley: Chichester.

Trott, P. (1998) *Innovation Management and New Product Development*, Financial Times/ Prentice Hall: Harlow.

Verona, G. (1999) 'A Resource-Based View of Product Development', *Academy of Management Review* 24(1): 132–42.

Warner, M. (1997) *Re-designing Health Services. Reducing the Zone of Delusion*, The Nuffield Trust: London.

Wernerfelt, B. (1984) 'A Resource-based View of the Firm', *Strategic Management Journal* 5: 171–80.

Notes

[1] The terms design and new product development are often used interchangeably in the literature and will be used in this way here.

3 Service structure: Understanding inter-organisational relationships and networks

Introduction

The design and delivery of health care within modern health systems is concerned to a significant degree with the management of a complex set of inter-organisational and inter-professional relationships. This reflects the increasing scope and complexity of the demands confronting modern health care organisations, the addressing of which extends beyond the boundaries of the individual organisation or profession. A key ongoing challenge facing health policy makers and managers is hence to develop effective mechanisms to manage – that is, coordinate and structure – these relationships and achieve what Klein (1994) referred to as the seamless delivery of care. Indeed the successive reforms and reorganisations of the NHS have to a significant extent been concerned with the reconfiguring of these relationships, with the objective of enhancing both the effectiveness and efficiency of service delivery. The NHS, in common with the health systems of other post-industrial economies, has consequently been characterised by the introduction of alternative structural arrangements or governance mechanisms at the system level, that is, hierarchical, market- and network-based models of organisational governance, in pursuit of the goal of improved health care delivery (EHMA, 1998).

Reflecting the centrality of inter-organisational relationships to the delivery of health care, understanding the nature and dynamics of such complex relationships is critical to the effective management of health care services from the initial design through to the delivery of services to the end user. Drawing on managerial, sociological and economic perspectives, this chapter will examine the nature and evolving dynamics of inter-organisational relationships in the NHS. Central to this is the examination of market- and network-based models of organisational governance, and the dynamics of relationships under such macro level governance frameworks. Examining such inter-organisational relationships within the context of predominantly competitive (market) and collaborative (network) policy regimes, the chapter considers the importance of broader organisational, professional and social networks in shaping patterns of organisational behaviour and inter-organisational interactions. Utilising this base, the chapter concludes with an examination of the relevance of conceptualisations of inter-organisational relationships derived from both public and private sector contexts in understanding the management of inter-organisational relationships in the delivery of health care. Collectively this provides the conceptual basis for the detailed examination of the structuring of service delivery within the NHS in Chapter 4.

Hierarchies, markets and networks: approaches to the organisation of health care

The complexity of modern health care delivery in terms of the need for effective integration raises fundamental challenges for policy-makers seeking to enhance both the efficiency and effectiveness of publicly funded health care systems. Consequently health care systems in post-industrial economies have witnessed near continuous structural change over the past two decades, as governments have sought to improve the delivery of health care in line with the increasing expectations of their population (Ranade, 1998; Powell, 1999). Against this backdrop in the United Kingdom the NHS has witnessed an evolutionary shift from being a monolithic internalised professional bureaucracy to being a decentralised grouping of separate managerially-led organisations, operating initially within a competitive market environment and subsequently within a collaborative network environment. That is the NHS, reflecting prevailing ideologies, has been portrayed as having been successively reorganised from a hierarchical organisation to a market based system to a network. Although this analysis has been challenged as too simplistic in that the NHS was never a conventional hierarchy, was never completely marketised and is unlikely to evolve into a network (Exworthy *et al.*, 1999), this distinction in the ideal type of organisational arrangement provides a valuable point of departure for examining the relevance of alternative approaches to the organisation of health care, that is, the role of alternative governance structures.

While the focus of this chapter is on the management of inter-organisational relationships under market and network policy contexts, in
attempting to understand the nature and dynamics of such relationships it is necessary to consider, albeit briefly, the nature of hierarchical
governance structures, given that the introduction of market governance was a response to the perceived failure of hierarchical governance within the NHS.

The concept of governance can be described as the processes and
mechanisms through which social coordination or order is established
within a society (Kooiman, 1993). Governance is not, however, solely a
political concept, but rather is equally concerned with the coordination
and ordering of economic activity (Rhodes, 1997). Reflecting this
economic dimension, a key function of governance mechanisms has been
seen as the organisation and allocation of economic resources (Scitovsky,
1992). The debate on governance structures has consequently revolved
to a significant degree around the relative efficiency of alternative mechanisms in coordinating economic activity, with the issue of transaction
costs being central to that debate. The early work of transactional
economists such as Williamson (1975, 1983) identified hierarchies and
markets as distinct ideal type governance or coordination mechanisms in
terms of the transaction costs incurred under each structure. A central
criticism of such analysis was that by concentrating exclusively on the
costs of transaction, the importance of social ties in shaping behaviour
was discounted, with such analysis offering an 'under-socialised' view of
market behaviour (Granovetter, 1985). The resultant intersection of
transaction cost economics and social network theory have seen the identification of a third ideal type governance mechanism, the network. As
such, the governance debate conceptually currently revolves around the
hierarchy, market and network distinction (Thorelli, 1986; Thompson *et
al.*, 1991), although the precise relationship between hierarchies,
markets and networks is open to conjecture. Operationally, the pursuit
of a 'third way' between markets on the one hand and hierarchies on the
other is central to the Labour government's reform of the public sector
from the late 1990s (Kirkpatrick, 1999). In understanding the organisation and delivery of health care, it is valuable to briefly highlight the key
features of each ideal type mechanism and the interrelationship between
these alternative organisational arrangements.

Hierarchies

Hierarchies are conventionally characterised by highly centralised decision-making and resource allocation processes, together with the existence of complex bureaucratic structures to implement such decisions.

The term 'command and control' is often used as shorthand to describe the effective operation of hierarchical structures. Within a hierarchy the autonomy of actors, both individuals and subsidiary units, is severely circumscribed, reflecting the existence of a direct employment relationship between the individual and the organisation. Reflecting this relationship, coordination within hierarchies is undertaken on the basis of bureaucratic routine and direct administrative control (Lowndes and Skelcher, 1998). While offering the benefit of direct control, hierarchies are increasingly viewed as stifling innovation due to the predominating emphasis on adherence to formal procedures and routines (Harrison, 1993). Public sector organisations in the United Kingdom, such as the NHS, have conventionally been viewed as archetypal hierarchical organisations (Ferlie and Pettigrew, 1996). The salient characteristics of hierarchies as governance mechanisms are outlined in Table 3.1.

Markets

In discussions of governance arrangements, the concept of market governance is usually defined in terms of neo-classical models of markets and market behaviour (Ferlie, 1992). Market governance is consequently anchored in concepts of exchange and competition, with price being the critical mechanism determining behaviour and through which the allocation of resources is determined. Contractual relationships between actors are thus the central characteristic of market-based governance. Central to the debate over the relative merits of hierarchical and market governance is the tension between adaptability and co-ordination. Whereas markets under the neo-classical paradigm are characterised by high levels of adaptability, they are equally characterised by low levels of coordination

Table 3.1 **Characteristics of governance mechanisms**

	Hierarchy	**Network**	**Market**
Normative basis	Employment	Complementarity	Contractual
Actor options	Dependent	Interdependent	Independent
Atmosphere	Formal, bureaucratic	Open, mutual benefits	Suspicion, measurability
Commitment	Medium	High	Low
Level of flexibility	Low	Medium	High
Communication	Procedures	Relationships	Prices
Conflict handling	Administrative control	Reciprocity	Litigation

Adapted from Powell, 1991

(Bradach and Eccles, 1991). In understanding market governance it is critical, however, to recognise the existence of alternative conceptualisations of markets and market behaviour derived from sociological, managerial and other strands of economic research (Ford, 1997). By placing emphasis on the centrality of long-term socially embedded relationships in shaping market behaviour these alternative perspectives on markets fundamentally alter the way in which markets as governance mechanisms may be understood. The salient characteristics of markets as governance mechanisms are outlined in Table 3.1.

Networks

The growing interest in networks as a mode of governance reflects the emerging critique of both hierarchies and markets as governance mechanisms. Anchored in shared objectives, networks are characterised by a web of interdependent relationships between organisations based on trust, loyalty and reciprocal exchange. Thompson *et al.* (1991) argue that whereas administrative control is the coordinating mechanism in a hierarchy and price fulfils that role in markets, trust and cooperation are the key drivers of networks. Perspectives, however, differ as to whether networks constitute a distinct form of governance in its own right (Podolny and Page, 1998) or whether they are a hybrid form of coordination and organisation lying in the intermediate area between hierarchies and markets (Miles and Snow, 1996). Either way, it is evident that within public sector settings networks are perceived to offer a viable alternative to the polar extremes of hierarchies and markets as a basis for managing inter-organisational relationships, what has politically been articulated as the 'third way'. The salient characteristics of networks as governance mechanisms are outlined in Table 3.1.

In understanding the management and organisation of health care delivery at the macro level it is critical to recognise that these ideal type governance mechanisms are not mutually exclusive. Rather they may coexist both spatially and temporally (Flynn, 1997). Bradach and Eccles (1991) highlight the mixed modes of governance which occur in various organisational settings, for example the existence of status hierarchies in professional networks, the role of personal relationships in markets, and internal trading structures in hierarchies. Similarly Exworthy *et al.* (1999) argue in their critique of the conventional 'hierarchy to market to network' portrayal of change in the NHS that the marketisation occurring under the Conservative government in fact witnessed a strengthening of hierarchical control and the emergence of nascent network structures alongside the introduction of market structures.

Not only do such alternative ideal type governance mechanisms coexist within health care systems, but evidence from both the United

Kingdom and the Netherlands (Laing and Cotton, 1995; Boonekamp, 1994) suggests that the formal distinction between market and network based models of governance may in fact disguise significant commonality in the management of inter-organisational relationships under both policy regimes. This reflects the broader ongoing debate concerning the status of networks as a governance mechanism. Consequently the structural arrangements under which modern health care is delivered are significantly more complex than such ideal type models of governance would suggest, with the management of inter-organisational relationships being a particularly complex and critical aspect of health care delivery. In attempting to understand the process of health care management from service design through to delivery, it is necessary to examine the dynamics and operation of markets and networks in health care, and in turn the relationship between these two forms of governance.

Understanding markets in health care

The rationale for the introduction of a quasi-market mechanism into the NHS was outlined in Chapter 1, as were the key structural features of the resultant internal market. It is within this context that the nature of health care markets will be examined from a range of conceptual perspectives. Focusing on the rationale for the creation of the internal market in the NHS it is readily apparent, as Ferlie (1992) observed, that neo-classical economic theory enjoyed what amounted to virtually unchallenged intellectual primacy in shaping public policy during the 1980s and early 1990s. Inevitably given such intellectual hegemony the core tenets of neo-classical economic theory were to be massively influential in shaping the quasi-market structures and regulations developed within public sector services such as the NHS. Yet neo-classical economic theory offers only one perspective on, one understanding of, the nature and operations of markets and market behaviour. Indeed the neo-classical conceptualisation of markets has attracted trenchant criticism from emerging branches of economic theory (Williamson, 1983; 1991), sociology (Granovetter, 1985; 1992) and management (Hakansson, 1982; Ford, 1997). To arrive at any judgement on the performance of markets as a governance mechanism within health care, it is necessary to look beyond this single conceptualisation of the market to alternative perspectives on markets which may offer a more realistic understanding of the dynamics and operation of health care markets.

Economic orthodoxy: neo-classical perspectives on markets

Within mainstream neo-classical economic theory markets are perceived to be the most efficient means by which the allocation of economic resources can be coordinated between alternative demands. Specifically price, and in particular changes in price, determine the relative allocation of resources, with prices adjusting in line with demand to ensure that scare resources are allocated to the production of those goods and services demanded by society. Within this process, competition between alternative suppliers is viewed as the vital stimulus for efficiency in that resources, through contractual arrangements between buyers and sellers, will flow to efficient producers at the expense of inefficient suppliers of comparable goods (Scitovsky, 1992). The market is, as such, a neutral, dispassionate set of structural arrangements through which competition and prices determine patterns of production. Patterns of market behaviour may thus be viewed as being essentially determined by information on product price and quality, with producers constantly being forced to improve product value by the threat of purchasers switching contracts to alternative suppliers in pursuit of a superior value offer. The market is consequently a highly dynamic environment where change rather than stability is the norm.

Such a conceptualisation of markets, and hence market behaviour, is underpinned by a number of key assumptions (Hakansson, 1982). First, there are assumed to be a large number of competing suppliers, with suppliers constantly entering and exiting the market in response to prevailing market conditions. Similarly there are multiple buyers operating within the market, with buyers effectively competing for suppliers resources. Second, the behaviour of both parties, i.e. the buyers and sellers, is assumed to be motivated by their desire to maximise their individual benefit or 'utility'. This is typically framed in terms of the goal of profit maximisation. Associated with both of these assumptions is the existence of arm's-length adversarial relationships between buyers and sellers, mediated through formal contracts, reflecting the neutral nature of the market mechanism. Third both buyers and sellers are assumed to have complete and equal access to information on the price and quality of products. A key consequence of this assumption of the free availability of information is that buyers, but particularly sellers, incur minimal transaction costs in negotiating contracts. It has been argued that the competitive model of contracting introduced into the NHS was underpinned by such neo-classical assumptions (Mackintosh, 1993; Lapsley 1994), and that the widely reported problems associated with contracting and commissioning arrangements (Jebb, 1992; Carter, 1993) were primarily a result of such arrangements being anchored in an inappropriate conceptualisation of markets and market behaviour in health care.

Indeed it is readily apparent from successive studies that the operation of the internal market in the NHS did not resemble such a neo-classical model (Appleby *et al.*, 1993; Ranade, 1995; Flynn *et al.*, 1996). Typically there were few if any competing suppliers in a locality. Moreover, because of the high investment costs associated with service provision in the majority of medical specialties new suppliers were unlikely to move into the market. Such oligopolistic patterns of service provision were mirrored in the organisation of purchasing with there being a limited number of purchasers in any locality, a process which was accentuated by the development of group-based purchasing (Laing and Cotton, 1997). Together with the high degree of loyalty shown by the majority purchasers towards their existing suppliers, as a result of concerns about local service availability and the strength of professional relationships, these factors collectively limited the dynamism of the market. The internal market was thus characterised by stability rather than change, with change only occurring at the margins (Light, 1997). This stability was further accentuated by the poor provision of information on prices and quality by providers (Carter, 1993) and the ongoing high levels of government regulation given the political consequences of radical changes in patterns of contracting (James, 1997).

In reviewing the operation of quasi-markets in the public sector more broadly, Propper (1993) suggested that the operation of such markets was characterised by a number of common failures. These perceived failures included:

1. The existence of an imbalance of information between purchasers and providers;
2. The existence of barriers to new suppliers entering the market;
3. That evidence concerning service outcomes and performance was vague or uncertain;
4. Structural weaknesses with the organisation of the contracting process;
5. Doubts over the ability of purchasers to act effectively as the agents of service users;
6. Concerns over user empowerment and public accountability.

The first three of these perceived failures are characterised by Propper as representing fundamental 'market failures'. However, to define these issues as constituting 'market failures' per se is arguably to adopt an unduly narrow, and indeed inappropriate perspective, on the nature of public sector markets. Rather such outcomes may be viewed as an inevitable product of the nature of such markets, reflecting the underlying characteristics of the services being delivered, for example health or social services, and the resultant complexity of contract negotiation and management in such professional service contexts (Wistow *et al.*, 1996).

Challenging neo-classical orthodoxy: transaction cost analysis and social network theory

The dominance of neo-classical economic theory in the public policy debates of the 1980s does not presuppose that the resultant conceptualisation of markets and market behaviour is unchallenged. Alternative models of markets drawn from sociological and managerial perspectives, as well as from other branches of economic theory, provide at least equally valid conceptualisations of the function and nature of markets. Such conceptualisations are arguably of particular relevance in examining and understanding market behaviour in those public sector market, or quasi-market, contexts where the assumptions of competition and dynamism underpinning the neo-classical model of markets appear not to be valid (Ferlie, 1992; Lunt *et al.*, 1996).

Central to the critique of the conventional neo-classical conceptualisation of markets has been the challenge to the assumption of the inherent and uniform efficiency of markets, an assumption which lies at the core of mainstream neo-classical economic theory. Focusing on the costs of executing market transactions, it is argued that transactions, rather than being costless, inherently involve a variety of organisational and financial costs (Williamson, 1983; 1991). The level of such transaction costs reflects both the characteristics of the goods or services being exchanged and the structure of the market. Such transaction costs impact on the behaviour of market participants in terms of the approach to supplier selection, the extent of switching by purchasers, and the process of contract management. More broadly, the rejection of the view that market transactions are effectively costless raises fundamental questions over the universal efficiency of the market as a mechanism through which to coordinate economic activity. The central question is thus whether it is more efficient for a transaction to be undertaken externally through a market or internally through a hierarchy. Consequently under such a perspective, the appropriateness of markets as a mechanism for the coordination of economic activity in a particular field is ultimately determined by considerations of the costs inherent in market transactions relative to the costs inherent in hierarchical organisational arrangements.

Specifically, markets are perceived only to be efficient coordination mechanisms where high levels of competition exist which results in prices being forced down, where accurate market information is readily available and where there are minimal transaction costs (Le Grand and Bartlett, 1993). Where these structural market conditions are not met, market exchanges become increasingly costly and in turn inefficient, especially in market contexts where there is a need to safeguard against opportunistic behaviour through the negotiation and monitoring of detailed contracts (Kirkpatrick, 1999). This issue of the cost of contract negotiation and monitoring is particularly significant in circumstances where performance evaluation criteria are ambiguous and problematic to measure due to the characteristics of the product or service involved, as in the context of professional services. In such circumstances, many of which pertain to public sector services such as health and social care (Wistow *et al.*, 1996; Flynn *et al.*, 1996), the contracting process is likely to be complex and costly. Non-market governance mechanisms consequently offer more appropriate approaches to coordination in such circumstances.

Although the transaction cost perspective has offered a trenchant critique of the neo-classical model of markets, it remains anchored in the broader economic paradigm dominated by ideas of economically rational individualism. Reflecting this anchoring, transaction cost analysis has been challenged from a sociological perspective on the basis that it presents an 'undersocialised' view of markets and market behaviour (Granovetter, 1985). At the core of this perspective is the view that social relationships, and in turn trust, are central to exchanges between participants operating in a market. Accordingly, economic exchange cannot simply be reduced to competition among isolated, self-interested participants, but rather participants' behaviours are shaped by the network of social and professional relationships within which they operate. That is, market exchanges must be seen as socially embedded. Markets are thus not simply neutral, dispassionate mechanisms for resource allocation where participants operate at arm's length, but are highly socialised and political structures where complex webs of relationships link organisations (Granovetter and Swedberg, 1992). This conceptualisation of market behaviour fits with the view expressed by Boonekamp (1994) that the most appropriate approach to understanding health care markets is a 'socio-political' perspective that considers such markets as comprising a network of interrelated and interdependent parties. Consequently, in understanding market operation and behaviour the focus should be on the dynamics of the complex web of relationships between market participants, and in particular on the ability of such relationships to foster trust between market participants.

Trust can be viewed as the critical means by which participants seek to reduce the risk and uncertainty inherent in market exchanges (Morgan and Hunt, 1994; Selnes, 1998). That is trust can reduce the complexities, and hence risks and uncertainties associated with market exchanges, by acting as what Oliver (1997) describes as a simplification mechanism. In particular, trust, by reducing the threat of opportunistic behaviour, reduces the need to specify and monitor all possible contingencies through formal contract mechanisms. The development of long-term relationships and in turn trust is thus a critical means by which market participants are able to mediate exchanges. The role of trust as a mediating mechanism is especially pertinent in services, such as health care, where purchasers face asymmetrical access to performance information (Thakor and Kumar, 2000). This emphasis on the role of relationships and trust as a means of mediating market relationships in the sociological literature is echoed in the work of MacNeil (1985) in distinguishing between classical and relational approaches to contract law. Specifically, under conditions of uncertainty market participants move towards a relational mode of contracting where the contract is increasingly embedded in a set of social relationships. In turn it is the development of this relationship, rather than the initial formal contract, which provides the critical frame of reference in managing the interaction between the two parties.

Relational and network perspectives on markets

This emphasis on the critical role of market relationships and the concept of relational contracts is central to the developing managerial literature on market behaviour. Drawing on both transaction cost analysis and social network theory, the emergent managerial models of market behaviour are anchored in evidence of patterns of behaviour in business market environments (Ford, 1997). In such contexts, markets are commonly viewed as being characterised by a high degree of stability, extensive collaboration and mutual interdependence. Market participants develop complex long-term relationships with a limited number of suppliers, with short-term opportunistic behaviour being shunned in favour of the perceived long-term mutual benefit to be gained from such relationships. Over time these relationships evolve and deepen, becoming effectively institutionalised through the development of multiple cross-organisational links, with the associated increasing levels of inter-organisational trust reducing the costs of managing market transactions (Heide and John, 1990).

Such relational patterns of behaviour reflect the structural characteristics of business markets. The key structural characteristics include first, the relatively limited number of market participants, both buyers and sellers operating within the market, and second, the active participation of both buyers and sellers in the process of market exchange, specifically joint product development. Taken together both characteristics promote the existence of a network of strong social and professional ties between the two parties. In other words such relationships are strongly socially embedded. Third, the existence of a highly specific asset base restricts market entry and exit necessitates buyers focusing on managing their relationships with existing suppliers rather than developing relationships with new suppliers, that is switching suppliers. Finally, the requirement for long-term investment in innovation and the need for such innovation to occur downstream in the supply chain further encourages the pursuit of long-term relationships (Hakansson and Snehota, 1995).

The primary points of difference between such a relational view of markets and the conventional neo-classical conceptualisation of markets are summarised in Table 3.2.

Under the neo-classical perspective markets can be characterised as consisting of a mass of free floating atomistic actors colliding in occasional market transactions. Relational markets by contrast can be characterised as comprising complex molecular structures, that is, a number of actors locked together by a network of complex economic, social and professional bonds. Hence while the relational perspective places long-term buyer–seller relationships at the core of the market, the dynamics of the market are also shaped by the broader network of relationships in which actors are involved within the market (Araujo and Easton, 1996). These networks of market relationships have been described by Hakansson and Snehota (1995) as constituting a complex set of interconnected relations between organisations, and individuals in those organisations, which collectively form a structured system within the larger set of market actors. Such a network perspective on markets highlights the role of peripheral actors in shaping patterns of market behaviour and necessitates actors taking account of the potential impact of their behaviours on other actors within the network of which they

Table 3.2 Structural characteristics of markets

Neo-classical perspective	Relational perspective
Multiple competing buyers and sellers	Limited number of buyers and sellers
No entry or exit barriers	High entry and exit barriers – asset specificity
Maximisation of utility	Maximisation of utility may not be motivator
Perfect information	Imperfect information – information asymmetries
Zero transaction costs	Significant transaction costs

form a part. Equally such market networks provide actors with product or service information which in contexts such as health care is not readily available through formal channels, thereby providing the essential mechanism through which market exchanges are transacted. Business markets can consequently be viewed as being dominated by institutionalised networks of relationships, both inter-organisational and interpersonal, which effectively bind organisations together and preclude opportunistic patterns of behaviour.

In such market settings economic benefit, that is competitive advantage, for both sets of market participants, accrues through the creation and maintenance of collaborative relationships with a network of actors rather than through adversarial transactions with a single party (Nielson, 1996). For buyers the development of long-term collaborative relationships reduces transaction costs, both in terms of the initial evaluation of suppliers and subsequent monitoring of delivery. At the same time such relationships enable buyers to integrate suppliers into the process of product or service innovation, thereby enhancing quality. Similarly for sellers such relationship development offers the secure income stream necessary for investment in maintaining their technological base. Moreover, relationship specific investment by ensuring that the supplier delivers a unique, tailored product reduces the risk of the buyer switching to an alternative supplier. For both parties a situation of bilateral, even multilateral dependence (Bolton *et al.,* 1994) emerges, which when coupled to the increasing socio-professional links between staff in both parties, results in a progressive deepening of inter-organisational relationships. Central to this perspective on market behaviour is the dynamic and evolutionary nature of inter-organisational relationships, both at the dyadic buyer–seller level and at the network level.

As highlighted in the preceding discussion of the neo-classical perspective on markets, health care markets do not correspond in terms of either structure or patterns of behaviour to the neo-classical ideal. By contrast evidence from the operation of the NHS internal market suggests that health care markets correspond to the relational perspective on markets, with the structural characteristics of such markets meaning that the development of a relational approach to contracting is the rational approach for market participants to adopt. In particular health care markets exhibit a high degree of interdependence between participants. Both service providers and purchasers are surrounded by a number of stakeholders with whom they will have to work over the longer term (Boonekamp, 1994). In other words many market relationships in health care are in fact predetermined in that there are only a limited number of alternatives, forcing the focus of market activity to be concerned with the maintenance of such relationships. This pattern of behaviour is reinforced by health care markets being geographically constrained.

In health care this imperative for the development of long-term relationships is further strengthened by the core characteristics of such services. Specifically professional services like health care are characterised, *inter alia*, by high levels of intangibility, heterogeneity and inseparability (Shostack, 1977). Professional services are intangible in that they have no physical dimension (Parasuraman *et al.*, 1985). Rather services are performances that can be experienced only when they are delivered. Heterogeneity refers to the problem of achieving standardisation, or homogeneity, in the delivery of professional services. With services being performed by autonomous professionals, each service delivery episode is unique. This is accentuated by the production and consumption of services being inseparable, that is, the buyer is directly involved in the production of the service (Sheth and Parvatiyar, 1995).

Collectively these characteristics fundamentally impact on the ability of buyers to evaluate professional services. In examining the purchasing of professional services Ziethaml *et al.* (1990) use the term 'credence services' to describe such services. For buyers credence services present the problem that such services cannot be evaluated prior to purchase. Indeed, service performance may be impossible to evaluate even after consumption, due to both the technical complexity of such services and the long-term nature of such service outcomes. Professional services consequently constitute high-risk purchases in that conventional informational approaches to risk reduction are of only limited value. Critically, organisational buyers face similar complexities as consumers purchasing such services (Hart and Hogg, 1998; Laing and Lian, 2001). Confronted with such characteristics, buyers place reliance on the development of long-term relationships with service providers as a means of reducing the risk associated with purchasing professional services (Thakor and Kumar, 2000). Alongside such long-term buyer seller–relationships, buyers also rely on broader market networks to provide second-hand experiential evaluation of service providers as a basis on which to select professional service providers.

It is evident from the preceding discussion that markets can thus embrace different types of exchange format, and that markets are not uniformly characterised by exploitative and opportunistic patterns of behaviour based on short-term profit objectives. Moreover in many settings, such as health care, there are clear economic and managerial arguments which promote relational patterns of behaviour and indeed collaboration within inter-organisational networks, rather than competition between autonomous organisations. The prevailing pattern of market behaviour in any market environment is ultimately the product of the dynamic balance between the relative benefits of competitive and cooperative behaviour to the market participants. The balance between competition and cooperation is, however, fundamentally influenced by the nature of the prevailing regulatory regime within that market context. Consequently the management of markets at the policy level is concerned primarily with developing the 'rules of the game' under which inter-organisational relationships develop.

Understanding networks in health care

The conventional neo-classical perspective on value was that value creation is a zero sum game being generated through an adversarial pattern of market behaviour, with buyers playing sellers off against one another in pursuit of organisational advantage. However, there has been an increasing shift towards the idea that value actually emanates from long-term relationships and single sourcing (Gadde, 1999). The logical next step to creating value, according to Campbell and Wilson (1996), is combining resources synergistically to provide improved performance or lower costs. Such synergistic combinations would take the form of directed networks that are specifically created to produce unique value packages. It is within this evolving context that the nature and role of networks as an approach to the coordination of health care delivery must be examined.

Defining networks: neither hierarchy or market

Networks have become an increasingly central theme within management. This interest in networks reflects the seemingly efficient governance of transactions and the scope for learning and innovation within such structures (Bianchi, 1995). The public sector has not been immune to the spread of network concepts, with such concepts being seen as offering policy makers an alternative to the hierarchy–market dichotomy. However, despite the increasing significance attached to networks as an approach to the organisation and coordination of economic activity, understanding of the specific nature, operation and appropriateness of network forms remain limited (Child and Faulkner, 1998). In examining the contribution of network concepts to management, Nohria (1992) argues that the proliferation in the use of the concept across a diverse range of academic fields, from sociology to management, in fact poses the threat of eroding its value as a coherent analytical framework. Although Araujo and Easton (1996) do not feel that such proliferation in usage is necessarily a source of weakness, they nevertheless acknowledge that the term network has acquired the character of a umbrella, being in effect a catch-all term under which a variety of theoretical developments in management, and the social sciences more broadly, seek refuge. As a result securing a common definition, or even common terminology, is problematic. The terms utilised to define networks include phrases like 'clusters of organisations', 'patterned relationships', 'informal inter-organisational collaborations' and 'lateral or horizontal patterns of exchange'. An indication of the range of differing terms and descriptions used in defining networks perspectives is provided in Table 3.3.

Allowing for such definitional complexity, it is nevertheless evident that the concept of a network is used to denote a distinctive form of organisational arrangements that do not fit the conventional market–hierarchy dichotomy. In this regard the key feature of networks is that coordination is achieved through less formal and more egalitarian means than in either markets or hierarchies, and that information exchange is more extensive than occurs within market settings and less restricted than in hierarchies (Hudson and Hardy, 1999). This reflects the centrality of what Sako (1992) describes as obligational contractual

Table 3.3 **Conceptualising networks**

Author/s	Term used	Description of network concept
Alter and Hage, 1993	Inter-organisational networks	Clusters of organisations forming non-hierarchical collectives of legally separate units.
Dubini and Aldrich, 1991	Networks	Patterned relationships among individuals, groups and organisations.
Flynn, Williams and Pickard, 1996	Networks	Extended chains of connections and linkages between organisations and professionals.
Gerlach and Linco, 1992	Alliance capitalism	Strategic long-term relationships across a range of markets.
Granovetter, 1994; 1995	Business groups	Collections of firms bound together by a range of formal and/or informal ties.
Hakansson and Snehota, 1995	Networks	A set of interconnected relations involving people and organisations forming a structured system within a larger set of actors.
Jones, Hesterly and Borgatti, 1997	Network governance	Select, enduring, structured set of organisations involved in product/service delivery based on implicit, open-ended agreements.
Kreiner and Schultz, 1993	Networks	Collection of informal inter-organisational collaborations.

relationships in networks, as distinct from the adversarial contracting characteristic of neo-classical markets. That is, contractual arrangements are embedded in a network of long-term social and professional relationships. MacNeil (1985) has suggested that the 'entangling strings' of reputation, friendship, interdependence and altruism thus constitute the critical building blocks of network relationships.

Such social exchanges or relationship in turn entail unspecified obligations that result in actors going beyond what might be encompassed by any formal contract, in the belief that their investment in the relationship will be rewarded in the longer term. Central to this is that actors trust one another to exercise judgement and discretion when resolving unfolding issues that are not addressed within the contract. Networks are generally viewed as operating on the basis of reciprocity, trust and expectations of longevity in the relationship. As such, it is socially rather than legally binding ties which hold networks together. Trust and cooperation are thus core to the operation of networks, with networks being characterised as essentially trust-based structures (Podolny and Page, 1998). Trust lies at the core of network operations because it is the mechanism that lowers network 'transaction cost', thereby making the network economically viable. This emphasis on inter-organisational trust creates an environment characterised by enhanced information exchange, knowledge-sharing and creativity compared to that occurring in market or hierarchical settings, yet which at the same time retains the elements of competition and power bargaining more conventionally associated with markets and hierarchies (Jones *et al.*, 1997).

Networks being agglomerations of separate organisations, each possessing their own identity and objectives, results in an inherent tension within networks between the desire for autonomy and the acknowledgement of dependency. That is, there is continuous tension between individual organisational strategy and the broader network strategy. Specifically network participants are frequently engaged in conflict over resources, with networks as a result being characterised as much by the exercise of power and the existence of dependency relationships as by trust and cooperation (Morgan, 1990). As a result there is inherent tension and instability within networks given the likelihood of divergence in organisational interest, with the participating parties commuting between cooperation and competition dependent on organisational self-interest (Carney, 1998). However, in certain contexts, notably professional services, organisational behaviour and network development may rather be driven by the existence of broader norms or values. Given that such norms, particularly when based on a professional ethos, are common across a range of organisations, their existence is likely to result in far greater unity of purpose, and hence stability, than is the case where network formation is purely interest driven.

Network formation and development

Mirroring divergence in definitions of networks, there is comparable divergence over the conditions and reasons for network formation. On the one hand there is an attribution of network formation to the fact that networks enable organisations to lower the costs of conducting 'transactions', that is coordinating activities (Jarillo, 1990). At the core of this argument is the contention that networks are more efficient than a hierarchy because they do not possess the bureaucratic inefficiencies associated with hierarchies, and are more efficient than markets because they do not incur transaction costs. On the other hand the development of inter-organisational trust is viewed as the core factor behind network development. Specifically organisations form or enter a network to share information, and hence develop mutual under-standing and trust as part of a longer-term interest in building collabo-rative ventures that will achieve the objectives of the individual organisations (Smith Ring, 1997). Under such a perspective the network is an efficient organisational form because of the central role of trust in lubricating interactions.

These two perspectives usefully exemplify the primary derivation of network concepts from both transaction cost economics and sociology. Jones *et al.* (1997) offer a valuable perspective in synthesising such economic and sociological perspectives on network formation. Linking transactional cost analysis and social network theory, they identify four conditions under which network formation is likely. First, situations where demand is uncertain yet supply is largely fixed and stable. For organisations in such circumstances, networks offer the opportunity both to safeguard levels of inputs and outputs and to stabilise the market environment over the longer term. Second, situations charac-terised by customised exchanges with high human asset specificity, such as professional services. Linked to this, networks have particular value in those markets where value cannot be precisely determined and where outcome measures are subjective. Third, situations where complex tasks requiring multiple inputs occur under significant time constraints, that is under conditions of high interdependency. More specifically from an industrial network perspective, Hakansson and Johanson (1993) argue that networks are critical mechanisms for coordination in environments characterised by multiple, deep and dynamic inter-organisational inter-dependencies. Fourth, situations where there are frequent multidimen-sional exchanges among the parties comprising the network. In this regards networks are frequently spatially constrained, emerging in environments that are naturally bounded by geographical, cultural or political factors within which there is extensive and deep interaction between actors (Smith Ring, 1997).

Operationally within such contexts the formation of networks is driven by a number of organisational factors. As previously highlighted, a key driver behind network formation and development is organisational self-interest. Organisations look at network participation largely in terms of the ability of networks to safeguard and advance their organisational objectives. Acknowledging the role of such behaviours, it is possible to identify a number of specific objectives which drive network formation from the stand point of participating organisations.

The existence of such a diverse range of organisational objectives highlights the potential instability within networks, with organisations entering networks with very different objectives and expectations. This highlights the dynamic and evolutionary nature of networks; their role and composition changes as a coherent and common network objective emerges. Evidence from the private sector suggests that networks seldom emerge without a substantial history of cooperation between at least some of the organisations involved. The development of boundary-spanning structures such as networks are typically preceded by a slow drifting together of organisations over time, building trust and enabling common goals to evolve (Hertz, 1996). Through such learning the activities and behaviours of individual actors are eventually modified and

Table 3.4 **Classification of network development drivers**

Revenue driver	Participants motivated by short-term financial considerations, e.g. the need for cost savings.
Value added driver	Longer-term financial considerations of improving quality and reducing failure costs, e.g. prevent users 'falling through gaps'.
Obeying orders driver	Instructions from above rather than on the basis of local needs, e.g. formation of LHCC/PCG.
Relationship driver	Desire to build relationship in its own right because perceived to have long-term future benefits, e.g. scope for innovation.
Learning driver	Transfer of knowledge between actors providing benefits to both supplying and receiving actor, e.g. clinical networks.
Network driver	Focus is on the consequences of action/inaction on relationships elsewhere in the network, e.g. cost of being outside the network.

Adapted from Ford *et al.*, 1996

adapted to fit with the activities of other actors, so that joint productivity is increased. This in turn has the effect of deepening the interdependency of the actors in the network (Hakansson and Johanson, 1993).
However, the extent to which such network development is realised
depends at least partially on the degree to which the core activities of
network participants are complementary or overlapping, with complementary actors drifting together and overlapping actors drifting away.

In health care more specifically, the development of networks can be
viewed as being primarily the product of three interconnected forces.
First, the nature of the service and the technology of service delivery.
Given the increasing complexity of service provision the delivery of
health care spans multiple organisations more and more, for example
primary care, secondary/tertiary care and long-term nursing care. As a
result networks are formed around groups of service providers involved
in the delivery of a particular service in order to avoid service users
falling into the gaps between the organisations involved in their care
(Hall, 1987). The parameters of a network are not, however, simply
delineated by the technical characteristics of service delivery in terms of
the activities comprising the delivery process. Rather the boundaries are
determined by how the actors involved have chosen to delineate each
activity. Consequently network structures are not determined by intrinsic technical imperatives but by the attitudes of the participating parties
and the way in which they perceive interdependencies (Hakansson and
Johansson, 1993). In health care the differing construction of LHCCs
across the NHS in Scotland, encompassing diverse sets of organisations,
highlights the critical role of actors in determining the parameters of the
network.

Second, external pressures for developing collaborative service
provision. Health care organisations are typically dependent on a
limited number of major organisations for funding, either government
agencies or insurance companies. Such organisations frequently
demand, under the threat of financial sanction, the establishment of
service delivery networks to enhance efficiency. However, the extent to
which such externally mandated network development is ultimately
effective is debatable, in that such 'forcing' of network development
potentially results in issues of ideological differences and power relationships not being addressed, eroding the basis for the formation of
inter-organisational trust. Third, the delivery of health care is often
characterised as a cooperative venture by health care professionals.
Health care professionals typically portray themselves as unselfish
professionals dedicated to the interests of service users. Consequently
health care professionals possess a normative set of values regarding
what constitutes appropriate patterns of behaviour between organisa-

tions. Structuring inter-organisational relationships on a competitive basis does not correspond with this prevailing altruistic ethos. Rather networks emphasising collaborative solutions are in more tune with the attitudes of health care professionals. The existence of such normative values, what is termed the concept of network latency, are equally important in network development beyond the confines of health care in that they limit organisational opportunism, a critical factor in limiting network costs.

Network costs and failure

The majority of the literature on networks has focused on conceptualising network forms and contrasting the operation of such forms of organisation to markets and hierarchies. Networks are almost uniformly presented in a positive light, emphasising the comparative strengths of networks in terms of facilitating cooperation, learning and innovation and governance of transactions (Bianchi, 1995). Such descriptions of networks tend to ignore the costs and risks associated with this form of organisation. Yet the market–hierarchy debate from which much of the network literature emerged is primarily concerned with the comparative costs of alternative organisational forms. As Ebers and Grandori (1997) argue, it is critical in undertaking any comparative analysis of networks as governance mechanisms to acknowledge the costs associated with developing and maintaining networks. The costs associated with information exchange and negotiation, preventing opportunistic behaviour and conflict resolution are central to network operations, and may in effect be regarded as constituting network transaction costs. Consequently in considering the potential contribution of network forms to the delivery of health care services it is necessary to determine the nature and determinants of network costs.

Kirkpatrick (1999) in reviewing the relative contributions of markets, hierarchies and networks in the public sector in the United Kingdom, argues that it is possible to identify three major potential sources of 'transaction' costs within networks. First, the cost of developing the inter-organisational trust which lies at the core of networks. Such trust is anchored in socio-professional links and reflects the long-term process of interaction between organisations (Hakansson, 1982). There is as such a significant time cost associated with the 'creation' of trust. However, in professional services such as health care key actors within separate organisations have well-established professional networks which can provide the trust necessary for the development of inter-organisational networks. Second, network organisations, being coalitions of organisations, are inherently unstable resulting in significant costs being associated with maintaining the coherence of organisations. As already highlighted, the existence of multiple competing goals and expectations raises the risk of networks being pulled in different directions, in that actors within a network will seek to position themselves so as to be able to exert influence over the network and secure their narrow organisational objectives. In addition where network benefits are intangible or long-term, maintaining motivation and enthusiasm among actors requires active management (Hudson and Hardy, 1999). Third, the development of the level of trust necessary for the effective functioning of networks creates conditions under which suboptimal behaviours may result. At one level contracting parties within a network becoming too close raises the prospect of inefficiencies as a result of collusion (Ring and Van der Ven, 1994). At another level close personal ties and hence trust may result in inappropriate and inefficient patterns of behaviour, with considerations of friendship taking precedence over organisational interests (Uzzi, 1997). Such problems reflect the highly embedded nature of relationships within networks, and the risk that relationships develop an existence of their own without reference to the economic benefit delivered. Taken together both aspects raise fundamental questions over the extent to which trust-based mechanisms provide effective governance structures, particularly in a context characterised by strong personal and professional ties.

Managing market and networks in health care

The structuring of inter-organisational relationships is central to the overall management of health care delivery. For policy makers the challenge is to establish a framework which offers the optimal balance between centralised control and operational flexibility. For health care professionals the challenge is to manage relationships within such a structural framework in a manner which optimises the delivery of care to patients. Within this context this chapter has provided an overview of the governance frameworks under which such relationships may be managed. The following chapter builds on these themes and examines in detail the way in which inter-organisational relationships have developed in the NHS under different policy regimes, and the implications for service delivery. In so doing it evaluates the suitability of such frameworks for the delivery of complex modern health care services.

References

Appleby, J., Smith, P., Ranade, W., Little, V. and Robinson, R. (1993) 'Competition and the NHS', in Tilley, I. (ed.) *Managing the Internal Market*, Paul Chapman: London.

Araujo, L. and Easton, G. (1996) 'Networks in Socio-Economic Systems: A Critical Review', in Iacobucci, D. (ed.) *Networks in Marketing*, Sage: Thousand Oaks.

Bianchi, M. (1995) 'Markets and Firms: Transaction Costs Versus Strategic Innovation', *Journal of Economic Behaviour and Organisation* 28: 183–202.

Bolton, M., Malmrose, R. and Ouchi, W. (1994) 'The Organisation of Innovation in the United States and Japan – Neoclassical and Relational Contracting', *Journal of Management Studies* 31(5): 653–79.

Boonekamp, L. C. M. (1994) 'Marketing for Healthcare Organisations: An Introduction to Network Management', *Journal of Management in Medicine* 8(5):11–24.

Bradach, J. and Eccles, R. (1991) 'Price, Authority and Trust', in Thompson, G., Frances, J., Levacic, R. and Mitchell, J. (eds) *Markets, Hierarchies, Networks: The Co-ordination of Social Life*, Sage: London.

Campbell, A. J. and Wilson, D. T. (1996) 'Managed Networks: Creating Strategic Advantage', in Iacobucci, D. (ed.) *Networks in Marketing*, Sage: Thousand Oaks.

Carney, M. (1998) 'The Competitiveness of Networked Production: The Role of Trust and Asset Specificity', *Journal of Management Studies* 35(4): 457–79.

Carter, N. (1993) *Explaining Extra Contractual Referral Price Differences*, Health Care Financial Management Association: Southampton.

Child, J. and Faulkner, D. (1998) *Strategies of Co-operation: Managing Alliances, Networks and Joint Working*, Oxford University Press: Oxford.

Ebers, M. and Grandori, A. (1997) 'The Forms, Costs and Developing Dynamics of Inter-organisational Networking', in Ebers, M. (ed.) *The Formation of Inter-Organisational Networks*, Oxford University Press: Oxford.

EHMA (1998) *The Impact of Market Forces on Health Systems*, European Health Management Association: Dublin.

Exworthy, M., Powell, M. and Mohan, J. (1999) 'The NHS: Quasi-market, Quasi-hierarchy and Quasi-network?' *Public Money and Management* 19(4): 15–22.

Ferlie, E. (1992) 'The Creation and Evolution of Quasi-Markets in the Public Sector: A Problem for Strategic Management', *Strategic Management Journal* 13: 79–97.

Ferlie, E. and Pettigrew, A. (1996) 'Managing Through Networks: Some Issues and Implications for the NHS', *British Journal of Management* 7(Special edn): 81–99.

Flynn, R., Williams, G. and Pickard, S. (1996) *Markets and Networks: Contracting in Community Health Services*, Open University Press: Buckingham.

Flynn, N. (1997) *Public Sector Management*, Harvester Wheatsheaf: Hemel Hempstead.

Ford, D., McDowell, R. and Tomkins, C. (1996) 'Relationship Strategy, Investments and Decision Making', in Iacobucci, D. (ed.) *Networks in Marketing*, Sage: Thousand Oaks.

Ford, D. (1997) *Understanding Business Markets*, 2nd edn, Dryden Press: London.

Granovetter, M. (1985) 'Economic Action and Social Structure: The Problem of Embeddedness', *American Journal of Sociology* 91: 481–510.

Granovetter, M. (1992) 'Economic Institutions and Social Construction', *Acta Sociologica* 35(3): 3–11.

Granovetter, M. and Swedberg, R. (1992) *The Sociology of Economic Life*, Oxford University Press: Oxford.

Grey, B. (1986) 'Conditions Facilitating Inter-Organisational Collaboration', *Human Relations* 38(10): 911–36.

Hakansson, H. (ed.) (1982) *International Marketing and Purchasing of Industrial Goods: An Interaction Approach*, Wiley & Sons: New York.

Hakansson, H. and Johanson, J. (1993) 'The Network as a Governance Structure', in Grabner, G. (ed.) *The Embedded Firm: On the Socio-Economics of Industrial Networks*, Routledge: London.

Hakansson, H. and Snehota, I. (1995) *Developing Relationships in Business Networks*, Routledge: London.

Hall, R. H. (1987) *Organisations – Structures, Processes and Outcomes*, Prentice-Hall: Englewood Cliffs.

Harrison, A. (1993) *From Hierarchy to Contract*, Policy Journals: Newbury.

Hart, S. and Hogg, G. (1998) 'Relationship Marketing in Corporate Legal Services' in Hogg, G. and Gabbott, M. (eds) *Service Industries Marketing: New Approaches*, Frank Cass: London.

Heide, J. and John, G. (1990) 'Alliances in Industrial Purchasing: The Determinants of Joint Action in Buyer-Supplier Relationships', *Journal of Marketing Research* 27: 24–36.

Hertz, S. (1996) 'Drifting Closer and Drifting Away in Networks: Gradual Changes in Interdependencies in Networks', in Iacobucci, D. (ed.) *Networks in Marketing*, Sage: Thousand Oaks.

Hudson, B. and Hardy, B. (1999) 'In Pursuit of Inter-Agency Collaboration: What is the Contribution of Research and Theory', *Public Management: International Journal of Research and Theory* 1(2): 235–60.

James, A. (1997) 'Beyond the Market in Public Service', *Journal of Management in Medicine* 11(1): 43–50.

Jarillo, J. C. (1990) 'Comments on "Transactions Costs and Networks"', *Strategic Management Journal* 11: 497–9.

Jebb, F. (1992) 'First-Wave Lessons Prove Vital for Hospital Contracts', *Fundholding* 11(6): 18–19.

Jones, C., Hesterly, W. S. and Borgatti, S. P. (1997) 'A General Theory of Network Governance: Exchange Conditions and Social Mechanisms', *Academy of Management Review* 22(4): 911–45.

Kirkpatrick, I. (1999) 'The Worst of Both Worlds? Public Services without Markets or Bureaucracy', *Public Money and Management* 19(4): 7–14.

Kooiman, J. (ed.) (1993) *Modern Governance*, Sage: London.

Laing, A. W. and Cotton, S. (1995) 'Towards an Understanding of Health Care Purchasing: The Purchasing Behaviour of GP Fundholders', *Journal of Marketing Management* 11(6): 583–601.

Laing, A. W. and Cotton, S. (1997) 'Inter-Organisational Purchasing Networks in the NHS', *European Journal of Purchasing and Supply Management* 3(2): 83–91.

Laing, A. W. and Lian, P. (2001) *Inter-Organisational Relationships in Professional Services: Towards a Typology of Inter-Organisational Relationships*, Institute for the Study of Business Markets Working Paper 10/2001, Penn State University.

Lapsley, I. (1994) 'Market Mechanisms and the Management of Health Care', *International Journal of Public Sector Management* 7(6): 15–25.

Le Grand, J. and Bartlett, W. (1993) 'Introduction', in Le Grand, J. and Bartlett, W. (eds) *Quasi-Markets and Social Policy*, Macmillan: London.

Light, D. (1997) 'From Managed Competition to Managed Co-operation', *Millbank Quarterly* 75: 297–341.

Lowndes, V. and Skelcher, C. (1998) 'The Dynamics of Multi-Organisational Partnerships: An Analysis of Changing Modes of Governance', *Public Administration* 76: 313–33.

Lunt, N., Mannion, R. and Smith, P. (1996) 'Economic Discourse and the Market: The Case of Community Care', *Public Administration* 74: 369–91.

Mackintosh, M. (1993) 'Economic Behaviour and the Contracting Outcome Under the NHS Reforms', *Accounting, Auditing and Accountability Journal* 6(3): 133–55.

MacNeil, I. (1985) 'Relational Contract', *Wisconsin Law Review* 3: 483–526.

Miles, R. E. and Snow, C. C. (1996) 'Organisations: New Concepts for New Forms', in Buckley, P. J. and Michie, J. (eds) *Firms, Organisations and Contracts*, Oxford University Press: Oxford.

Morgan, G. (1990) *Organisations and Society*, Macmillan: London.

Morgan, R. M. and Hunt, S. D. (1994) 'The Commitment-Trust Theory of Relationship Marketing', *Journal of Marketing* 58: 20–38.

Nielson, C. C. (1998) 'An Empirical Examination of the Role of 'Closeness' in Industrial Buyer-Seller Relationships', *European Journal of Marketing* 32: 441–63.

Nohria, N. (1992) in Nohria, N. and Eccles, R. G. (eds) *Networks and Organisations – Structures, Form and Action*, Harvard Business School Press: Massachusetts.

Oliver, A. L. (1997) 'On the Nexus of Organisations and Professions: Networking Through Trust', *Sociological Inquiry* 67(2): 227–45.

Podolny, J. M. and Page, K. L. (1998) 'Network Forms of Organisation', *Annual Review of Sociology* 24: 57–76.

Powell, W. (1991) 'Neither Market nor Hierarchy: Network Forms of Organisation', in Thompson, G., Frances, J., Levacic, R. and Mitchell, J. (eds), *Markets, Hierarchies, Networks: The Co-ordination of Social Life*, Sage: London.

Powell, M. (1999) 'New Labour and the "Third Way" in the British NHS', *International Journal of Health Services* 29: 353–70.

Parasuraman, A., Zeithaml, V. A. and Berry, L. (1985) 'A Conceptual Model of Service Quality and its Implications', *Journal of Marketing* 49: 41–50.

Propper, C. (1993) 'Quasi-Markets: Contracts and Quality in Health and Social Care', in Le Grand, J. and Bartlett, W. (1993) *Quasi-Markets and Social Policy*, Macmillan: London.

Ranade, W. (1995) 'The Theory and Practice of Managed Competition in the NHS', *Public Administration* 74: 639–56.

Ranade, W. (1998) *Markets and Health Care: A Comparative Analysis*, Longman: London.

Rhodes, R. A. (1997) *Understanding Governance*, Open University Press: Buckingham.

Ring, P. S. and Van der Ven, A. H. (1994) 'Development Processes of Co-operative Inter-organisational Relationships', *Academy of Management Review* 19(1): 90–117.

Sako, M. (1992) *Prices, Quality and Trust: Inter-Firm Relations in Britain and Japan*, Cambridge University Press: Cambridge.

Scitovsky, T. (1992) *The Joyless Economy: The Psychology of Human Satisfaction*, Oxford University Press: New York.

Selnes, F. (1998) 'Antecedents and Consequences of Trust and Satisfaction in Buyer Seller Relationships', *European Journal of Marketing* 32: 305–22.

Sheth, J. N. and Parvatiyar, A. (1995) 'The Evolution of Relationship Marketing', *International Business Review* 4(4): 397–418.

Shostack, G. L. (1977) 'Breaking Free of Product Marketing', *Journal of Marketing* 41: 73–80.

Smith Ring, P. (1997) 'Processes Facilitating Reliance on Trust in Inter-organisational Networks', in Ebers, M. (ed.) *The Formation of Inter-Organisational Networks*, Oxford University Press: Oxford.

Thakor, M. and Kumar, A. (2000) 'What is a Professional Service? A Conceptual Review and Bi-National Investigation', *Journal of Services Marketing* 14(1): 63–82.

Thompson, G., Frances, J., Levacic, R. and Mitchell, J. (eds) (1991) *Markets, Hierarchies, Networks: The Co-ordination of Social Life*, Sage: London.

Thorelli, H. B. (1986) 'Networks: Between Markets and Hierarchies', *Strategic Management Journal* 7: 37–51.

Uzzi, B. (1997) 'Networks and the Paradox of Embeddedness', *Administrative Science Quarterly* 42: 35–67.

Williamson, O. (1975) *Markets and Hierarchies, Analysis and Anti-Trust Implications*, Free Press: New York.

Williamson, O. E. (1983) *Markets and Hierarchies*, Free Press: New York.

Williamson, O. E. (1985) *The Economic Institutions of Capitalism,* 1st edn, Collier MacMillan: London.

Williamson, O. E. (1991) 'Comparative Economic Organisation', *Administrative Science Quarterly* 36: 269–96.

Wistow, G., Knapp, M., Hardy, B., Forder, J., Kendall, J. and Manning, R. (1996) *Social Care Markets: Progress and Prospects*, Open University Press: Buckingham.

Zeithaml, V., Parasuraman, A. and Berry, L. (1990) *Delivering Quality Service*, Macmillan: New York.

4 Service structure: managing inter-organisational service delivery

Introduction

The structuring of the complex networks of inter-organisational relationships underpinning modern health care systems is central to the efficient and effective delivery of services. As highlighted in Chapter 3 the structuring of these relationships is one of the primary challenges facing health care policy makers, with these relationships being structured at the macro level on the basis of either 'competitive' market or 'collaborative' network frameworks. Yet these policy regimes cannot be viewed as mutually exclusive, with inter-organisational collaboration occurring under 'competitive' market regimes and competition occurring under 'collaborative' network regimes (Flynn *et al.*, 1996; Exworthy *et al.*, 1999). Indeed, despite the imposition of alternative policy frameworks, the underlying nature of the relationships between various organisational actors within health care may be viewed as remaining remarkably constant. Such consistency in the face of changing organisational topography is indicative of the central role played by informal socio-professional ties in shaping the reality of inter-organisational relationships in professional service settings such as health care. Although one should avoid the adoption of an 'over-socialised' view of organisational relationships, in understanding the management of inter-organisational relationships in the delivery of health care it is important to examine the nature of the connection between informal socio-professional ties and formal organisational links.

In developing a systemic understanding of the structuring of health care services, the primary focus of this chapter will be on the specific nature and format of the relationships which have emerged under different policy frameworks in the NHS. Understanding the complex operational dynamics of inter-organisational relationships is critical to the effective management of such relationships and in turn to the design and delivery of health care services. Central to this is an examination of the constituent building blocks of these relationships, that is both the formal exchanges occurring between the constituent organisations and the informal ties which exist between professionals in these organisations. Adopting an analytical framework derived from business to business markets, this chapter specifically provides an in-depth examination of the changing nature and dynamics of inter-organisational relationships across the primary–secondary care divide, as well as within the primary care sector. In this regard the shift in emphasis from conflict to co-operation between primary and secondary care and from isolation to integration within primary care will be critically examined. From this analysis of inter-organisational dynamics, the chapter concludes with an examination of the changing role of patients, and other service users, in the overall management of such relationships. This provides the context within which the patient's perspective on the design and delivery of health care services is examined in Chapter 5.

Conceptualising inter-organisational relationships in health care

The specific structure and dynamics of inter-organisational relationships are a product of the local environment within which the constituent organisations operate. Although externally imposed macro level governance frameworks dictate the broad parameters within which inter-organisational relationships develop, the actual format of the specific relationship is a product of both environmental factors and the nature of the constituent organisations themselves. The resultant pattern of interaction between the organisations in turn shapes the long-term pattern of development of that relationship. Consequently in understanding the development and hence management of inter-organisational relationships, it is necessary to analyse both the nature of the interaction between the constituent organisations and the context within which that interaction occurs. In examining the nature of such organisational interaction, concepts developed from research into patterns of business to business market behaviour provide a robust conceptual framework within which inter-organisational relationships in health care settings can be analysed.

Anchored in transaction cost economics and social network theory, at the core of this body of research is the analysis of the dynamics of organisational interaction and the impact of such interaction processes on the development of inter-organisational relationships (Ford, 1999). Although the primary focus of this conceptual framework is on buyer–seller relationships, reflecting the derivation of this work from business to business market contexts, the framework nevertheless provides valuable insights into understanding the operational dynamics of inter-organisational relationships more broadly. Specifically, subject to adaptation it provides an appropriate framework for conceptualising inter-organisational relationships in health care. An adaptation of the framework to examine primary–secondary care relationships is illustrated in Figure 4.1. This framework however, can equally be applied to other inter-organisational relationships in health care.

Central to any inter-organisational relationship are the characteristics and behaviours of the constituent actors, that is the *interacting parties*. The process of interaction and relationship development depends significantly on a number of core characteristics of the interacting organisations. These include formal organisational characteristics such as size, structure, strategy and culture as well as previous experiences of relationships with other organisations. Additionally the characteristics, experiences and expertise of the individuals in each

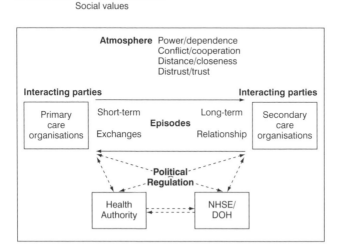

Adapted from Laing and Cotton, 1996

Figure 4.1 **Understanding inter-organisational interaction**

organisation influence the tenor of interaction and hence relationship development (Campbell, 1985). Focusing on the primary–secondary care relationship, conventionally the key feature of this interaction has been the disequilibrium in terms of size and resources between the parties. Secondary care organisations are generally large complex organisations possessing considerable financial strength, depth of managerial expertise and clearly articulated organisational strategy and procedures. By contrast, primary care organisations have generally been relatively small with limited managerial expertise and a weak strategic perspective. Inevitably this imbalance has fundamentally affected both the structure and the tenor of the relationship between the parties, significantly affecting the shape of future relationships. Moves towards developing collaborative structures within primary care – fundholding consortia, primary care groups and related structures – can in part be viewed as a response by primary care professionals to addressing this imbalance and hence reconfiguring the primary–secondary care relationship (Laing and Cotton, 1997).

The process of interaction between the constituent organisations encompasses a complex range of encounters or *episodes* which collectively shape the development of a relationship. In analysing inter-organisational relationships there is an inevitable tendency to focus on the formal organisational interactions encompassing episodes such as meetings and negotiations, information exchange and service or product delivery as the key influences on relationship development. Given the complex nature of professional services such as health care, tangible processual episodes rather than service delivery episodes, can constitute the critical bases on which the performance of the other organisation is evaluated and hence the development of the relationship depends (Bostrom, 1995). Under GP fundholding, for example, a key factor affecting satisfaction with secondary care organisations was the efficiency of the billing process. Clearly the outcomes of such formal interactions are central to relationship development, in that the underlying rationale for the existence of a relationship is the delivery of benefits to the interacting organisations. Yet to focus on this formal interaction is to adopt an under-socialised view of the nature of organisational relationships (Granovetter, 1985). This is particularly critical in health care given the strong socio-professional relationships that exist between professionals across different sectors of the NHS due to shared training and working experiences (Flynn, 1992). Consequently the informal interactions between individuals in the interacting organisations play a major role in determining the nature and development of inter-organisational relationships. Critically such socio-professional relationships inform initial decisions regarding which secondary care organisations the primary care organisation will develop a relationship with. It is these repeated formal and informal interaction episodes which collectively provide the basis for, and determine the nature of, the relationship between the interacting organisations.

Taken together, the characteristics of the interacting parties and the process of interaction generate the *atmosphere* within which the relationship develops. This must be seen as a two way process, in that the atmosphere is a product of the interaction process but at the same time influences the interaction process. The atmosphere can be characterised in terms of the prevailing power–dependency relationship, the state of conflict or cooperation, the closeness or distance, and the level of trust or distrust between the interacting organisations. Of these characteristics the concept of closeness is core to relationship development in that it is instrumental in promoting inter-organisational trust (Nielson, 1998). Closeness in a relationship is a complex multidimensional construct encompassing various aspects of the process of interaction. These process aspects include the time orientation of the relationship, that is the perceived duration of the relationship, the degree of customisation through investment in relationship-specific assets, the level of co-ordination in terms of objective setting, the formality of communication, and the strength of socio-professional bonds in a relationship. Taken collectively such factors generate an atmosphere which promotes or inhibits relationship development. However, to view the atmosphere as simply a product of the interaction between the organisations involved is to adopt a narrow dyadic perspective and ignore the broader network context within which the organisations are embedded. Specifically the respective relationships which the interacting organisations have with other actors will contribute, as inhibitors or promoters, to the pattern of relationship development. In the context of the NHS the relationship between primary and secondary care organisations is significantly affected by the respective relationships which they have with the relevant health authority locally and the NHS Executive nationally, in that the influence of political control and 'regulation' constrains their freedom of manoeuvre and in turn influences the trajectory of relationship development.

Such political regulation can more broadly be viewed as constituting a key dimension of the *environment* within which inter-organisational relationships are framed. The environment is the broader context in which the interacting organisations are situated, encompassing the prevailing governance structures as well as the dominant social values. Whereas in many organisational contexts the environment exerts only a general and diffuse influence over relationship development, in publicly funded health care systems the influence of the environment is more

direct. Specifically, politically driven changes in the prevailing governance system, that is from market to network, will inevitably impinge
on the process of relationship development. For example the imposition
of quasi-market mechanisms may have constrained relationship development as a result of regulation designed to promote competitive
patterns of behaviour, while the introduction of a network approach to
management may promote relationship development. Equally in a
professional field like health care, the dominant social values directly
influence the process of organisational interaction and hence the pattern
of relationship development. The NHS, as with many publicly funded
health care systems, is widely perceived as being characterised by a
strongly cooperative and collectivist ethos (Collins *et al.*, 1994). Such an
ethos is inimical to competitive market-based relationships, rather
favouring collaborative relational approaches to service delivery. In this
context the strength of the dominant social values may be viewed as
promoting the development of long-term relationships in the face of a
governance structure which, at least initially, was antipathetic to relational patterns of behaviour.

The development of inter-organisational relationships in health care is
thus a product of the complex and ongoing process of interactions occurring within a particular environment. It follows in turn that inter-organisational relationships are dynamic and evolutionary. However, to view
inter-organisational relationships as passing through a discrete and
predictable 'life cycle' towards increasingly close and embedded relationships (Sharma, 1994) is to ignore the inherent variability and unpre-
dictability of relationship development. Rather it is more appropriate to
consider relationships as corresponding to a number of non-linear 'ideal
type' formats. Specifically inter-organisational relationships can be
viewed as existing along a spectrum ranging from transactional, i.e.
short-term arm's-length relationships to embedded, i.e. close long-term
relationships. Critically, organisations do not necessarily progress
sequentially through such relationship formats. Indeed organisations can
move in either direction along the spectrum, and move from one end of
the spectrum to the other, without passing through the intermediate
formats, as a result of changes in the environment and internal changes in
the interacting parties. The prevailing relationship format is ultimately
the result of the particular organisational and environmental circumstances as well as the dynamic of interaction between the organisations at
any given point in time. A representation of alternative relationship
formats in terms of their salient characteristics is outlined in Table 4.1.

In seeking to manage inter-organisational relationships it is vital to
recognise that relationships cannot be viewed as uniform, but rather
encompass a range of formats, each of which poses distinct character-

Table 4.1 **Characteristics of alternative relationship formats**

		Elementary relationship	Interactive relationship	Embedded relationship	Partnering relationship	Integration
1	**Trust**	Low	Medium	High	Very high	Very high
2	**Closeness**	Arm's length	Close	Interactive	Embedded	Internal
2a	**Time orientation**	Short term	Medium term	Long term	Long term	Long term
2b	**Level of socio-professional ties**	Low	Medium	High	Very high	Very high
2c	**Nature of communication**	Very formal	Formal	Informal	Informal	Very informal
2d	**Nature of coordination**	Unilateral	Negotiated	Consultative	Consultative	Set by provider
2e	**Level of customisation**	Low	Medium	High	Very high	Total
2f	**Nature of boundaries**	Rigid	Permeable	Blurred	Merged	None
2g	**Nature of secondary relationships**	Arm's length	Arm's length	Close	Interactive	Embedded
3	**Organisational Policy**	Rigid	→	→	→	Flexible
3a	**Level of interal service expertise**	Low	Medium	High	High	Very high
3b	**Formality of selection**	High	Medium	Low	Low	Very low
3c	**Extent of service evaluation**	High	Medium	Low	Low	Very low

Adapted from Laing and Lian (2001)

istics and hence managerial challenges. The relationship characteristics identified above provide basic indicators against which the format and evolution of inter-organisational relationships may be assessed. It is against this analytical framework that the evolving nature and dynamics of primary–secondary care relationships within the NHS will be examined.

Managing primary–secondary care relationships: conflict or cooperation?

The management of the primary–secondary care relationship is central to the effective delivery of health care services in that primary care acts as the formal gatekeeper to secondary care services. Yet evidence suggests that the interface between these two sectors has been the most complex and problematic inter-organisational relationship to manage within the NHS (Haggard, 1993). Successive reforms of the NHS have sought to reconfigure this relationship by changing the basis on which the two parties interact in order to improve the delivery of services. Critically, however, the primary–secondary care relationship is as much a professional divide between primary care generalists and secondary care specialists as it is a service divide. As such at the core of this relationship is the balance of both professional and organisational power between primary and secondary sectors. Conventionally the secondary care sector has enjoyed dominance, both in terms of organisational resources and professional status. Glennester *et al.* (1994), in describing the initial changes wrought by the internal market, reported the apocryphal story of how prior to the introduction of the internal market general practitioners sent Christmas cards to consultants in order to ensure that their patients were treated, but subsequent to the market reforms the process was reversed as consultants sought to protect the flow of patients to their units. Whether apocryphal or not, it effectively encapsulates the constantly shifting power dynamics of this relationship at the organisational level.

At the core of this uneasy relationship is the perception among primary care professionals that as the agents for their patients they have a valid role in influencing the nature and format of service delivery in secondary care, while the perspective of secondary care professionals is that services need to be designed on the basis of their technical expertise. In essence the tension in the relationship is the classic tension between consumer expectations, as articulated by primary care professionals, and the producer judgement, in this case of secondary care professionals. Pratt and Adamson (1996) elegantly sum up the primary–secondary care relationship as being characterised by 'mutual irritation'. In this the relationship can be characterised as a marriage of necessity where the primary concern of each party is the management of the existing relationship, rather than searching for new organisational partners (Wilkinson and Young, 1994). That is, the focus in the relationship is on securing adaptations in the existing relationship rather than divorcing the partner organisation. While in part reflecting the structural characteristics of the NHS, i.e. the existence of local monopoly providers due to geographic constraints, it also reflects the impact of the embedded professional relationships which cut across the primary–secondary care divide.

In understanding the operational dynamics of the primary–secondary care relationship, it is critical to recognise that both primary and secondary care organisations do not operate in isolation, but rather function within broader networks of organisations and interest groups. Collectively these networks of secondary relationships impact on the dynamics of the focal primary–secondary care relationship. Such networks are characterised by multidimensional relationships between the constituent parties, encompassing managers and clinicians professional links, interdependencies in the service delivery process, and patient interfaces with multiple organisations. This reflects both the multidisciplinary nature of modern health care services and the essentially integrated nature of the NHS. Consequently, the operation of the primary–secondary care relationship is dependent on the dynamics of the relationships between other organisations and non-organisational actors in that particular network. In this regard the critical secondary relationships that require to be managed include those with health authorities, social services, neighbouring primary and secondary care organisations, professional bodies and community groups.

Such networks of secondary relationships uniformly underpin the primary–secondary care relationship within the NHS. However, the nature and impact of such networks can vary significantly. Gummesson (1996) argues that it is possible to view networks as being in dynamic equilibrium, in that any network will be characterised by a particular balance between competition, collaboration and regulation. Consequently different networks will exhibit significantly different patterns of interaction, due to differences in the specific balance between these three forces. The balance between competition and collaboration in a particular network is dependent on the objectives and behaviours, and hence relationships, of the constituent parties in that network. Although the networks faced by primary and secondary care organisations in different localities may appear structurally similar, the equilibrium of that network, and hence the nature of the primary–secondary care relationship, is determined by the nature of the interaction between the constituent parties. In other words the atmosphere within the network is a major influence on the nature and tenor of the primary–secondary care relationship. The management of the primary–secondary care relationship is consequently concerned with the broader management of the networks of which the organisations form an integral part.

At the core of the networks within which primary and secondary care organisations are anchored are the strong socio-professional ties which exist between clinicians across formal organisational boundaries. Such professional ties have a direct impact on the behaviour of the organisations in which clinical professionals operate and in turn the dynamics of the formal relationships between their respective organisations. Reflecting on evolving patterns of primary–secondary care interaction under the internal market, a number of studies highlighted the highly relational nature of market behaviour (Laing and Cotton, 1996; Llewellyn and Grant, 1996; Robinson, 1996). What makes such relational patterns of behaviour particularly notable is that the prevailing regulatory framework was designed to promote dynamic, short-term arm's-length contracting. Although (as outlined in Chapter 3) this in part reflects the complexity of health care services and the structure of the quasi-market, it must equally be viewed as a product of the socio-professional links that exist across the primary–secondary care interface. One of the defining characteristics of the health care professions is the close socio-professional links that exist between professionals working in different sectors of the health service (Flynn, 1992). Based on shared education, training and membership of professional bodies, these ties cut across imposed organisational boundaries and shape the nature of inter-organisational relationships. Harrison (1995) suggests that these professional ties may take precedence over affiliation to externally imposed organisational and managerial structures.

Alongside the underlying resource and status tensions which characterise the primary–secondary care interface at the organisational level, such embedded socio-professional ties shape the particular dynamics of primary–secondary care relationships. Whether relating to the process of referral at the individual patient level, or commissioning negotiations at the broader organisational level, the interplay of these two factors is critical in determining the nature of that relationship. Focusing on the commissioning interface between GP fundholders and self-governing NHS Trusts as a well-documented exemplar of the primary–secondary care relationship, it is possible to identify a number of generic operational themes emerging in this relationship. In reviewing the nature of this interface, Fischbacher and Francis (1999) use the term 'multiplex relationship' to describe the multifaceted and complex nature of the interaction. Although typically characterised as a purchasing relationship, within this overarching context such relationships involved multiple organisational interfaces including information exchange, shared training, and service redesign. Although collectively these separate interfaces or strands determine the overall nature of the primary–secondary care relationship, the dynamics of the individual strands of this relationship may vary. In other words, conflict and cooperation can coexist within the overall primary–secondary care relationship.

Examining these strands individually provides a robust understanding of the dynamics and nature of the overall primary–secondary care relationship. Turning initially to the overarching purchasing relationship, the dominant feature was the stability of existing primary–secondary care relationships. Although the explicit aim of the market reforms was to offer primary care organisations the opportunity to 'stimulate hospitals to be more responsive to the needs of GPs and their patients', this did not result in significant switching of contracts by primary care purchasers. Rather the predominant approach among primary care organisations to poor secondary care service provision was to work with the existing secondary care provider rather than seek a new supplier (Ellwood, 1999). Typically this resulted in joint investment in service developments and formation of alliances between primary and secondary care organisations. Where new suppliers were sought this was typically viewed as a mechanism by which to secure the desired changes in service provision (Fischbacher and Francis, 1998). Such loyalty to existing secondary care providers in situations where the market was not geographically constrained and alternative NHS secondary care providers existed, highlights the importance of professional ties in determining patterns of primary–secondary care interaction. More specifically, the central role of socio-professional ties in shaping patterns of primary–secondary care interaction is evident from the reliance placed by primary care professionals on their professional links with secondary care professionals in determining both which secondary care organisations to contract and the tenor of the contracting process (Laing and Cotton, 1996).

This critical role of professional ties in shaping primary–secondary care interaction is further highlighted by the patterns of information utilisation and exchange within the contracting process. The most striking aspect of the process of interaction is the overwhelming reliance placed on informal non-organisational sources of information, with particular importance being attached to direct personal knowledge and experience of the key professionals responsible for service delivery (Farmer and Chesson, 1998). Such personal knowledge was substantially based on long-established professional contacts with secondary care professionals occurring through membership of professional bodies and shared training. These professional contacts are critical in both the initial establishing of relationships and the subsequent maintenance of that relationship. The durability of these ties is central to the durability of relationships at the inter-organisational level. By contrast little or no weight is placed on the formal service information provided by secondary care organisations. Indeed such information is widely discounted as being of little value in informing primary care decision-making, given concerns with the accuracy and comparability of data, and whether such data offered a robust basis on which to assess service quality. In part this reflects that this information is typically managerially rather than professionally generated. The reliance of primary care organisations on professional sources of information in shaping relationships is evident from Table 4.2.

Table 4.2 **Primary care information utilisation**

	0 No importance	1 Little importance	2 Some importance	3 High importance	Overall importance (rating)*	Ranking
Promotional material from providers	9	9	7	1	26	8
Seminars/presentations from providers	8	8	7	4	34	5
Health Authority literature	5	13	8	0	29	6
Professional publications	8	9	9	0	27	7
Outcome of previous referrals to consultant	0	0	7	20	74	1
Personal knowledge of consultant	0	0	11	16	70	2
Word of mouth: other GPs	1	2	15	9	59	4
Word of mouth: other health professionals	1	7	13	6	51	= 3
Word of mouth: patients	2	3	11	11	59	= 3

Adapted from Laing and Cotton, 1996

It is evident that secondary care organisations increasingly recognise the central role played by professional ties and contact in shaping the behaviour of primary care organisations, and that they are developing 'link schemes' to facilitate professional contact and information exchange (Laing and McKee, 2001). A major element of this is an effort to bridge the knowledge and experience gap between professionals operating in both sectors, as a means by which distrust and distance can be reduced. Increasingly there is an acknowledgement that despite the existence of strong professional ties, the professionals in these two sectors inhabit very different worlds. From the primary care perspective there is recognition that secondary care services are constantly changing, and if the referral process is to be managed effectively there is a need for ongoing training from secondary care professionals. Similarly, secondary care professionals' lack of exposure to primary care during initial training is seen as failing to provide an understanding of the challenges facing primary care professionals. This lack of mutual understanding is core to the dynamics of the primary–secondary care relationship. Fischbacher and Francis (1999), for example, observe the benefit of shared training and subsequent changes in behaviour in terms of referral and discharge letters on the quality of primary–secondary relationships. Shared education by exposing both parties to the reality of the working environment faced by each other is critical in reducing the distrust and latent conflict which has typically characterised primary–secondary care relationships at an organisational level. As such shared training constitutes an increasingly core strand of the primary–secondary care relationship, and is central to the evolution from an arm's-length to more integrated relationship between primary and secondary care organisations.

Reflecting the evolving nature of the primary–secondary care relationship, alongside such shared training is the increasing occurrence of service development partnerships and alliances between primary and secondary care organisations. Given the 'boundary-spanning' nature of the demands confronting health care professionals, the development of collaborative partnerships, notably between primary and secondary care, is increasingly central to effective service delivery (Hudson and Hardy, 1999). For both primary and secondary care organisations inter-organisational collaboration is increasingly the most effective way in which service failures can be addressed. Typically involving joint provision of funding, examples of such cross-organisational service developments include the provision of secondary care outpatient clinics in primary care centres and the provision of pre- and post-operative care in primary care (Singer, 1999). Such adaptations and developments in service provision effectively lock the parties together. At the same time through working together primary and secondary care organisations are able to influence other critical actors within the network, notably health authorities, in order to secure changes in the environment beneficial to both parties.

The primary–secondary care relationship comprises a complex multidimensional and dynamic set of interfaces. Conventionally characterised at the organisational level as an uneasy arm's-length relationship based on mutual distrust, it is evident that the underlying nature of this relationship is changing with growing emphasis on co-operation and the development of boundary-spanning partnerships. Critically this shift is independent of policy, occurring under a policy regime which explicitly separated primary care (purchasing) and secondary care (provision) functions. Rather this evolution reflected the complexity of modern health care, the interdependent nature of primary and secondary care services, and embedded socio-professional ties. However, it is evident that despite such developments, tensions over professional boundaries, funding arrangements, and the operational management of the interface remain a source of 'mutual irritation' in this relationship. Consequently the primary–secondary care relationship continues to be a marriage of necessity – one in which the partners have developed a grudging respect, if not affection.

Developing primary care relationships: isolation or integration?

Over the past three decades primary care has undergone radical organisational change. From the dominance of single-handed practices and small partnerships operating largely in isolation from one another, primary care is increasingly dominated by large group practices working in collaboration. Associated with the integration of additional health professionals into the primary care team and the appointment of a professional managerial cadre in primary care organisations, this shift reflects both the increasing complexity of the environment facing primary care and the need to enhance service provision (Laing *et al.*, 1998). The central feature of this process of development has been the erosion of established boundaries, initially professional boundaries but subsequently, and more significantly, organisational boundaries. For primary care which has conventionally been characterised by a high degree of professional and organisational autonomy, both from central regulation and from other primary care organisations (Calnan and Williams, 1995), this erosion of boundaries has presented fundamental challenges to primary care professionals and managers. In particular the pressure to break down formal organisational boundaries has confronted primary care professionals with a conundrum of how to reconcile organisational self-interest with longer-term service development. Consequently the critical influence on the evolving nature of relationships between primary care organisations is the tension between the desire for independence and increasing interdependency in service provision.

At the core of the changing relationships between primary care organisations has been the emergence of integrative network-type structures encompassing a number of primary care organisations within a given locality. Originally anchored in operational efforts to address specific local issues, such as out of hours service provision and the purchasing of secondary care services, the development of these boundary-spanning network-type structures has subsequently become a central plank of government policy in respect of primary care. The following extract from *Designed to Care* (1997) illustrates the central role assigned to such emergent structures by policy makers, 'General medical practitioners and their teams are increasingly aware of the advantages of working together ... practices are forming alliances, creating the foundations for new primary care organisations, which will overcome the artificial boundaries.' These new network-type structures require a fundamental realignment of the relationships between primary care organisations from one based on isolation to one characterised by increasing integration. In understanding the dynamics of the evolving relationships between primary care organisations, and in particular the development of these boundary-spanning structures, the operation of 'purchasing consortia' as an early exemplar of network-type organisation in primary care, offer valuable insight into the issues confronting professionals working in Primary Care Groups and Local Health Care Co-operatives.

The development of network-type purchasing organisations in primary care represents a significant step in moving away from the isolationist tradition of primary care. Driven by the operational realities of the quasi-market environment, the development of such purchasing consortia, and related structures, constituted collaborative attempts to manage the complex and turbulent environment facing individual primary care organisations (Laing and Cotton, 1997). Although the format of such collaborative structures varied widely, they were underpinned by a number of common objectives centred on the desire to address the power imbalance between primary and secondary care organisations. Specific common objectives included, first, achieving economies of scale and effectiveness in management, second, reducing the workload of primary care professionals, third, sharing experience and expertise to enhance service quality, and fourth, adopting a locality-wide perspective on service provision (Maclean, 1996; Paynton, 1996). These articulated objectives reflect the range of sectional interests that are conventionally viewed as driving the formation of network type organisations. Critical sectional interests include:

- *Interests of users*: network development is inspired by the need to optimise care provision, with network formation securing more effective linkage of supply and demand.
- *Interests of organisations*: individual network members view networks as a means of securing economies of scale and sharing of administrative overheads.
- *Interests of network*: network members share common interests in managing the environment, with the network serving as a means of handling uncertainty.

For the constituent primary care organisations, and the individual professionals, there were clear benefits to be derived from membership of such collaborative network-type organisations. The recognition of clear benefits serves not only as the driver behind the initial development of such structures, but also provides the motive force maintaining the structure. As outlined in Chapter 3, without clearly articulated benefits and an acceptable cost-benefit tradeoff for participating organisations, durable inter-organisational collaboration is unlikely and the resultant network-type structures are potentially unstable (Ebers and Grandori, 1997; Hudson and Hardy, 1999). This later point is particularly critical in the context of both Primary Care Groups and Local Health Care Co-operatives where the initial development was externally mandated (Grey, 1986) through government policy, with the result that the early development of such structures has been concerned with identifying the net benefits to individual primary care organisations of membership (Hopton and Heaney, 1999). Alongside the existence of measurable benefits, the effectiveness and indeed survival of network-type structures is dependent on the way in which they are structured and managed.

The mandate and authority of network-type organisations is ultimately based on the consent and commitment of the participating organisations. As a consequence the emphasis in the development of such structures is on ensuring effective representation of all participating organisations. In examining the operation of purchasing consortia, this requirement typically resulted in the adoption of cellular structures, in which local groups of primary care organisations nominated representatives to serve on what can be described as the executive group of the consortium. Although widely viewed as an appropriate structure, there is evidence of an appreciation among participating organisations that structural representation did not necessarily ensure equality of access to, or influence over, the actual decision-making processes (Laing and Cotton, 1997). Specifically organisations or professional groups that were directly represented on the central executive were perceived by those organisations or professions not directly represented as possessing greater influence. While this did not necessarily result in the representative's organisations having or exercising more power per se, by receiving information more rapidly these organisations were able to take a lead in shaping strategy formulation. This reflects the argument that communication links ultimately constitute the reality and substance of network-type organisations (Piercy and Cravens, 1995). In this regard effective communication was widely perceived to be the 'glue' which held such organisations together. Together with communication, research suggests that the professional networks, expertise and personality of representatives, together with the geographic distance of organisations from the centre of the network, may be seen as further contributors to differences in power and influence between participating primary care organisations (D'Souza, 1995). What both aspects clearly highlight is the critical role of informal links and relationships to the de facto operation of network-type organisations. Collectively these perceptions highlight the underlying tensions and instability inherent of network-type structures where the mandate is derived from the participating organisations and where diverging expectations require to be reconciled. Given the increasingly central role of these organisational structures in the delivery of health care, the problems and challenges experienced in purchasing consortia and related structures are set to be the key organisational and managerial issues facing primary care professionals and emerging organisations.

Drawing on this evidence of the development and operations of purchasing consortia as an early exemplar of network-type organisations in primary care, and the broader literature on networks examined in Chapter 3, it is possible to identify a number of specific influences on the development of network-type organisations within primary care. First, environmental conditions have a major impact on the development of network structures, particularly in terms of cohesion. External pressure, for example the threat of financial repercussions, may force organisations into a network. This is encapsulated in the idea of centripetal forces pushing participating organisations together. However, organisations equally have a range of relationships with actors outside of the network which on occasions require priority, pulling individual organisations away from the network. This is encapsulated in the idea of centrifugal forces pulling participating organisations apart. Consequently network structures are characterised by ongoing tension between pressures for independence and interdependence.

Second, the number of participants in a network, together with the geographic spread of participants, fundamentally impacts on the nature and development of network structures. The more the network expands in terms of number of members, the more the chance of rapid decision-making diminishes. At the same time, with increasing numbers of members decisions tend to be driven down to the lowest common denominator, restricting the ability of the network organisation to develop radical solutions. Despite the scope of modern communications, distance continues to matter in the formation and maintenance of networks. At least distance continues to affect the relationships between the individuals representing their respective organisations. Logically when organisations are located close to one another, it is more likely that representatives will meet in the course of their broader professional activities, enabling informal communication and the development of personal trust.

Third, the characteristics of the participating organisations affect network development. Network structures in health care frequently consist of organisations that perform different functions within the service 'supply chain'. As a result differences in ethos, ideology and culture affect the development of such network-type structures. However, although the participating organisations differ in terms of goals and sources of income, they are functionally complementary, hence limiting the risk of fundamental boundary conflict. Problems within network structures are more common when the participating organisations have significant overlap in service provision and market coverage, and hence face difficulties in reaching consensus as to the boundaries of their respective activities. More specific differences in terms of structural characteristics of the participating organisations, the size of the organisations, the degree of professionalism, and the degree of centralisation, all affect the development and functioning of a network-type structure.

Fourth the personal characteristics and behaviours of individual representatives have a direct bearing on the formation and sustainability of network-type structures. The development of networks is easier where there are strong personal relationships between the members of the various organisations, because the functioning of networks in part depends on the degree to which organisational representatives are able to 'get along'. Beyond social ties, professional networks provide a valuable platform on which network-type organisations can be developed. In this regard the role of social and professional bonds is as critical in shaping the development and operation of network structures as they are in ensuring the effective operation of market structures. However, in the same way as personal ties can impact negatively on the operations of markets, strong personal ties can compromise the performance of network-type structures through resulting in suboptimal patterns of inclusion and exclusion in decision-making processes.

The management of relationships between primary care organisations is increasingly core to the delivery of health care services. Although the erosion of the boundaries between primary care organisations can be viewed as part of an ongoing trajectory of development, the emergence of new boundary-spanning network-type organisations not only shifts such relationships from the periphery to centre stage but also presents primary care professionals and managers with an increasingly complex task. The underlying tensions and inherent instability characteristic of such new organisational forms pose fundamental questions for policy-makers seeking to enhance the provision of health care through reconfiguring the structuring and delivery of primary care services.

Patients and inter-organisational relationships: exclusion or empowerment?

At the core of the management of inter-organisational relationships within modern health care systems is the efficient and effective delivery of services to patients. The underlying rationale for the ongoing recon-figuration of relationships between the constituent elements of the health care system is to achieve a seamless delivery of services to patients across organisational boundaries. This emphasis on the effec-tive integration of health care delivery across organisational boundaries is articulated in successive policy documents '... our modern NHS must care as well as it cures. We will improve the patient's journey from GP surgery to outpatient clinic, from hospital to home' (Scottish Executive Health Department, 1999). The centrality of patient interest in the reorientation and reconfiguration of health care delivery reflects the emphasis placed by policy makers from the late 1980s onward on the empowerment of service users within public sector services (Keaney, 1999). In this regard Griffiths (1988), in the context of health care, argued that 'the interests of the consumer have to be central to every decision taken by the health authorities and their management. It is not a bolt on option to be used occasionally'. Given this emphasis on the empowerment of patients, in examining the dynamics of inter-organisational relationships in health care it is critical to review the extent and pattern of involvement of patients in the management of such key service delivery relationships.

In reviewing the nature of patient involvement two aspects of the primary–secondary care relationship patient must be examined. These are first, the individual referral process and second, the commissioning process. Turning initially to the individualised referral process, data suggests that in the majority of cases patients are typically not involved, at least formally, in decisions regarding choice of hospital and consul-tant (Mahon *et al.*, 1994). A critical issue in this regard is the distinction between the direct formal involvement and indirect informal involve-ment of patients in decision-making as part of the broader consultation process. At the same time, recent research suggests that only slightly over half of all patients expect to be consulted by primary care profes-sionals in decisions regarding the choice of hospital for treatment, with involvement being ranked eighth in terms of expectations of primary care service delivery (Laing and Hogg, 2002). From the perspective of primary care professionals, although there is an acknowledgement of the importance of patient views with the majority of primary care professionals acknowledging that an awareness of patient views influ-enced referral decisions, patient views would to date appear ultimately to take second place to professional judgement. However, within the specific context of the individual referral process, the increasing availability of information on treatment options, as well as hospital and consultant performance data, has the potential to fundamentally alter the respective roles of patients and professionals and hence the dynamics of primary–secondary care relationships (Hogg *et al.*, 2002). This changing role of patients in clinical decision-making, the balance between patient and professional power, and the changing nature of the service encounter is examined in Chapter 6.

Turning to the broader commissioning process occurring at the organisational level, patterns of patient involvement to a significant degree mirror that occurring at the individualised referral level. It is evident from Table 4.2 that in the commissioning process primary care professionals placed significant weight on the information received from patients in shaping decisions. However, in the majority of cases such information was largely derived from the fragmented and potentially unrepresentative experiences of primary care professionals with individual patients. There has traditionally been a lack of formal mechanisms to secure more representative patient views at the policy level within primary care organisations. Those primary care organisations that have sought to develop more formal representative mechanisms to facilitate direct patient input into decisions regarding secondary care service provision reported a deep-seated lack of patient interest and apathy beyond the context of individual or family need (Laing and Cotton, 1996). Where patients participated in such formal mechanisms there was concern about the extent to which those participating were representative of the patient population, as the following view illustrates: 'Only the articulate patients, the chattering classes, ever seem to get involved in influencing the practices purchasing plans, the rest are generally happy so long as they get their pills and appointments' (Laing *et al.*, 1998).

Such limited patient participation must in part be viewed as reflecting the long-established paternalistic ethos of the NHS and the challenge involved in changing patient expectations. This is reinforced by ongoing questioning of the value of patient input by primary care professionals in terms of whether patients can make informed judgements about the quality of care offered by secondary care organisations, even where they had direct personal experience of service delivery. Underpinning this concern among primary care professionals is the perceived influence of the media on patient views of health care and consequently their ability to participate in decisions regarding secondary care provision (Brindle, 1996; Diem *et al.*, 1996). In this regard health care mirrors other complex professional services, where the informational asymmetries between service professionals and service users fundamentally affect the ability of users to participate in decisions regarding service design and delivery (Gabbott and Hogg, 1998). As such patients can currently best be viewed as peripheral actors in the management of relationships between primary and secondary care organisations. However, the increasing availability of information, both as a result of policy initiatives to empower patients and as a result of the increasing penetration of the Internet, erodes such informational asymmetries and offers patients increasing opportunities to actively participate in the management of primary–secondary care relationships. This empowering of patients and the implications for health care professionals will be examined in Chapter 6.

Managing health care relationships: organisations, professionals and patients

A complex network of interconnected relationships underpins the delivery of health care services in modern health care systems. Comprising formal organisational links, informal socio-professional ties, and patient interfaces with multiple organisations, understanding the operational dynamics of these relationships is central to the efficient and effective management of such services. Within this context this chapter has specifically examined the evolving nature and dynamics of relationships between primary and secondary care organisations, and among primary care organisations. The central theme in both sets of relationships is the critical role played by socio-professional ties in facilitating the effective operation of service relationships at the organisational level. By contrast patients as service users have to date had little input into and influence over the development and management of such relationships. In examining the changing behaviour of patients within the health care delivery process, the following chapters will provide the basis for considering the evolving role of patients in the management of inter-organisational relationships in health care.

References

Bostrom, G. O. (1995) 'Successful Co-operation in Professional Services', *Industrial Marketing Management* (24): 151–65.

Brindle, M. (1996) 'Television Programme Distorted Danger of Diagnostic Radiology', *British Medical Journal* 312: 1163.

Calnan, M. and Williams, S. (1995) 'Challenges to Professional Autonomy in the United Kingdom? The Perceptions of General Practitioners', *International Journal of Health Services* 25(2): 219–41.

Campbell, N. (1985) 'An Interaction Approach to Organisational Buying Behaviour', *Journal of Business Research* 13: 495–509.

Collins, C., Hunter, D. J. and Green, A. (1994) 'The Market and Health Sector Reform', *Journal of Management in Medicine* 8(2): 42–55.

Diem, S., Lantos, J. D. and Tulsky, J. A. (1996) 'Cardiopulmonary Resuscitation on Television – Miracles and Misinformation', *New England Journal of Medicine* 20: 1578–82.

D'Souza, M. F. (1995) 'The Multifund and Outcome Research', *International Journal of Epidemiology* 24(3): S113–8.

Ebers, M. and Grandori, A. (1997) 'The Forms, Costs and Developing Dynamics of Inter-organisational Networking', in Ebers, M. (ed.) *The Formation of Inter-Organisational Networks*, Oxford University Press: Oxford.

Ellwood, S. (1999) 'GP Fundholder Admissions and the New NHS', in Davies, H. T. O. *et al.* (eds) *Controlling Costs: Strategic Issues in Health Care Management*, Ashgate Publishing: Aldershot.

Exworthy, M., Powell, M. and Mohan, J. (1999) 'The NHS: Quasi-market, Quasi-hierarchy and Quasi-network?' *Public Money and Management* 19(4): 15–22.

Farmer, J. and Chesson, R. (1998) 'GP Fundholding and Purchasing: Evidence Based Decision Making', *Health Bulletin* 56(1): 476–83.

Fischbacher, M. and Francis, A. (1998) 'Purchaser Provider Relationships and Innovation: A Case Study of GP Purchasing', *Financial Accountability and Management* 14(4): 281–98.

Fischbacher, M. and Francis, A. (1999) 'Relationships in Health Care Commissioning: A Case Study of Glasgow', in Davies, H. T. O. *et al.* (eds) *Controlling Costs: Strategic Issues in Health Care Management*, Ashgate Publishing: Aldershot.

Flynn, R. (1992) *Structures of Control in Health Management*, Routledge: London.

Flynn, R., Williams, G. and Pickard, S. (1996) *Markets and Networks: Contracting in Community Health Services*, Open University Press: Buckingham.

Ford, D. (1999) *Managing Business Relationships*, John Wiley and Sons: Chichester.

Gabbott, M. and Hogg, G. (1998) *Consumers and Services*, John Wiley and Sons: Chichester.

Glennester, H., Matsaganis, M., Owens, P. and Hancock, S. (1994) 'GP Fundholding: Wild Card or Winning Hand', in Robinson, R. and Le Grand, J. (eds) *Evaluating the NHS Reforms*, Kings Fund: London.

Granovetter, M. (1985) 'Economic Action and Social Structure: The Problem of Embeddedness', *American Journal of Sociology* 91: 481–510.

Grey, B. (1986) 'Conditions Facilitating Inter-Organisational Collaboration', *Human Relations* 38(10): 911–36.

Griffiths, R. (1988) 'Does the Public Service Serve? The Consumer Decision', *Public Administration* 66: 195–204.

Gummesson, E. (1996) 'Relationship Marketing and Imaginary Organisations: A Synthesis', *European Journal of Marketing* 30(2): 31–44.

Haggard, E. (1993) 'Integrating Primary and Secondary Care', in Cook, H. and Garside, P. (eds) *Managing NHS Trusts*, Longman: Harlow.

Harrison, S. (1995) 'Clinical Autonomy and Planned Markets: The British Case', in Saltman, R. and Von Otter, C. (eds) *Implementing Planned Markets in Health Care*, Open University Press: Buckingham.

Hogg, G., Laing, A. and Winkelman, D. (2002) *The Internet Empowered Consumer*, Working Paper Glasgow Caledonian University Division of Marketing 04/02.

Hudson, B. and Hardy, B. (1999) 'In Pursuit of Inter-Agency Collaboration: What is the Contribution of Research and Theory, Public Management', *International Journal of Research and Theory* 1(2): 235–60.

Keaney, M. (1999) 'Are Patients Really Consumers?', *International Journal of Social Economics* 26(5): 695–706.

Laing, A. W. and Cotton, S. (1996) 'Purchasing Health Care Services: Information Sources and Decision Criteria', *Journal of Marketing Management* 12: 783–802.

Laing, A. W. and Cotton, S. (1997) 'Inter-Organisational Purchasing Networks in the NHS', *European Journal of Purchasing and Supply Management* 3(2): 83–91.

Laing, A. W., Joshi, R., Marnoch, G., McKee, L. and Reid, J. (1998) 'The Buying Centre: Patterns of Structure and Interaction in Primary Care', *Service Industries Journal* 18(3): 20–38.

Laing, A. W. and Lian, P. (2001) *Inter-Organisational Relationships in Professional Services: Towards a Typology of Inter-Organisational Relationships*, Institute for the Study of Business Markets Working Paper 10/2001, Penn State University.

Laing, A. W. and McKee, L. (2001) 'Willing Volunteers or Unwilling Conscripts? Professionals and Marketing in Service Organisations', *Journal of Marketing Management* 17(5–6): 559–76.

Laing, A. W. and Hogg, G. (2002) 'Political Exhortation, Patient Expectation and Professional Execution: Perspectives on the Consumerisation of Health Care', *British Journal of Management* (in press).

Llewellyn, S. and Grant, J. (1996) 'The Impact of Fundholding on Primary Health Care: Accounts from Scottish GPs', *Financial Accountability and Management* 12(2): 125–40.

Maclean, H. (1996) 'The General Practice Consortium: The Future of Fundholding', in Meads, G. (ed.) *Future Options for General Practice*, Radcliffe Medical Press: Oxford.

Mahon, A., Wilken, D. and Whitehouse, C. (1994) 'Choice of Hospital for Elective Surgery Referrals: GPs and Patients Views', in Robinson, R. and Le Grand, J. (Eds) *Evaluating the NHS Reforms*, King's Fund Institute: London.

Nielson, C. C. (1998) 'An Empirical Examination of the Role of "Closeness" in Industrial Buyer-Seller Relationships', *European Journal of Marketing* 32: 441–63.

Paynton, D. (1996) 'The City Multi-fund: A Mechanism for Primary Care Locality Development', in Meads, G. (ed.) *Future Options for General Practice*, Radcliffe Medical Press: Oxford.

Piercy, N. F. and Cravens, D. W. (1995) 'The Network Paradigm and the Marketing Organisation', *European Journal of Marketing* 29(3): 7–34.

Pratt, J. and Adamson, L. (1996) 'Boundaries in Primary Care', in Gordon, P. and Hadley, J. (eds) *Extending Primary Care*, Radcliffe Medical Press: Oxford.

Robinson, R. (1996) 'The Impact of the NHS Reforms 1991–1995: A Review of Research Evidence', *Journal of Public Health Medicine* 18(3): 337–42.

Scottish Executive Health Department (1997) *Designed to Care; Renewing the National Health Service in Scotland,* The Stationery Office: Edinburgh.

Scottish Executive Health Department (1999) *Making it Work Together*, HMSO: Edinburgh.

Sharma, D. (1994) 'Classifying Buyers to Gain Marketing Insight: A Relationship Approach to Professional Services', *International Business Review* (3): 15–30.

Singer, L. (1999) 'Primary Care Groups of Fundholding', *Clinician in Management* 8(1): 8–12.

Wilkinson, I. F. and Young, L. (1994) 'Business Dancing: Understanding and Managing Business Relations', *Asia-Australia Marketing Journal* 2(1): 67–79.

5 Understanding health care consumers

Introduction

The idea that service users should be viewed as consumers, enjoying the same rights in respect of public services – such as the NHS – as they have with regard to private sector organisations has been central to government policy towards the public sector. Thus the application of commercially derived marketing concepts has driven the development of most public sector services in the last 20 years. The underlying assumption behind such initiatives has been that encouraging consumerist patterns of behaviour among individual service users, when coupled to the provision of information on performance and service standards, would allow the operation of market forces to drive standards upwards. Put simply, the marketing concept places the customer at the centre of the exchange relationship and offers market forces, where the consumer drives demand, as the mechanism for improvement; thus competitiveness drives change. The effectiveness of such initiatives however, is ultimately dependent on the willingness of consumers to change their established patterns of behaviour and exercise the rights and accept the responsibilities given to them. As Butler and Collins (1995: 89) observe: 'Much of the change in the public sector revolves around the attempts by governments … to educate citizens to act like consumers'.

Such policy initiatives must be seen within the context of the broader socio-economic and increasingly technological changes occurring since the early 1980s, developments that have impacted on the expectations and behaviours of consumers in all walks of life. Central to these socio-economic trends has been the decline in the idea of community and citizenship values and a corresponding increase in emphasis on the rights of the individual (Abercrombie, 1994). The challenge for service providers, therefore, is to understand the motivation of the individual and what Campbell (1989) refers to as the 'puzzle' of modern consumerism.

Consumers and health care

The rise of modern (and postmodern) consumerism has been extensively documented. Gabriel and Lang (1995), for example, discuss at length the reasons why the consumer has become part of daily reality in Western developed economies. It has been suggested that the ideas and rhetoric of marketing have been used to legitimise change in both public and private sector organisations, offering markets as the solution to a wide range of problems (Brownlie *et al.*, 1999). Traditionally the marketing concept views consumers as rational, sovereign and seeking to maximise the benefits of personal acts of choice (du Gay and Salaman, 1992). More recently attention has turned to ways in which consumers interpret the signs and symbols of consumption and relate to each other through the 'processes and practices' of consumption (Brownlie *et al.*, 1999: 8). This process, referred to as 'commodification', is predicated upon the idea that all goods and services are in some way commodities that can be traded, the implication being that consumers will use the same criteria to choose a doctor as they would any other product. The service provider's assumed response to this is to reorientate towards the consumers' wants and expectations. Service providers in all walks of life are constantly exhorted to put the customer first, that the customer is 'king' and that these customers have increasing expectations of the services they will receive. For the NHS, which has traditionally emphasised its responsibilities to rather than the rights of its consumers, this requires a refocusing of services to put the patient, rather than the system, at the heart of the organisation. An understanding of consumers and consumer behaviour is therefore imperative.

Although the structural and cultural basis of the NHS has altered over the last 50 years, the fundamental purpose of health care for the individual remains the same – the delivery of health or 'well-being'. This is an abstract concept and one that is difficult for the individual to assess and impossible for the professional to guarantee. Well-being is more than simply the outcome of health care, it is a partnership between the individual and professional that requires both to play a part. This recognition of the active role of the patient and the structural changes that were introduced to solidify patients' rights were designed to force this change in the role of the individual from 'patient' to 'consumer' (Leavey *et al.*, 1989).

The idea of the patient as consumer remains problematic for professional groups for many reasons, however this subject is beyond the scope of this text. What is clear is that the twenty-first century consumer can apply the same criteria to health care provision that they use in other service contexts, and that health care providers need to understand these criteria and respond to them in designing and delivering services. This chapter considers how consumers choose and consume services and the implications of this for the design and delivery of health care.

Consumers and services

It has become axiomatic to state that most of our knowledge of consumers is based on tangible goods. Since the 1960s a growing literature has examined services as a separate product category and latterly has attempted to understand how the characteristics of services effect consumer behaviour. Clearly health care is a service industry and as such understanding how consumers interact with other services will assist in this context. Health care is, however, unique. Consumers can not choose whether or not they become customers of the service, at some point inevitably individuals need health care whether in the form of treatment or prevention. The efficient and effective organisation, payment, management and evaluation of health care systems is problematic for all western democracies. The NHS, with its core tenet of treatment free at the point of entry, has become a cultural icon and one which consumers defend fiercely. Clearly this changes the nature of consumer interaction as price, a central concept in understanding consumer behaviour in most consumption decisions, is removed. Understanding the health care consumer in the UK may therefore be different from, for example, the US consumer (see for a discussion Gabbott, Hogg and John, 1998). The following section considers the applicability of current consumer understanding to the NHS and the usefulness of this theory in this context.

As with most knowledge, consumer behaviour research has moved through a number of phases, each building on the last and moving our understanding forward. There are three broad strands of research allied closely to the root disciplines of economics, psychology and anthropology. These can be summarised as the information processing perspective (the cognitive consumer) and behavioural perspective (the learning consumer) and the postmodern/experiential perspective (the feeling consumer).

The cognitive consumer perspective is based on the idea that the individual consumer, when faced with a decision, will adopt a structured and logical approach to solving the 'problem'. This approach assumes consumers will use information to establish, assess and evaluate the potential benefits associated with the alternatives available and then make a rational and conscious decision. The learning or experiential consumer perspective is based upon a view that consumer behaviour is determined by an individual's response to different stimuli, in particular the responses characterised by approach/avoidance. Consumers are able to learn rewarding and punishing behaviour through the experience of consequences. This type of behaviour, most graphically described by Pavlov's experiments on dogs in 1927, is based on the assumption that there is a systematic relationship between experience and subsequent behaviour i.e., rewarding behaviour is repeated. Those who subscribe to the idea of a feeling consumer reject any form of structure to the consumption experience. The constructs of 'choice', 'decision' and 'learning' are inherently modern and are rejected in favour of consumption motivated by fantasy, pleasure, hedonism and self-identity. From this postmodern perspective consumer research is best directed toward the analysis of transitory experience, where style becomes more important than utility. Whilst this approach has interesting implications for many consumption decisions, its relevance to health care is more problematic. In order to discuss consumer behaviour in health care, therefore, this chapter concentrates on the cognitive approach; the following chapter relates this to consumer learning. This is not to say that the other approaches are either invalid or inappropriate to the consideration of health services, rather the cognitive/information processing approach offers a clear framework to structure the discussion.

The cognitive consumer

Whilst recognising that there are a number of influences on behaviour, the idea of a cognitive consumer is based upon a sequence of tasks characterised as a problem-solving exercise. The problem is formulated as a desired outcome where the consumer must evaluate the components of the environment in order to construct a solution or course of action to achieve the desired outcome. This problem solving behaviour comprises a number of distinct stages.

Like most models, these stages are a simplification of reality but they assist in structuring the discussion. The first stage is the growing recognition of a need or want that can be satisfied through some form of consumption. This stage in the process is characterised in mechanistic terms by a sense of tension experienced as the consumer recognises their current 'state' in comparison with an 'ideal state'. In health care terms this amounts to a recognition that the current state is problematic, called for the sake of simplicity 'illness', and that by visiting a health care professional, most usually a doctor, some form of advice or treatment will provide a solution to the problem. Alternatively the consumer may recognise that their lifestyle or habits are having a detrimental

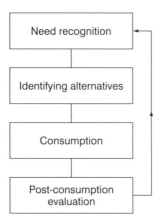

Figure 5.1 **The decision process**

effect on their health and that in order to improve their well-being changes to their current state are required. An important distinction here is in the recognition that not all needs will be translated into goal-orientated behaviour, e.g. consumers may recognise a need to eat five portions of fruit and vegetables a day, but not be motivated to do anything about it. Alternatively consumers may be concerned about certain symptoms but do nothing about them for whatever reason. Need recognition can therefore be influenced by education and information, as well as more obvious triggers.

The second stage in this simplistic model of consumer behaviour is the identification of alternatives, which may meet the need and their detailed evaluation. This process can be divided into an information search phase (where consumers collect information about alternative courses of action), followed by an evaluation stage where they engage in a form of attribute algebra to arrive at a ranking of the possible alternatives. For example, faced with a set of symptoms the consumer may decide on self-medication, advice from an alternative therapist, changes to diet or lifestyle, or a visit to a doctor or other health care professional. This requires a balancing of the information that the consumer has about symptoms, previous experiences, self-knowledge and confidence, attitudes towards traditional and complementary therapies, availability of treatments and services. In other circumstances this would also include a comparison of different service providers: what is unique in the case of health care is that the cultural and structural constraints of the system mean that this need recognition and information search do not lead to provider decisions, these are made infrequently and on a rather different basis than other service decisions.

Consumer involvement

As a social psychological construct, involvement is described by Koziey and Anderson (1989) as part of a person's individual cognitive map which affects their model of reality and gives form to their behaviour in everyday situations. It has been described as an 'individual difference variable', i.e., each consumer has a differing level of involvement. Involvement had been identified as a causal or motivating factor with direct consequences upon consumer behaviour (see Krugman, 1965, 1967; Mitchell, 1981; Kassarjian, 1981; Zaichowsky, 1985; Mittal, 1989). As a general definition, involvement is a motivational variable reflecting the extent of personal relevance of the decision to the individual in terms of basic goals, values, and self concept (Zaichovsky, 1985; Celsi and Olson, 1988). In practice, and depending upon their level of involvement, consumers are likely to differ with respect to a number of decision process dimensions. It is important in this context because whatever the definition of involvement health care is a high involvement product. As a result, when discussing consumer choice of either primary or secondary care, consumers will be both interested in, and involved with, the decision.

Choice of health care providers

The historical and political decisions that lead to the structure of the NHS are beyond the scope of this chapter. The result, a system where general practitioners (GPs) act as the first point of contact for health care services and as gate keepers to secondary care, is important for several reasons. First, consumers are not required to make complex decisions about which specialist service will address their need, or to access hospital services directly, except in an emergency. This makes the initial decision, choice of GP, the crucial point of entry to the system. Second, as GP lists were until relatively recently geographically restricted the choice was generally made between few undifferentiated providers. Although these geographic restrictions were lifted, practical considerations mean that few of us have a realistic choice of more than a few providers. Third, when access to secondary care is required the decision is influenced by the GP, who has professional expertise on which to base the decision. Each of these points has important implications for consumer behaviour.

Choice of GP

Choosing a GP is a decision unlike any other service provider. First, most of us will have been registered with a GP since birth, and only change when circumstances force us to. Although the reforms of the NHS promoted increased patient choice, both the structural constraints in the system of registration on which GP remuneration is based and the cultural constraints of the consumer, result in very little switching. Consumer behaviour literature provides that in order to make a choice consumers have three requirements: information about the alternatives available, grounds for discrimination between the alternatives and motivation to make a choice. In choosing a GP all three of these requirements can be questioned.

In consumer behaviour terms there are two main types of information – internal and external. Internal information is memory, previous experience of the service, service category or individual provider. As most of us have had very little experience of GP practices – patients tend to switch doctors within practices rather than the practice itself – consumers have a very limited range of previous experiences on which to draw (Schleglmilch *et al.*, 1992). External information can be divided into tangible, factual information that is verifiable and common to all consumers, and subjective, interpersonal information from others who have had experience of the service. When the White Paper makes reference to the provision of more information to encourage choice it is the former, tangible factual information contained in Practice Information Leaflets that is referred to. The nature of this information is such, however, that it can only provide facts about, for example, the range of services provided, age, sex qualifications of the doctors and practice accessibility. This type of information does not give any indication of the experience of using the practice or of the primary purpose of health care, the doctors' ability to cure illness. In these circumstances Murray (1991) suggests consumers will look to personal sources of information such as asking friends, relatives or other respected individuals. This supports the work of Zeithaml (1981), who suggests that the need for experience information prompts a reliance on word of mouth sources, as they are perceived to be more credible and less biased. However, this information is subjective and requires an understanding of the criteria that the individual giving the information is using as a basis for assessing the service.

Fundamentally, what is being sought from a GP is not health care per se, but health. The individual patient is not competent to assess this aspect even after treatment; it is possible for the patient to know that his or her symptoms have been relieved, but not always to know if he or she has been cured or even if the symptoms have been treated in the most beneficial way. In these circumstances that patient relies on the credence of the doctor, the trust that a patient has in the doctor's ability to cure illness. The nature of the credence relationship between doctor and patient and the psychological effect of that credence in treating patients has been discussed by a number of authors (see for instance Zeithaml, 1981; John, 1992). Trust is a complex interpersonal construct which has a number of facets, including knowledge, situation and experience. It is, however, very difficult to define and impossible to quantify. The outcome of trust, however, is cooperation, a willingness to engage in behaviour in the belief that it will have a beneficial outcome. This in itself may act as a placebo, improving the likelihood of a successful outcome. When recommending a doctor or practice the nature of the trusting relationship between the professional and the patient is central and yet poorly understood.

The crucial task for the prospective patient is to identify which aspects of the information that is available to him/her are most reliable in predicting the doctor's ability. This distinction between the 'cure' dimensions or the outcome of health care and the 'care' dimensions or the way in which the service is delivered is important in understanding consumer behaviour. This simplistic framework has been used to describe the basis of health care evaluation, where the technically complex 'cure' dimension is assessed on the basis of the more familiar 'care' experience. In other service contexts models have been presented which have similar bases, despite different terminology. For instance, Grönroos (1991) refers to technical vs. functional aspects, Zeithaml (1988) uses an intrinsic vs. extrinsic distinction, Lawson (1986) a motivation vs. hygiene model and Iacobucci *et al.* (1994) describe 'core' and 'peripheral' aspects of the service. Although the word pairs may not be entirely interchangeable, there are strong conceptual parallels. The issue in health care is that the individual consumer, or patient, does not have the technical knowledge to assess the 'cure' dimension, even after service delivery. The patient may know that his/her symptoms have been relieved, but not that he/she has been cured, or that the treatment was the most effective available. A patient has an investment in believing in the ability of the doctor to deliver health, the psychological effects of which have been explored by Frank (1968) and Shapiro (1959). The implication is that faced with this impossibility of evaluating outcome, patients will use other criteria to assess the cure dimension. In these circumstances, *how* the service is delivered is used to evaluate *what* was delivered, i.e. clinical competence is inferred from the process of care. The evaluation of health care is discussed in greater detail in Chapter 7. It is important in this context, however, as it is the individual's assessment of their doctor or practice which forms the basis of recommendation.

Choice of hospital

The second level of choice for consumers comes when illness requires more specialised treatment, which is delivered in hospital. The theory of the market is that this will be motivated by a cognitive assessment of where the 'best' service will be available. Immediately consumers are faced with the same problem as choice of GP – what constitutes 'best' for the consumer and how can this be assessed. The paternalistic approach of the NHS over the last 50 years gave the decision about what is best for the patient to the doctor. The spirit of the reforms however, is that patients will adopt the consumerist role and exercise choice of hospital. Research conducted by Laing and Hogg (2002) has demonstrated that patients are not exercising this choice. The clear expectation of patients in this research was that health care professionals should refer patients to the hospital that would provide the best treatment in terms of anticipated outcome, with convenience and patient choice being as lesser considerations. This suggests a focus on service outcome rather than process dimensions in making service decisions regarding the provision and utilisation of health care services. What is of particular significance is that a consistent minority of respondents to this survey rated customer service issues as 'unimportant' compared with more obviously medical issues such as length of time allocated to consultations and clarity of diagnosis. Over 20 per cent of respondents did not consider that service users, i.e. patients, should expect to have a choice of hospital and moreover did not believe that patient convenience should be a factor in shaping referral decisions.

Although patients want high standards of service from health care professionals in terms of the care they receive, the most important aspect of the service encounter remains the medical outcome, the 'cure'. This highlights one of the critical paradoxes apparent in patterns of service user behaviour in health care. Specifically the outcome dimension in health care is overridingly important, indeed can literally be a case of life or death. It has conventionally been argued, however, that in professional services where the consumer cannot evaluate the outcome, for example legal and financial services, they use the process of delivery of the service as a proxy (Parasuraman *et al.*, 1991). The data suggests that this is not the case in health care. Arguably the service users' emotional investment in believing that the doctor both has the medical knowledge (expertise) and the patients' interest at heart (altruism), expertise and altruism being antecedents of trust, leads to a relationship-based trust that militates against conventional consumerist patterns of behaviour.

This 'rejection' of conventional consumerist patterns of behaviour on the part of many patients to taking responsibility for decisions regarding their health, suggests that patients prefer such decisions to be taken by 'experts'. Indeed emerging evidence on Internet usage by consumers suggests that despite increased availability of health care information, patients continue to seek direct professional guidance in decisions regarding their utilisation of health care services (Hogg and Laing, 2002). Such patterns of behaviour mirror that reported by health professionals when using health services of which they have extensive professional knowledge, with such 'expert' consumers seeking professionals '... who would dominate, who would tell me what to do, who would in a paternalistic manner assume responsibility for my care' (Inglefinger, 1983).

Such willing dependency on the part of service users must be seen as reflecting the high emotional impact of illness on service users, and hence their vulnerability at key points in the decision-making process regarding their use of health care services (Strasser *et al.*, 1995). Inevitably this emotional vulnerability will impact on the ability and willingness of service users to behave in a consumerist manner. It can consequently be argued that the status of health care as a 'distress purchase' fundamentally impacts on users behaviour. Over the past ten years increasing attention has been given in service marketing theory to the development of relationships and the importance of the interpersonal relationship between service consumer and service provider. Clearly this relationship varies according to the characteristics of the industry, but is particularly applicable to the health care consumer as the dynamics of the doctor–patient relationship are so important. Liljander and Strandvik (1995) identify a number of bonds that tie service providers and consumers to each other in a mutually beneficial relationship. Although the economic bond is not as important in a public service, many of the others are.

The perceived comparative strength of these bonds links the consumer to the service provider and determines the relationship between the two. This is not to suggest that the consumer perceives these individual bonds as tying them, but that the relationship between doctor and patient is dependent on the commitment the parties have to each other.

Consumption of health care: the service encounter

Once the choice of service provider has been made the consumer/patient must access the service. In traditional consumer behaviour this would be referred to as the consumption stage and in services this is called an encounter. Health care services are fundamentally an interpersonal interaction between an individual, whose role is the patient, and the professional. The prime relationship is usually characterised as the doctor–patient relationship but it is acknowledged that this could be

Table 5.1 **The Liljander-Strandvik Relationship Model.**

Knowledge bond	Knowledge of patients medical history, family etc. that militates against switching.
Geographical bond	Limited possibilities of going elsewhere because of travel constraints.
Social bond	Bond that builds up as patients become familiar with their doctor which allows them to trust and to talk openly about symptoms.
Cultural bond	Shared beliefs or expectations of the health care system or cultural norms within specific subcultures.
Ideological bond	Common preference for particular treatments or behaviours, e.g. home birth.
Psychological bond	Belief in the doctors ability.
Time bond	Investment in the relationship over time and encounters.
Technological bond	Availability of particular specialist equipment or diagnostics.
Legal bond	The duty of care and confidentiality that a medical professional owes the patient.

Adapted from Liljander-Strandvik, 1995

with a number of health care professionals – for simplicity the professional will be referred to as doctor. This interaction is the central encounter, the situation where the consumer comes into contact with the service provider, and is critical because it provides what Carlsson (1987) refers to as the 'moment of truth', the instance when the consumers' expectations, past experiences, and previous information about the service are validated by first-hand experience. There are a number of characteristics of such encounters that assist in explaining the dynamic of the relationship.

First, encounters are purposeful, i.e., the patient visits the doctor for a reason. Medicine acknowledges that these reasons are not always clinical and that frequently the declared purpose of the visit is not the underlying reason, however within every encounter there are degrees of 'task' as opposed to 'non-task' interaction. Task interaction refers to the core purpose of the visit and non-task to the socio-emotional aspects of any interaction between two individuals. This will vary between patients, but in general whilst some non-purposeful and altruistic social exchange is part of the service, the patient expects to leave the encounter having addressed the reason for going. It is clear that when the participants in an encounter are human and physically proximate as they are during a medical consultation, they are involved both consciously and subconsciously in social action, defined by Blumer (1953) as 'taking each other into account'. The richness of communication in this context is indicated by Blumer as 'being aware of him (sic), identifying him, making some judgement or appraisal of him, identifying the meaning of his action, trying to find out what is on his mind, trying to figure out what he intends to do'. Interpretation of these cues is a vital part of the encounter; misinterpretation by the doctor may lead to incorrect diagnosis, misinterpretation by the patient may lead them to conclude that the doctor is uninterested or uncaring. As 90 per cent of social interaction occurs non verbally (Argyle 1994) this social element of the service encounter is vital.

Second, the encounter provides behavioural boundaries and roles, which each party to the encounter adopts. Traditionally doctor–patient encounters have been dominated by a power imbalance, which dictates that the doctor, as keeper of specialised knowledge, controls the conduct of the encounter and regulates the time and conduct of the consultation. Within the encounter roles normally adopted by the patient in everyday life are suspended in favour of an alternative hierarchy based on the knowledge asymmetry, which has motivated the encounter. These roles may be reversed when the doctor becomes the consumer in other circumstances, but for the duration of the consultation the dominant party is the professional. This information asymmetry may indeed be changing with the increased information available to patients, especially over the Internet (See Chapter 6), but the doctor remains the gatekeeper to access to prescription drugs, specialised equipment and procedures. The roles played within the encounter may also breach the common social rules of everyday life, for example, most doctor–patient encounters require that the normal rules regarding personal space and physical contact between acquaintances are breached.

Third, whilst the individual encounter is a discrete event it will fit into a pattern of such encounters that define the doctor–patient relationship. These encounters may be infrequent, or in the case of chronic conditions, extremely regular: each builds into the overall schema and has an affect on future encounters. Finally the encounter will be dominated by the nature of the relationship or trust that exists between the two parties that was discussed above. Importantly the existence of trust not only increases cooperation, but implies the possibility of 'forgiveness' when an encounter goes wrong. Patients build a sense of ownership of their doctors, referring to 'my' doctor, and as a result minor service failures are unlikely to cause a breakdown in the relationship.

Servicescapes

Doctor–patient encounters do not take place in a vacuum; patients visit the medical premises, either practices in the case of primary care or hospitals and clinics in the case of secondary care. Indeed it is becoming increasingly infrequent that doctors visit patients in their own home. As a result the surroundings in which the encounter takes place play a vital role in the consumption experience. Within this environment are the tangible instruments of service delivery or the signs, symbols and artefacts that are associated with the service. There are a number of dimensions of the servicescape that affect consumer behaviour but for the purposes of this discussion two will be examined in detail, the effect of surroundings on consumer experience and the role of cues.

A number of studies have attempted to investigate the role of the service environment and impact upon the consumers' perception (see for example Bitner, 1992), working in retail environments can be categorised as either encouraging positive approach responses (enjoyment, returning, attraction, exploration) or negative avoidance responses (not to enjoy, not to return, not to explore etc.). In such a rich environmental context – physical design, smell, sound, activity of service providers etc. – environmental influence becomes very confused making it difficult to separate the effect of the environment from other service issues. For the health care consumer, service environments are of concern in terms of their layout, their ambient conditions and their physical content.

Layout   This would include the arrangement of desks, entrance and waiting areas, size and shape of furniture, and obvious process paths, such as signposting, ease of access etc. For example, a professional sitting behind a desk is more intimidating than one sitting alongside a patient.

Ambiance   This includes physical ambiance such as temperature and humidity as well as lighting, colour, sound and smell. Consumers have expectations that hospitals will be well lit, clean and bright and are put off by a shabby, uncomfortable or cold place.

Content   This aspect would include whether the space contained complex equipment or not, whether it contained office furniture or trolleys, was sterile or dirty etc. Consumers are aware that certain complex equipment may be necessary for treatment, but their lack of understanding of the technical details means that they fear much of the equipment and are uneasy or nervous faced with things that they don't understand.

These factors may not impinge on the service or the likelihood of a 'cure', but they provide the wrong cues and therefore effect the consumer's perception of the service they are getting. A distinction can be made between the consumer-dominant domain such as waiting rooms, the employee-dominant domain or the 'behind the scenes' areas that patients do not enter or only enter in particular circumstances usually in the company of a professional, and the exchange domain where the main interaction between patient and health care professional takes place. Each will have a different emphasis in terms of layout, ambiance and content.

These environmental issues are important; space modifies and shapes behaviour and affects consumers through the stimulation of the senses, thereby affecting perceptions, attitudes and images which can all effect the consumption experience. For example, Maslow and Mintz (1953) suggested that the aesthetic appeal of physical surroundings can affect individual mental states, Sommer (1969) cites research that indicates that raising light levels can increase interpersonal communication, and increasing natural light levels can enhance mood.

The second important role of the environment in determining the consumers' view of the service is the way that consumers perceive and interpret cues. A cue is a piece of information that conveys meaning, either intentionally or unintentionally. As consumers we constantly interpret cues in our surroundings and use them to make judgements. The cues are learned and regularly updated according to how reliable they have proven to be, for example, uniform is used to imply authority, a white coat to signify a doctor, or the country of origin of a product to convey reliability. In the health care environment there are a number of cues that patients use to reassure themselves that they can place their trust in the professionals. These may have some practical function, e.g. stethoscope, be based on dress or uniform or be part of the furniture and fittings such as examination couches, but together they help the consumer locate his or her place within the encounter. In many cases the traditional cues associated with the medical world are either outdated or inappropriate, but consumers only acquire new cues through experience. The acquisition of this experience is discussed in more detail in Chapter 6, particularly in relation to the role of television and the Internet in determining consumers' expectations of health care experiences. The point is that cues may indeed be a poor predictor of a successful outcome or no longer salient, but they remain powerful in the minds of consumers, especially in situations of high uncertainty which characterises most health care interactions.

Implications for health care providers

Clearly consumers of health services are also consumers of other service industries and as such use the same criteria to evaluate the services they receive. Although consumers may be prepared to make some allowances for the demands of a publicly funded service, there is increasing evidence that this does not extend far. The NHS has been a constant political issue with all major political parties claiming to be able to offer solutions and to champion the patient. As a result the standards of care and the inevitable lapses in service provision are constantly being brought to the attention of the general public. As we are all possible customers of the NHS, probably involuntarily, these stories are of concern. As in most walks of life, bad service experiences are more memorable and make a better story than good experiences, therefore one 90-year-old lady left on a trolley is a story, one hundred treated well is not. This is important not only for the provision of services; crucially it has an effect on the ways in which consumer expectations are influenced. The formation of expectations is discussed at more length in the following chapter. In terms of consumer behaviour, however, developments in other service provision has an inevitable effect on health care consumers.

Research has demonstrated that consumers are increasingly demanding of service providers, more likely to complain and less loyal to their providers. This growth of consumerism has been slow to reach the NHS for several reasons, both structural and cultural. The nationalised system militates against choice, although the procedures for changing GP were simplified and some efforts were made to deregulate the primary care market, there remains a reluctance on the side of consumers to switch. Reasons for this reluctance are not difficult to understand, as patients have a vested interest in believing in the ability of their doctors to make them better – and the placebo effect shows the importance of this belief. Most consumers choose their GP on the basis of geography, i.e. nearest to home or on the recommendation of friends and relatives, and switch only when forced by, for example, moving house. Similarly, in the case of secondary services there is a high reliance on expert opinion in choosing who or where to be referred to. Indeed outside of the major urban conurbations there is little realistic choice – strategic provision of services necessitates that not every hospital can provide a full range of services. As a result there are very few opportunities to acquire skills in decision-relevant information in the same way as would occur in other services. Choice of GP is a high risk decision, in the extremes a life or death decision, and as a result one that is generally avoided except when absolutely necessary. This goes some way to explaining the reluctance on the part of consumers to exercise positive choice. This does not, however, imply that service providers can ignore the voice of the consumer in designing and delivering services. Indeed it appears that without the market mechanism, choice is simply limited to not going back to a service provider who does not provide a satisfactory service, the consumer is more likely to complain.

Conclusion

The commitment to placing the service user at the core of the health care delivery process has been a consistent policy theme across successive governments in the last 20 years. Although the philosophical and organisational approaches to such reorientation have varied, the objective of refocusing service delivery on the consumer has remained core to health care policy. In marketing terms the focus of health policy has been on exhorting a shift in service delivery away from a producer orientation toward a consumer orientation (Ames, 1970). Central to this shift has been the need to change the behaviours of both parties involved in the service delivery process, that is service providers and consumers, given the inseparability of production and consumption in professional services such as health care (Zeithaml and Bitner, 1996). Most importantly, there has been a need to change patients' expectations of the service delivery, together with their role in that process, and professionals' execution of service delivery in terms of the management of service encounters.

To this end, consumers have been consistently exposed to messages encouraging consumerist expectations and behaviours in respect of the delivery of health care services. Such messages can be seen as being reinforced by the impact of broader socio-economic changes encouraging a more individualistic, consumerist culture. Yet the striking theme to emerge from the research in this area is the relative unwillingness of consumers to articulate consumerist expectations or behaviours in respect of health care services and hence renegotiate the service encounter. There are clear indications that assumptions regarding the willingness of consumers to act in a consumerist manner in respect of health care services may be ill-founded. The flaws in assumptions based on experience from other professional service settings arguably reflect the intersection of two critical factors in respect of health care services. First, in contrast to other professional service settings there is a high degree of emotional vulnerability associated with the utilisation of health care services (Jadad, 1998). This vulnerability leads to interaction based on dependency, which militates against the emergence of conventional consumerist patterns of behaviour, and rather results in relationships based on trust. Second, consumers are aware that publicly funded health services constitute public rather than private goods (Bocock, 1997) and consequently continue to exercise 'private constraint' (Butler and Collins, 1995) in their interactions with health care professionals. It is thus questionable whether encouraging consumerist patterns of behaviour can constitute an effective lever for changing the behaviour of health care professionals.

Evidence of professional reaction to re-engineering initiatives aimed at reorientating the health care delivery process suggests that NHS professionals, like consumers, have not responded to consumerist policies with universal enthusiasm. In part this reflects the top-down managerialist process of implementation adopted in a significant proportion of hospitals. In this regard such initiatives can be seen as mirroring the experience of other of re-engineering programmes in the public sector, where the lack of progress can be directly attributed to the failure to develop professional ownership of the change process at the operational level (Willcocks *et al.*, 1997).

Equally, however, there may be more substantial grounds for professional resistance to the reorientation of service provision. Specifically the reorientation of health care delivery and the concomitant empowerment of service users can be seen as fundamentally challenging the expertise and autonomy of professionals in the delivery of services. In particular these changes have forced health care professionals to give weight to processual aspects of service delivery alongside conventional outcome considerations. By the same token, the reconfiguration of the service encounter and the emphasis on user input may be viewed as a distraction from the core objective of a public health care system such as the NHS – enhancing the health status of the population. As with the reaction of service users to the promotion of consumerist patterns of behaviour, such professional reaction raises fundamental questions over the role and validity of private sector derived management concepts such as marketing within a public sector setting.

This chapter has attempted, within an acknowledged simplistic model of consumer choice behaviour, to illustrate the main influences on health care consumers as they choose providers and interact with the system. The model has two other crucial stages, the evaluation of provision and assessment of satisfaction/dissatisfaction and the influence of this evaluation on future health care related behaviour. Before addressing these crucial issues for the future of health care provision, Chapter 6 considers some of the main influences on health care consumers that effect their consumption and the changing nature of these influences in the twenty-first century.

References

Abercrombie, N. (1994) 'Authority and Consumer Society', in Keat, R., Whiteley, N. and Abercrombie, N. (eds) *The Authority of the Consumer*, Routledge: London.

Ames, B. C. (1970) 'Trappings versus Substance in Industrial Marketing', *Harvard Business Review*, July–August, 93–102.

Argyle, M. (1994) *Bodily Communication*, Routledge: London.

Bitner, Mary Jo (1992) 'Servicescapes: The Impact of Physical Surroundings on Customers and Employees', *Journal of Marketing* 56: 57–71.

Blumer, H. (1953) 'Psychological Import of the Human Group', in Sherif, M. and Wilson, M. (eds) *Group Relations at the Crossroads*, Harper and Row: New York.

Bocock, R. (1993) *Consumption*, Routledge: London.

Brownlie, D., Saren, M., Wensley, R. and Whittington, R. (1999) 'Marketing Disequilibrium: On Redress and Restoration' in Brownlie, D., Saren, M., Wensley, R. and Whittington, R. (eds) *Rethinking Marketing: Towards Critical Marketing Accountings*, Sage: London.

Butler, J. (1993) 'A Case Study in the National Health Service: Working For Patients' in *Markets and Managers*, Taylor-Gooby, P. and Lawson, R. (eds) Open University Press: Buckingham.

Butler, P. and Collins, N. (1995) 'Marketing Public Sector Services: Concepts and Characteristics', *Journal of Marketing Management* 11: 83–96.

Campbell, C. (1989) *The Romantic Ethic and the Spirit of Modern Consumerism*, Blackwell Publishers: Oxford.

Carlsson, A. (1987) *Moments of Truth*, Ballinger: Cambridge.

Celsi, R. L. and Olson, J. C. (1988) 'The Role of Involvement in Attention and Comprehension Processes', *Journal of Consumer Research* 15: 210–24.

du Gay, P. and Salaman, G. (1992) 'The Cult(ure) of the Customer', *Journal of Management Studies* 29(5): 616–33.

Frank, J. (1968) 'The Influence of Patients and Therapists' Expectations on the Outcome of Psychotherapy', *British Journal of Medical Psychology* 41: 349–56.

Gabbott, M., Hogg, G. and John, J. (1998) 'The Healthcare Consumer' in Gabbott, M., Hogg, G. (eds) *Consuming Services*, Wiley: London.

Gabriel, Y. and Lang, T. (1995) *The Unmanageable Consumer*, Sage: London.

Glasgow Caledonian University Division of Marketing 04/02.

Grönroos, C. (1991) *Strategic Management and Marketing in the Services Sector*, Studentlitteratur: Lund, Sweden.

Hogg, G., Laing, A. and Winkelman, D. (2002) *The Internet Empowered Consumer*, Working Paper.

Iacobucci, D., Grayson, K. and Ostrom, A. (1994) 'The Calculus of Service Quality and Customer Satisfaction' in Swartz, T. and Brown, S., (eds) *Advances in Services Marketing and Management* Vol. 3, JAI Press: Connecticut.

Inglefinger, F. J. (1983) 'Arrogance', *New England Journal of Medicine* 303: 1507–11.

Jadad, A. (1998) 'Promoting Partnerships: Challenges for the Internet Age', *BMJ* 319: 761–4.

John, Joby (1992) 'Patient Satisfaction: The Impact of Past Experience', *Journal of Health Care Marketing* 3: 56–64.

Kassarjian, H. (1981) 'Low Involvement – A Second Look', in Monroe, K. B. (ed.) *Advances in Consumer Research*, Vol. VIII, Ann Arbor, MI.

Koziey, P. and Anderson, T. (1989) 'Patterning Interpersonal Involvement', *Journal of Psychology* 123(3): 217–35.

Krugman, H. (1967) 'The Measuring of Advertising Involvement', *Public Opinion Quarterly* 30: 583–96.

Krugman, H. E. (1965) 'The Impact of Television Advertising: Learning Without Involvement', *Public Opinion Quarterly* 29: 349–35.

Krugman, H. E. (1967) 'The Measuring of Advertising Involvement', *Public Opinion Quarterly* 30: 583–96.

Laing, A. W. and Hogg, G. 'Political Exhortation, Patient Expectation and Professional Execution: Perspectives on the Consumerisation of Health Care', *British Journal of Management* (In Press).

Lawson, R. (1986) 'Consumer Satisfaction: Motivation Factors and Hygiene Factors', Marketing Discussion Paper, University of Otago, NZ. Referenced in Iacobucci *et al.* (1994) op. cit.

Leavey, R., Wilkin, D. and Metcalfe, D. (1989) 'Consumerism and General Practice', *BMJ* 298: 737–9.

Liljander, V. and Strandvik, T. (1995) 'The Nature of Relationships in Services', in *Advances in Services Marketing and Research* Vol. 4, JAI Press: Greenwich CT.

Maslow, A. and Minz, Z. (1953) 'Effects of Aesthetic Surroundings', *Journal of Psychology* 14: 247–54.

Mitchell, A. A. (1981) 'Dimensions of Advertising Involvement in Advances', in Monroe, K. B. (ed.) *Consumer Research* Vol. 8, Association for Consumer Research: Ann Arbor, MI.

Mittal, B. (1989) 'Measuring Purchase-Decision Involvement', *Psychology and Marketing* 6: 147–62.

Murray, K. (1991) 'A Test of Services Marketing Theory: Consumer Information Acquisition Activities', *Journal of Marketing* 55: 10–25.

Parasuraman, A., Berry, L. and Zeithaml, V. A. (1991) 'Understanding Customer Expectations of Service', *Sloan Management Review* Spring pp. 39–48.

Schleglmilch, B., Carman, J. and Moore, S. Anne (1992) 'Choice and Perceived Quality of Family Practitioners in the United States and the United Kingdom', *The Service Industries Journal* 12: 263–84.

Shapiro, Allen (1959) 'The Placebo Effect in the History of Medical Treatment: Implications for Psychiatry', *American Journal of Psychiatry* 116: 298–304.

Sommer, R. (1969) *Personal Space: The Behavioural Basis of Design*, Prentice Hall: New York.

Strasser, S., Schweikhart, S., Welch, G. E. and Burge, J. C. (1995) 'Satisfaction with Medical Care', *Journal of Health Care Marketing* 15(3): 34–42.

Willcocks, L. P., Currie, W. and Jackson, S. (1997) 'In Pursuit of the Re-engineering Agenda in Public Administration', *Public Administration* 75: 617–49.

Zaichowsky, J. L. (1985) 'Measuring the Involvement Construct', *Journal of Consumer Research* 12: 341–52.

Zeithaml, V. and Bitner, M. J. (1996) *Services Management*, McGraw Hill: New York.

Zeithaml, V. A. (1988) 'Consumer Perceptions of Price, Quality and Value: A Means End Model and Synthesis', *Journal of Marketing* 52: 2–22.

Zeithaml, V. A. (1981) 'How Consumer Evaluation Processes Differ Between Goods and Services' in Donnelly, J. H. and George, W. R. (eds) *Marketing of Services*, Chicago: AMA.

6 The changing consumer

Introduction

Chapter 5 described in some detail a simple decision choice model of consumer behaviour and examined some of the key features of the health consumption decision and the way in which consumers interact with the system. The disadvantage of this model is that it is static and does not take account of the myriad influences on consumers. In fact as individuals we are constantly revising our expectations about services in line with our everyday experiences. A more comprehensive model of consumer behaviour would also take account of the impact on the decision process of psychological variables and, importantly, consumer learning. Learning is conceptually linked to attitudes, personality and individual motives; in the context of health care however, it is important because it plays a central role in the development of expectations about the service which impacts directly on consumer evaluation. In this chapter the role of learning on consumer decision-making and the impact of this on the formation and development of expectations about health care services are discussed; however, as we enter the twenty-first century it is particularly important that we consider the impact of technology on the consumer decision process. In this chapter two main technologies that alter the nature of the health care encounter are considered. The first is now considered to be an old technology, but one that plays an increasing role in everyday life – television. The second, the Internet, has the potential to have a radical influence on the doctor–patient relationship as the traditional roles based on information asymmetry are challenged.

Learning

Learning can be described as a change in behaviour occurring as a result of past experience (Assael, 1992). The concept is broad and complex but for the purposes of this discussion two schools of thought can be identified, the cognitive, which views learning as a conscious mental activity, and the behavioural school which approaches learning as an unconscious response to stimuli. The two are not as clearly defined as this categorisation would suggest, for example the simplest form of cognitive learning is rote learning, memory through repetition of, for example, an advertising jingle. This type of learning involved little conscious thought and may be argued to be a form of conditioning characteristic of behaviourist approaches. Another form of cognitive learning, vicarious learning, is also closely linked to the behaviourist school. Grounded in social theory, vicarious learning describes the way in which consumers learn particular behaviours, patterns or form expectations by observing the behaviour of others. Based in part on the theory of conformity, individuals adopt patterns of behaviour that they believe are expected of members of a social group. Consumers therefore learn how to behave in particular situations by observing what others, particularly those who appear to be knowledgeable, are doing. From this individuals develop schemata and scripts to govern behaviour in particular settings. Thus consumers are aware of the roles that they are expected to play during service encounters. As Foxall *et al.* (1998) state, complex behaviours do not generally appear spontaneously, but can be explained as a chain of successive acts that in behaviourist terms constitute reinforcement leading to the 'shaping' of behaviour. Consumers build up learning histories based on their experiences and knowledge that determine their response to new situations. These learning histories are the foundation for expectations.

Expectations

In interacting with any service we have a number of assumptions, or expectations, of both what will happen and how it will happen. The role of expectations in determining the consumers' evaluation of health care is discussed in detail in the next chapter. This chapter is concerned with the formation of expectation, i.e. how do patients as consumers develop their assumptions about health services. An expectation is a belief about what will happen based on an individual's learning history. A number of differing types of expectation have been identified including ideal expectations, what the consumer thinks *should* happen; normative expectations, i.e. what the consumer thinks will *actually* happen; and deserved expectations, what the consumer thinks *ought* to happen. As services are made up of bundles of benefits, these expectations relate to all parts of the service encounter, but for simplicity can be divided into process and outcome – how the encounter will take place and what will happen (Grönroos, 2001).

The expectations of certain services are obvious, for example the outcome expectation of window cleaning services is simply clean windows; the process expectations are minimal. In other services the problems in identifying precise outcome expectations implies that a greater emphasis will be placed on process. For example, in the previous chapter the outcome expectation of medical care was described as cure, however it not possible for individuals to know with any certainty that they have been cured, or even that their symptoms have been treated in the most efficacious way. As a result patients rely on the process, or care, elements of the service to imply the cure (John, 1992). It is not suggested, however, that this separation of expectations into process and outcome is as deliberate or dichotomous in the minds of consumers who are unlikely to apply such distinctions. Rather, expectations are generally more easily defined and understood if these distinctions are made.

Grönroos (2001), following Ojasalo (1999), identifies a category of 'fuzzy' expectations. These are expectations that the consumer has but which have not been consciously formulated. They perceive that something is needed but do not clearly know what. If these expectations are not met the consumer is disappointed without really knowing what is missing. In understanding expectation formulation these expectations are important as they may lead to consumers feeling unhappy or frustrated, yet it is difficult to identify where these expectations come from or how they can be managed.

When considering how expectations can be managed a number of factors have been identified in the academic literature as impacting on expectations, for example, the consumers previous experience (learning) about both the particular type of service (product category) and the specific provider; information search about the service in general and the provider in particular; communication controlled by service providers e.g. advertising and promotion; expert opinion both from within the organisation if it is available and from impartial sources; personal purchaser characteristics; price of the service; and finally the service itself including its essentiality and the importance to the consumer (Swartz and Brown, 1991; Parasuraman, Zeithaml and Berry, 1991; John, 1992). In discussing health care some of these factors are more relevant than others. There is no price expectation in health care and little or no advertising, the service is extremely important to consumers, but there is a very high reliance on experts directing and influencing decision making. When considering expectations as an influence on consumption behaviour it is vital to understand how expectations are formed. To date much work in this area has concentrated on internal consumer learning, the role of experience on future behaviour. What has not been considered is external learning, i.e., what consumers learn from the popular media, and in particular that most powerful of media, television, in determining what consumers expect from particular service providers.

The role of television in shaping consumer expectations

Whilst the marketing literature is replete with examples of the effect of television advertising on consumers, little attention has been paid in the literature to the role of television programmes, both factual and drama, in shaping consumer expectations. Lavin's (1995) study of the radio soap opera in creating consumers in the 1930s traces a link between the role models of 'real life' attaining the American Dream via consumption and the behaviour of the American public. These programmes blurred the boundaries between programming and advertising and impacted upon consumers' desires and tastes. At that time, Lavin argues, radio was 'a basic instrument for the national, day to day dissemination of a single consumption ideology' (1995: 87). In the twenty-first century however, the role of broadcast media in influencing consumers is more complex. Mass consumption and the associated ideologies are well established, the debate is now how we can identify the effect of broadcast media and its role in the shaping of social change. The question raised by Curran and Seaton (1991) is whether mass entertainment changes society, or merely reflects the changes made by others. This discussion of whether the media audiences interpret media artefacts and incorporate them into their world view (see Willis, 1990) or media reflects the everyday life of its audiences is a central theme of cultural studies (see for example Fiske, 1989; Golding and Murdock, 1996).

Broadcasting in Britain has evolved as a 'quasi-public' institution (Golding and Murdock, 1997: 23) which has traditionally adopted a role of both educating and entertaining, for example, *The Archers* was originally designed to provide the Ministry of Agriculture with a means of disseminating information about farming developments. Whilst there has been a change in this conception of broadcasting following the enterprise culture of the 1980s which has been reflected in the BBC's increasing emphasis on ratings, and more recently the need to meet the challenge of new technologies, the prevailing culture is still one of paternalism. Terrestrial television companies, both private and publicly funded, are carefully regulated in terms of the balance of their output. However, the arrival of satellite, pay per view and digital television is causing a slow transformation in the structure, habits and predictability of audiences. A BBC policy document in 1995 recognised this change suggesting that audiences are 'more discerning, more aware of their power … less willing to be patronised or talked down to…'. The media consumer is, therefore, an increasingly powerful force in determining programming, both content and policy. As a result Blumler and Gurevitch (1997) suggest that in order for media to maintain their position in society they must be closely attuned to the spirit of the times.

From an alternative perspective, however, Golding and Murdock (1997: 29) point out that, 'People depend in large measure on the cultural industries for the images, symbols and vocabulary with which they respond to the social environment'.

Indeed social systems and media systems are profoundly interdependent. Research with children and adolescents has shown that the media is a primary source of socialisation (Rosengren, 1994). For example, in a BBC Radio programme (BBC Radio 4, 8 October 1998) it was suggested that the television programme *Grange Hill* had changed childrens' expectations of school and acceptable behaviour within school. Much of the work in this area is linked to political economy and the effect of media news on political attitudes, although there is an acknowledgment that the resolution of issues presented in fictional programmes influences how these issues are viewed in the 'real' world. Thus when instigating the government's literacy campaign, a key part of the strategy announced by the Secretary of State for Education was the inclusion of literacy in the storyline for *Brookside*. O'Donohoe (1998) argues that in the course of our everyday lives we absorb a great deal of information from our general media encounters, indeed it is clear that, as Van Zoonen (1998) argues, in certain circumstances viewers do not have any choice but to interpret media as being true to reality.

It is evident that television programmes about the medical profession and health care generally have had an enduring appeal. From early programmes such as *Dr Kildare* and *Dr Finlay's Casebook* in the 1950s to the current programmes such as *Casualty*, *Peak Practice*, *Cardiac Arrest* and *Dangerfield*, medical programmes have been popular. Ten million viewers watch *Casualty* on a regular basis with *Peak Practice* and *Dangerfield* (which combines medicine with the other perennial favourite of the viewing public, crime) attracting large and regular audiences. In terms of factual programmes, series such as *The Pulse*, *Children's Hospital* and *Making Babies* are dedicated entirely to medical matters, whilst other documentaries like *Panorama* also regularly feature medical issues. As a result it is likely that a large proportion of the population will at some time have watched programmes with a medical theme or focus. This fascination with medical programmes that do not always reflect the actuality of medical treatment is of concern to doctors (see Crayford, 1997; Brindle, 1996 and Diem *et al.*, 1996). It has been suggested that the demands of drama and good television override actual fact. This discussion is not concerned with the validity of individual storylines in terms of medical practice, but with the effect that watching these types of programmes has on viewers' expectations of the both the care and cure dimensions of medical services they receive when they take on the role of patient.

Research by Hogg *et al.* (1999) indicated that consumers who enjoy TV programmes based in health care settings had significantly different expectations about the care they will receive from health care professionals than those who claimed not to watch these programmes. Importantly, results indicate that watchers of TV programmes have higher expectations of their GP surgeries on all dimensions of service, including availability of specialist clinics, the waiting room decoration, the politeness/helpfulness of receptionists, toys to keep the children amused, even the way the doctor is dressed. The only exceptions to this were waiting times and convenience of surgery hours. More importantly, they had *lower* expectations that the doctor would be able to make them better or cure them than non-viewers, or that the doctor would have time to listen or explain clearly to them what is wrong and the necessary treatment. When it comes to their satisfaction, however, viewers of these programmes are significantly more likely to be satisfied with the service they receive and the medical treatment they receive. Given the dominant conceptualisation of satisfaction as a comparison of expectations and perceptions (see Chapter 7) this is interesting. Television appears to be persuading viewers that doctors are not able to provide levels of service that they subsequently experience, resulting in higher levels of satisfaction than non-viewers. Considering that the trust between a doctor and patient is a crucial element in medical care and the success of certain treatments (see John, 1992) this is an important conclusion. The role and responsibility of media producers to present an accurate reflection of reality can be at odds with dramatic requirements. This is highlighted in the conclusions of Crayford *et al.* (1997) paper on death rates in soap operas and the Diem *et al.* (1996) paper on the unrealistic success rate of cardiopulmonary resuscitation in *ER*. At the same time concerns have been raised by media commentators about the pressures placed on producers to include government approved 'messages' within storylines (*The Message*, BBC Radio 4, 4 February 2000) potentially comprising artistic integrity, if not dramatic effect.

In this process the blurring of the boundaries between factual and fictional programming characterised by the rise of the docu-drama, so-called 'infotainment' must arguably be seen as a particularly significant development. For many consumers it is reasonable to postulate that such television programmes provide a critical mechanism by which they acquire information about, and develop expectations of, the nature of products and in particular services of which they have no direct personal experience. In the increasingly atomistic society characteristic of postmodern western economies, television may in fact be viewed as providing the second hand experience of products and services, which consumers once secured from others in the community within which they lived. With the ever-increasing pervasiveness of television due to developments such as multi-channel digital broadcasting, this can be viewed as a critical research field in advancing our understanding of consumer behaviour in service industries.

This raises critical managerial issues in respect of the management of the service encounter, in particular the management of what may be characterised as the pre-encounter or prelude. Consumers' pre-encounter comprises both conscious and unconscious information gathering. The unconscious dimension may be characterised by the acquisition of information regarding the nature of services, gathered in the course of everyday life. This type of vicarious learning is crucial to understanding consumers' reaction to health care provision. Increasingly, however, patients are actively and consciously gathering information about their conditions and using that information to impact upon the nature of the encounter. The so-called 'information revolution' engendered by the Internet places consumers in an entirely new position that potentially changes the nature of the health care encounter.

The Internet empowered consumer

Cognitive learning theory is predicated upon a highly involved consumer actively searching for information that will lead to a reasoned decision about consumption behaviour. When this information is highly technical or complex, the individual is forced to turn to professionals to assist and clarify. Health care has long been viewed as the archetypal professional service (Wilson, 1994). The consumer is inexpert, lacking both diagnostic skills and knowledge of treatment options, while the professional is the expert possessing the relevant technical skills and knowledge. As a consequence of such informational asymmetries there is an inbuilt power imbalance in the service encounter, with the consumer engaging with the professional from a position of dependency, and the professional determining what is in the consumer's best interest on the basis of his or her professional judgement (Parsons, 1975). The analogy has been that of supplicant and priest: 'The consumer's only right is to have access to the health care system, to the secular church: once that has been achieved, it is for the professional providers to determine what treatment is appropriate' (Klein, 1995: 307).

The consumer is viewed in such circumstances to be passive, to be a patient by displaying patience, and to defer to the expert judgement of the professional and limit his or her involvement to consenting to the professional's preferred option. Neuberger (2000: 7) argues that the traditional relationship between doctor and patient was one of 'deference, obedience and instruction'. Although the balance between the two parties varies according to the nature of the medical situation (Szaz and Hollender, 1956), the format of the service encounter has been one in which power resides with the professional on the basis of his or her knowledge and access to information.

Internet information

The Internet has the power to change this relationship. The information revolution engendered by the Internet in terms of consumer access to specialist technical information, formerly the preserve of professionals, has fundamentally changed the informational asymmetries which have conventionally characterised the delivery of professional services (Jadad, 1998). Professional dominance and power in the service encounter has conventionally been based on the existence of an imbalance in knowledge and expertise between the professional and the service user (Wilson, 1994). The Internet, with its breadth of information and, more significantly, its scope for interaction among consumer communities through providing virtual discussion forums, has the potential to redress these informational asymmetries and empower consumers to challenge the established dominance of service professionals.

Taking the form of both formal information 'sites' and informal discussion forums, a key component in the exponential growth of the Internet has been the proliferation of health care information (Smith, 1999). This information revolution engendered by the Internet raises fundamental questions regarding the future shape of the health care service encounter. The format of the health care service encounter has evolved in light of the impact of increasing consumer education, declining social barriers between professionals and their clients, and the impact of popular media on consumers, as well as changes in public policy towards consumer rights. It is, however, the Internet-driven information revolution that is seen as marking the key change in the relationship between patient and professional (Jadad, 1998). Specifically the explosion in the availability of health care information through the Internet offers the prospect of changing the balance of power between health care consumer and professional. Detailed and comparative health care information is no longer the preserve of the professional, but is increasingly accessible to consumers.

Validity of information

Pressure on primary care services has led health care professionals to provide an increasing number of services which consumers can use before, or instead of, visiting a doctor. One example is NHS Direct, which is both a telephone and an Internet-based service designed to provide medical advice. Whilst most medical practitioners agree that these services are useful, there have been concerns raised over the advice given. Indeed it has been suggested that the increasing number of self-diagnostic opportunities may be counterproductive as potentially serious conditions are misdiagnosed. The medical profession is therefore split between supporting measures that reduce pressures on the service and condemning inappropriate advice. The number of unregulated Internet sites providing patient information intensifies this dichotomy. That consumers have an appetite for such Internet-based information about health care is evident from the US, where it has been estimated that 38 per cent of the general Internet user population actively seeks information about health and medicines (FIND/SVP, 1996).

This image of Internet-empowered consumers is reinforced by anecdotal accounts in the letters pages of journals such as the *British Medical Journal* and *New England Journal of Medicine* from health care professionals describing consumers arriving for a consultation armed with reams of Internet printouts (see Coiera, 1996; Eysenbach and Diepgen, 1998). Problems have been identified, however, in the veracity of the information patients gather. For example, an article in *The Sunday Times* (12 March 2000) suggested that of 41 pages giving advice on treating a child, only four gave advice that an independent doctor considered appropriate. Indeed, as patients make increasing use of Internet sites for obtaining information, the nature and reliability of the information becomes increasingly important. Analysis of 423 randomly chosen health care sites based in the US and Europe (160 information sites, 148 news groups, and 115 e-mail discussion groups) suggested that commercial organisations that might provide biased information, because they have interests in the sale of related products and services, own more than half the sites reviewed (FIND/SVP, 1996 http://www.findsup.com). Only 48 per cent of the sites were owned by acknowledged 'credible' authorities such as professional organisations, medical schools, or government agencies (Hogg *et al.*, 2002). The challenge facing consumers utilising the Internet to gather information on health care service options is to evaluate the veracity of divergent views on service alternatives.

Health care professionals acknowledge this issue of the quality of health care information on the Internet as a major challenge in managing the behaviour of Internet-empowered consumers. In seeking to address this issue certain Internet sites contain restrictions, which can be either geographic (e.g. 'This information is for UK residents only') or professional restrictions (e.g. 'This information is for medical professionals only'), but unless there is a detailed registration process these restrictions are ineffectual. The anarchic nature of the Internet, together with the increasing questioning of professional judgements by consumers, must raise doubts about the realistic effect of such initiatives. Consequently, questions over the veracity of information accessed by consumers have a significant impact on the evolving role of the professional within service encounter. The role of the health care professional may be seen as shifting from one of information provision to one of information evaluation and verification.

Consumer motivation

It is important when evaluating the use of information by consumers to assess their motivation for information acquisition. The consumer's root motivation for medical information can be described as a 'survival need'. Such a 'survival scenario' is based on psychological theory, which states that 'decisions in which we have a personal stake in the outcome are rooted in changes in body states that arouse emotions' (Wolfe, 1998). Thus, faced with a situation in which individuals perceive a problem with their health, certain consumers may be a consumer who is motivated to seek help and information about their condition. This is not a universal reaction, since for many the complexity of medical information may lead them to place their trust in the advice of the doctor.

Clearly not all consumers have the same level of involvement with health care. It is possible to identify three groups of consumers in terms of the basis on which they interact with the service:

- *Passive consumers* are satisfied with current treatment and/or information provided by their doctor. They are not prone to seeking out alternative sources of information and usually have good relations with their current health care professionals.
- The *active consumers* are not completely satisfied with either their treatment and/or information provided. They will actively seek out information within their health care system and are willing to take control of their health care by voicing their opinion. They are not likely to go outside their current health care system for information. Active patients will also discuss experiences with other consumers within the context of their current health care system.

- The *high-involvement consumers* are not satisfied with their treatment and/or information provided. They will actively seek out information and take control of their own health care by voicing their opinion. They are willing to work outside their health care system and seek outside opinions. They are the most aggressive patient segment and have embraced the Internet as a primary medium of communication and as a means to compare health care systems.

It is readily apparent that the Internet provides consumers with access to an unprecedented diversity of health care information. Of particular significance, however, is the scope offered by the Internet for consumers to engage in discussion with both professionals and other consumers outside of the parameters of the primary encounter (i.e., the main service encounter between individual and his or her doctor). The existence of such bidirectional information forums, by providing consumers with the opportunity to develop their understanding of particular medical conditions and securing alternative opinions on both diagnosis and treatment, arguably has the greatest potential to reconfigure the health care service encounter.

Consumer communities

The global nature of the Internet not only offers consumers access to unidirectional information on health care from beyond the confines of their national health care system but also develops global communities of consumers with shared interests engaged in bidirectional information exchange. At one level these can be viewed simply as the extension of conventional nationally-based support and pressure groups. However, such Internet communities (IC) or computer-mediated communities (CMC), can be considered to have lower barriers to participation than traditional information sources in terms of factors such as time and commitment and importantly the patient can remain anonymous and therefore protect their privacy. These communities offer consumers the opportunity to compare health care systems, diagnosis and treatment as well as offer mutual support and 'counselling'. In addition, because of the evolving expertise of the 'members' of such communities, they have the potential to provide a mechanism for consumer education. These community forums take the form of interconnected chat rooms, personal websites, e-mail lists, and bulletin boards.

The most prevalent form of such 'virtual community' interaction is chat rooms. These health care communities can be characterised as communities of relationship, centred on the emotional and informational ties associated with illness. Within such chat rooms a host monitors the postings and helps to stimulate the conversations. By controlling what is posted and who is allowed into the chat rooms they effectively regulate and 'manage' the communities. While the range and power of the host varies, they play a critical role in shaping the nature of the information exchange undertaken in a manner akin to that of an editor. Consumer communities also take the form of e-mail discussion groups or list boxes. As with the chat rooms, these are loose affiliations based on the shared experience of an illness. The absence of a host monitoring the list, however, changes the dynamic of this form of community from that found in chat rooms. The key feature of this type of forum would appear to be that they offer the consumers a decentralised, almost anarchic network of information gatherers around the world rather than a centralised managed forum. This is likely to provide consumers with greater diversity of information and experience, but equally place greater demands on the consumer to filter such information in comparison to the chat room community.

As health care consumers increasingly discover the power of Internet communities in terms of networking, they are increasingly exploring and comparing treatment options. These networks defy the conventional relationship and information boundaries of the 'primary' service encounter. A critical element underpinning the information provision role of such Internet-based communities is the linking of such forums to other health care information resources on the Internet via 'web rings' or interconnected site links. Such mechanisms allow consumers easy access to diverse resources related to particular conditions. These resources include personal web pages offering highly detailed and personal accounts of conditions and treatments which, in the absence of linking mechanisms, would not be as widely accessible to other consumers given the 'noise' of the Internet.

There are indications that these informal virtual communities are starting to develop outside the Internet environment to form real geographically based subcommunities. The process starts with consumers with similar interests forming virtual communities of relationship. These groups are then linking with other groups to form larger virtual communities which progress to forming into organisations with a shared 'local', i.e. health care system-specific, agenda. Finally these consumers, patients and primary caregivers develop the informational and organisational capacity to lobby health care systems with a unified voice. It can be argued that the Internet thus offers a low-cost start-up route for consumers to join communities of shared interest. As they mutate into more formal geographically-based groups they have the potential to influence local health care systems in a way in which traditional pressure groups were unable to, through their access to international networks of information and support.

Clearly the Internet has significant implications for the level of consumer pressure that can be applied on both health care professionals and governments. Large groups of consumers can meet and mobilise through Internet community forums, the power of such forums being their collective ability to mobilise data from across a network of actors. This has important implications for areas such the drug formulary approval process. If a consumer in the UK finds that a drug is available in the US they can develop a coalition of consumers in the UK to bring pressure on the NHS for the acceptance of that particular drug. While such consumer pressure groups are not new in health care, what is new is the speed and ease of organisation and the breadth of information resources at their disposal.

Doctor–patient relationships

The increased accessibility of health care information to consumers via the Internet poses fundamental challenges for the delivery of health care services at two levels. First, at the strategic level, is the management of expectation and demand at a system-wide level. Second, at the operational level, is the management of the individual service encounter. At the strategic level this challenge is manifest in the growing power of consumer pressure groups and the increased transparency of health care systems, resulting in unprecedented individualised demands being placed on public health care systems. However, the impact of this challenge is most apparent and acute at the level of the consumer–professional interaction. 'Trying to juggle individual patients with decisions on resource allocation for a wider society leaves clinicians with conflicting moral obligations' (Toop, 1998).

For professionals, the ability of consumers to access information comparable to that available to professionals has fundamentally changed the format and dynamic of the service encounter. In particular, the role of the professional within the primary service encounter has shifted from being the pre-eminent provider of health care information to the interpreter and evaluator of information derived from multiple sources. Implicit in this is the shift of the health care professional within the primary service encounter from being the sole information provider and decision-maker, in varying degrees of consultation with the consumer, to being one of a number of advisors accessed by the consumer through parallel service encounters. In understanding this shift it is critical to place the impact of the Internet as an informational resource within the broader context of increasing consumerism in professional services arising from both socio-economic and policy trends. The Internet as an informational resource can thus best be viewed as facilitating the actualisation of latent consumerist behaviour in professional services.

This perceived professional resentment of consumers' adoption of a more active role in the process of diagnosis and treatment is a recurring theme among consumers in both the UK and US. In particular there is widespread concern with the negative reaction of health care professionals to increased consumer involvement in the service encounter. Such consumers do not perceive themselves to be either questioning the expertise of the professional or seeking to bypass the professional, but rather to be taking increased ownership of their particular condition. One potential explanation for this emerging tension in the consumer–professional relationship is that the consumer, despite lacking the underlying training, has an advantage because they are generally studying one condition, while the professional must keep up to date on a broad range of conditions and associated medicines and treatments. This is especially true of the NHS, where there is restricted access to specialist professionals due to the general practitioner playing a larger role in treatment and acting as the 'gatekeeper' to secondary care. This education conundrum underpinning the changing consumer–professional relationship is likely to continue as the pace and range of prescription drug treatments accelerates due to advances in drug development technology (i.e. biotechnology, genomic databases, computer-assisted drug design, and combinatorial chemistry). These new technologies are drastically reducing the time of screening compounds and finding targets for new drug development. This, in turn, is likely to lead to an increased number of potential prescription products entering the market.

Implications for health care providers

This chapter has concentrated on two relatively narrow but nonetheless important aspects of consumer learning. Television, whilst a passive push technology, is ubiquitous in modern western society and therefore inevitably plays a role in consumer learning, influencing the expectations that individual patients have of the service they will receive. The wider debate about the role of television in affecting behaviour is beyond the scope of this discussion. The argument is rather that the invasiveness of the medium means that consumers learn vicariously what they can expect from health care. Anecdotal evidence has shown that health concerns discussed in the media are immediately transferred to the doctors' waiting room and issues such as the safety of the MMR vaccine are of intense media interest. Health care is an inexact science, 'correct' treatment is a matter of professional judgement and as such consumers are ill-equipped to evaluate the outcome of treatment. As a result the dependence on process or the care dimensions of service are increasingly important for certain groups of consumers.

The Internet provides a totally different type of consumer learning. Clearly cognitive, this type of learning is based once again on the difficulties in evaluating health care treatment. These high involvement Internet-empowered consumers prefer to adopt a proactive approach to information acquisition and actively challenge the knowledge base of the professional. For health care professionals the significance of the Internet-empowered consumer is in redesigning the actual face to face encounter from a paternalistic, asymmetric exchange towards more participatory style (Toop, 1998). Consumers, both individually and collectively, need to be treated as co-producers (Wikstrom, 1996) within the service encounter. Consumers' desire to develop knowledge of particular conditions has scope for exploitation by health care professionals. Such exploitation of the consumer as co-producer would allow consumers to be connected with the process of health care delivery and enhance the capabilities of the health service professionals. The adoption of such consumer–professional partnerships, however, requires fundamental changes in the position of the service professional in the service encounter. Such fundamental reconfiguration requires a change in the prevailing professional culture of the entire organisation.

In terms of the diffusion of innovations, it is clear that once the power offered by access to specialist information is realised by the high involvement consumer it is unlikely to remain unused. Indeed consumers may use this informational power to assist friends and family members in maximising their input into the service encounter. Consumerist patterns of behaviour will arguably be transferred between consumers, that is from early adopters to laggards, thereby shifting the balance of consumers in the direction of more active participation in the service encounter.

Conclusion

The service encounter, what Carlsson (1987) described as 'the moment of truth', is the actualisation of the service, that is the intersection of service capacity and demand. The service encounter can thus be seen as the point at which the consumer can evaluate the service offering and the health care provider manage consumer perceptions (John, 1996). As a consequence the dynamics and management of the service encounter are central to the understanding of the consumers' perceptions of health care. However, this predominant focus on interpersonal interactions and their surrounding environment may place artificial boundaries on the nature of the service encounter. If health care providers are to improve their understanding of the consumer it is important to look outside of the interpersonal interaction to consider the attitudes, expectations and understanding of patients. The following chapter considers patients' evaluation of satisfaction and how this can be measured and managed.

References

Assael, M. (1992) *Consumer Behaviour and Marketing Action*, 4th edn, PWS: Kent, MA.

Blumler, J. and Gurevitch, M. (1997) 'Media Change and Social Change' in Curran, J. and Gurevitch, M. (eds) *Mass Media and Society*, Arnold: London.

Brindle, M. J. (1996) 'Television programme distorted danger of diagnostic radiology', *BMJ* 312(4): 1163.

Calzon, J. (1987) *Moments of Truth*, Ballinger Books: Cambridge, MA.

Coiera, E. (1996) 'The Internet's Challenge to Health Care Provision', *BMJ* 312: 3–4.

Crayford, T., Hooper, R. and Evans, S. (1997) 'Death Rates of Characters in Soap Operas on British Television: Is a Government Health Warning Required?', *BMJ* 315: 1649–52.

Curran, J. and Seaton, J. (1996) *Power without Responsibility: Press and Broadcasting in Britain*, 5th edn, Routledge: London.

Diem, S., Lantos, J. D. and Tulsky, J. A. (1996) 'Cardiopulmonary Resuscitation on Television – Miracles and Misinformation', *New England Journal of Medicine* 20: 1578–82.

Eysenbach, G. and Diepgen, T. L. (1998) 'Towards Quality Management of Medical Information on the Internet: Evaluation, Labelling and Filtering of Information', *BMJ* 317: 1496–502.

Fiske, J. (1989) *Understanding Popular Culture*, Unwin: London.

Foxall, G. R., Goldsmith, R. E. and Brown, S. (1998) *Consumer Psychology*, International Thomson Business Press: London.

Golding, P. and Murdock, G. (1996) 'Culture, Communications and Political Ecomony' in Curran, J. and Gurevitch, M. (eds) *Mass Media and Society*, Arnold: London.

Golding, P. and Murdock, G. (1997) 'Culture, Communications and Political Economy' in Curran, J. and Gurevitch M. (eds) *Mass Media and Society*, Arnold: London.

Gronroos, C. (2001) *Service Management and Marketing: A Customer Relationship Management Approach*, Wiley: London.

Hogg, G., Laing, A. and Tagg, S. (1999) The Role of TV Programmes in Determining Customer Expectations of Services', *Proceedings of the 28th EMAC Conference*, Berlin 11–14 May, 1086–95.

Hogg, G., Laing, A. and Winkelman, D. (2002) *The Internet Empowered Consumer*, Working Paper Glasgow Caledonian University Division of Marketing 04/02.

Jadad, A. (1998) 'Promoting Partnerships: Challenges for the Internet Age', *BMJ* 319: 761–4.

John, Joby (1992) 'Patient Satisfaction: The Impact of Past Experience', *Journal of Health Care Marketing*, 3: 56–64.

Klein, R. (1995) 'Big Bang Health Care Reform – Does it Work? The Case of Britain's 1991 NHS Reforms', *Millbank Quarterly* 73: 299–337.

Lavin, M. (1995) 'Creating Consumers in the 1930s: Irna Philips and the Radio Soap Opera', *Journal of Consumer Research* 22: 75–89.

Neuberger, J. (2000) 'The Educated Patient: New Challenges for the Medical Profession', *Journal of Internal Medicine* 247: 6–10.

Ojasalo, J. (1999) Quality Dynamics in Professional Services, Working Paper Swedish School of Economics, Centre for Relationship Management.

Parasuraman, A., Berry, L. and Zethaml, V. A. (1991) 'Understanding Customer Expectations of Service', *Sloan Management Review* Spring, 39–48.

Parsons, T. (1975) 'The Sick Role and the Role of the Physician Reconsidered', *Millbank Quarterly* 53: 257–78.

Rosengren, K. (1994) 'Media Use Under Structural Change', in *Media Effects and Beyond: Culture, Socialisation and Lifestyles,* Routledge: London.

Smith, D. (1999) 'The Free Access Revolution', *Marketing* 4 March, 14–15.

Swartz, T. and Brown, S. (1989) 'Consumer and Provider Expectations and Experiences in Evaluating Professional Services', *Journal of the Academy of Marketing Science* 17: 189–95.

Szaz, T. S. and Hollender, M. H. (1956) 'A Contribution to the Philosophy of Medicine', *Archives of Internal Medicine* 97: 585–92.

Toop, L. (1998) 'Primary Care: Core Values', *BMJ* 316: 1882–3.

Van Zoonen, L. (1997) 'Feminist Perspectives', in Curran, J. and Gurevitch, M. (eds) *The Media in Mass Media and Society*, Arnold: London.

Willis, P. (1990) *Common Culture*, OUP: Milton Keynes.

Wikstrom, S. (1996) 'The Customer as Co-Producer', *European Journal of Marketing* 30(4): 6–19.

Wilson, A. (1994) *Emancipating the Professions*, John Wiley and Sons: Chichester.

Wolfe, D. (1998) Wyatt, J. C. (1997) 'Commentary: Measuring the Quality and Impact of the World Wide Web', *BMJ* 317: 1881–4.

Zeithaml, V., Parasuraman, A. and Berry, L. (1991) 'Understanding Customer Expectations of Service', *Sloan Management Review* 39: 89–96.

7 Consumer evaluation of health care

Introduction

This penultimate chapter continues to focus on the final consumers of health care and addresses some key issues with respect to service evaluation. Usually described within the health care literature as the measurement of patient (or carer) satisfaction, a wealth of publications have focused on issues ranging from practical questionnaire design to ideological debates questioning the role of the consumer as evaluator. The value of patient satisfaction data as an evaluatory mechanism has been questioned by many, both within the NHS and elsewhere. The conceptual and methodological problems involved are well documented both in the health care and marketing/service quality literature, where for the latter, 'consumer satisfaction' represents a pivotal construct. Key issues from a range of literatures are synthesised here to provide a framework for discussion of the major decision areas and contingent problems involved in assessing consumers' evaluation of health care.

Why measure patient satisfaction?

A growing emphasis on consumerism, and the need for accountability within the public sector, has been paralleled by an increasing interest in gathering information from consumers. A decade ago Fitzpatrick (1990) argued that within the National Health Service these general currents gained specific and influential expression in the NHS management inquiry (1983) (the *Griffiths Report*), which emphasised the need to obtain systematic evidence of patients' satisfaction. In 1989, McIver and Carr-Hill reported that all but one region in the NHS had produced policy documents on quality assurance and customer relations, and that surveys of patient satisfaction appeared to be key components of this activity. Since the *Griffiths Report* a number of NHS initiatives have emphasised the role of patient opinion in service evaluation (see for example *Working for Patients*, Department of Health, 1989).

More recently, the Government's Performance Assessment Framework (Department of Health, 1997), outlined in the first chapter, includes an assessment of 'patient/carer' experience where a national survey will provide 'systematic and comparable information' for assessing the quality of care received. This focus amongst policy-makers reflects the role of the patient as both taxpayer and consumer, who therefore has a right to a quality service, and the centrality of the NHS as an indicator of political success. Other proponents of patient satisfaction measurement highlight the relationship between satisfaction and behaviour, either where a patient can choose between alternatives in terms of customer choice and switching behaviour (Gabbott and Hogg, 1995; Jun *et al.*, 1998) as an influence on decision-makers, for example, GPs purchasing health services or in terms of patients following medical advice, reattendence and health improvement. (Hopkins, 1990; Hudak and Wright, 2000). Finally, the relatively low cost of patient satisfaction measurement and the apparent simplicity with which questionnaire data can be collected, analysed and presented has been highlighted (Levois *et al.*, 1981).

Whilst many support the view that consumer opinion should be an input into decision-making and an important element in performance evaluation, there is also considerable concern with respect to the value of such information. Both practitioners and researchers have raised a number of issues involved in obtaining and evaluating patient satisfaction data.

Problems and issues in the measurement of patient satisfaction

Concern over the relevance of patient satisfaction research focuses upon a number of questions and issues:

Can consumers/patients evaluate the service which they receive?

Hopkins (1990) for example, while arguing the case for assessing patient satisfaction stated: 'It must be remembered that one can have a satisfied patient who has had inappropriate investigation, incorrect diagnosis, inappropriate therapy and a less favourable outcome than could have occurred with treatment of better quality' (1990: 55).

Similarly, Clare (1990: 106) argued:

The satisfied patient may well be satisfied with very little. Did we not all know physicians with substantial private practices and a clientele of adoring patients but to whom we fellow physicians, with our insiders' knowledge would not send our dog.

Although for some members of the medical profession the notion of user participation runs counter to shared professional beliefs (Crawford and Kessel, 1999), a key issue for others centres on what patients are capable of evaluating and specifically, their ability to evaluate the 'technical quality' of the service.

A number of studies (Rashid *et al.*, 1989; Smith and Armstrong, 1989; Jun *et al.*, 1998); have found differences between patients' evaluations of the quality of care and those of doctors, governments or administrators. Critics have used such findings to suggest that patients' assessments of care are ill-informed and inadequate measures. Others have challenged these views, citing studies which have indicated agreement between providers and consumers of health care, arguing that patients may be more capable judges than sceptics have implied (see for example Davies and Ware, 1988; Pascoe, 1983). Additionally, the need for service providers to be aware of the differences between their own and consumers' evaluations is highlighted in service quality models (Parasuraman *et al.*, 1985).

Do variations in satisfaction reflect consumer characteristics rather than differences in the standard of care?

Other critics of the usefulness of consumers' satisfaction ratings claim that variations in evaluations reflect respondent characteristics rather than differences in the quality of care. Researchers have replied to these criticisms by either describing the weakness of relationships in studies or by arguing for the probability that features of medical care and individual characteristics are related in the real world, thus groups of consumers are receiving different levels of care (see for example, Davies and Ware, 1988; Locker and Dunt, 1978; Fitzpatrick and Hopkins, 1983; Linn and Greenfield, 1984).

A challenge for patient satisfaction researchers therefore is to identify how and why patient characteristics impact on evaluation; whether these do reflect differences in the actual level of service delivery *or* differences in, for example, the expectations of different consumer groups. An additional factor, discussed later, relates to the extent to which patient characteristics impact on response biases, such as acquiescence (yea-saying), extreme responses etc.

Whose satisfaction is (and should be) being measured?

The emphasis on consumerism highlights the need for all sections of the public to have a voice in the design and evaluation of public services. One problem with all aspects of community involvement is the tendency for some groups not to be fully represented. Many patient satisfaction measures require not only a level of literacy but also considerable motivation to complete. The elderly, for example (although by no means a homogenous group [see Jones *et al.*, 1987]) may experience difficulties in responding to Likert scale formats (Smith, 1993) which form the basis of many of the well-documented patient satisfaction and service quality questionnaires discussed later.

Similarly, Godfrey and Wistow (1997) argue that mental health services present a particular challenge to user participation in decisions on treatment. Where the nature of the illness has been perceived as a rationale for discounting peoples' experience and therefore excluding them from both exercising choice and involvement in decision-making. Here too the need, for example, to administer questions orally may result in higher levels of satisfaction being recorded than when questionnaires are self-administered (see Levois *et al.*, 1981).

Finally, the role of other 'consumers' must be considered and in particular, those carers for whom medical/health care experiences have a significant impact. Ygge and Arnetz (2001), for example, have developed a questionnaire to measure parental satisfaction with paediatric hospital care, and the role of satisfaction in influencing these groups to ensure compliance with medical advice and attain beneficial outcomes has been emphasised (Taylor, 1996; Lewis *et al.*, 1986). For further discussion of issues relevant to the measurement of parent satisfaction see McNaughton (1994).

The failure of patient satisfaction measures to predict related behaviours

As previously discussed, proponents of patient satisfaction measurement emphasise a link between the satisfied patient (and others) and contingent behaviours such as compliance with medical advice. Similarly, the management literature emphasises the positive relationship between satisfaction, service quality and, for example, word of mouth recommendation and customer retention (Fornell, 1992; Zahorik and Rust, 1992; Gremler and Brown, 1999). The relationship between positive evaluations, intended and actual behaviour is complex and tenuous, and has been described both within a health care and wider context. Explanatory factors may include those attributable to the research process; for example, the respondent's wish to please the researcher, express rational views or avoid complex explanations. Additionally, intended behaviours are subject to future developments such as, environmental change, availability of alternatives, and changes in motivation of the respondent.

Research design problems

Even when it is agreed that patient satisfaction measurement is a useful input to service evaluation and design, the problems in operationalising such measures are considerable. Significant debate surrounds key questions – for example:

- What is patient satisfaction?
- What can, and should, be measured?
- What measurement problems should be anticipated?

These questions are addressed in Figure 7.1 and form the basis of the remaining sections of this chapter.

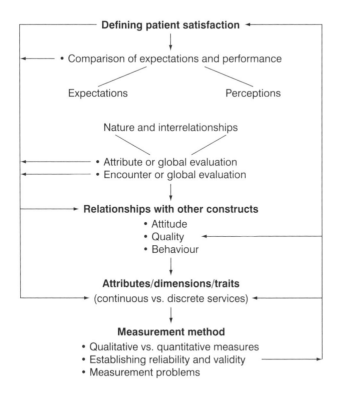

Figure 7.1 **Measuring patient satisfaction: key issues**

Defining 'patient satisfaction' and its relationship with other constructs: what is being measured?

The first stage in the measurement of consumer-related constructs is to define the phenomenon under investigation (Churchill, 1979); yet those concerned with the conceptualisation and measurement of patient satisfaction within the NHS generally agree that it is ill-defined. More recent concerns (see for example, Avis *et al.*, 1995; Hudak and Wright, 2000; Sitzia and Wood, 1997) continue to reflect those of earlier authors. Locker and Dunt (1978), for example, argued that it was rare to find the concept of satisfaction defined, and that there had been little clarification of what the term meant either to researchers who employed it or respondents who reported it. In 1990, Fitzpatrick stated:

> In view of the amount of effort that is currently being invested in conducting surveys of patient satisfaction in this country and elsewhere, it would be reasonable to expect that the concept of satisfaction had been clearly defined and that some effort has been made to measure the phenomenon with a degree of consistency. This is far from the case.

> (1990: 20)

A number of approaches for defining and conceptualising patient satisfaction have emerged in the medical/health care literature, and these reflect developments elsewhere, for example, in research focusing on consumer behaviour. Three major themes are:

Patient satisfaction as a comparison of expectations and performance

The premise that consumer satisfaction derives from a comparison of prior expectations with perceived performance levels is a dominant theme in both consumer behaviour and the medical and health care literature. Pascoe (1983) states that most patient satisfaction studies have used a discrepancy approach i.e. involving the subject's perception of what is expected, or valued, as the baseline for comparing actual outcomes.

The nature of expectations is however complex. Ross *et al.* (1987) in a review of the research focusing on the role of expectations in patient satisfaction, cite four studies of primary care where expectations have been defined specifically i.e. Noyes *et al.* (1974) – time spent, cost and pain; Burton and Wright (1980) – pain, mobility, deformity, and/or post-operative care; Ross *et al.* (1981) – waiting time, physician style, knowledge of family and technical quality of care and Rogers *et al.*

(1982) – improved physical function and decreased pain. Thus expectations in the patient satisfaction literature have been defined in terms of both process and outcome and later studies have developed the areas which patients evaluate when determining their level of satisfaction.

A second major focus is on the complex relationship between the patient's expectations, the perceived performance level and the reported level of satisfaction. The assumed definition of expectations is important here since researchers have adopted a variety of measures. Fitzpatrick and Hopkins (1983) for example, conceptualise expectations as predicted actions, whereas Miller (1979) has described a range of expectations i.e. a subjective ideal, a subjective sense of what one deserves, a subjective average of past experience in similar situations or some minimally acceptable level. Thompson and Sunol (1995) add 'unformed' to a classification also including ideal, predicted and normative expectations. They argue that 'while the concept of unformed expectations may seem a negation of the concept when using the definition of a belief it may actually be extremely prevalent in the health care context' (1995: 131).

Pascoe (1983), in describing the logical and empirical weakness of a discrepancy approach, argues that the subjective standard used for judging a health care experience may be one, or a combination of expectations. Further, he argues for a latitude of acceptance around these subjective standards which will result in generally satisfied consumers. Linder-Pelz (1982) has emphasised the patient's tendency to post-rationalise expectations following an encounter and underlying psychological traits, such as the need for consistency, have been highlighted by researchers (Levois *et al.*, 1981). In view of the many approaches adopted to measure expectations and the complexity of the disconfirmation process it is not surprising that studies have provided equivocal conclusions.

Patient satisfaction as attribute or global evaluation

Patient satisfaction researchers (see for example, Locker and Dunt, 1978; Hopkins, 1990) have noted that global measures of satisfaction are of little or no value, since patients will generally state that they are very satisfied with the level of care. However, questioning with respect to attributes of care will elicit varying levels of patient satisfaction.

Further discussion within the health care literature focuses on the multidimensionality of care, and a considerable amount of research has aimed to identify the dimensions, or factors, which consumers evaluate in their assessments of the standards of care. Here, health care research parallels that of the service quality, rather than consumer satisfaction, literature as discussed later.

Patient satisfaction as evaluation of an encounter or global evaluation

Singh (1991) describes how more recent research has regarded the episode (or situation) as a major source of variation in 'satisfaction' evaluations. Consequently, a patient's satisfaction with care would be better defined as an individual's evaluation of the quality of care in a specific medical care situation, and not as a global evaluation (or attitude) aggregated across episodes. Pascoe (1983) emphasises that in patient satisfaction research the domain should be clearly explicated and that one important measurement issue involves whether general health care (macro) or a particular service experience (micro) is being considered. He also criticises the conceptualisation of satisfaction as an expectancy – value attitude (as suggested by Linder-Pelz [1982]), emphasising the impact of the immediate experience rather than general values and expectations regarding the medical enterprise. Conversely, researchers (for example Godfrey and Wistow, 1997) have emphasised the need to adopt a more holistic approach, focusing on the individual patient rather than an aspect of the service. The decision with respect to the scope of the enquiry has important implications for the measurement method used (for example, critical incidents technique; diary etc); for the timing of evaluation and consequently for the interpretation of which construct has been measured (for example satisfaction or attitude). This last point is discussed in the next section, and other issues in later sections focusing on measurement methods.

Relationships between constructs

As indicated in the previous section, a failure to clearly define the scope and domain of 'patient satisfaction' will preclude:

- A reasoned evaluation of relationships, for example, between high levels of satisfaction and behaviours, such as conformance with medical advice;
- Comparison between research studies;
- A meaningful assessment of the reliability and validity of patient satisfaction measures.

The variety of measures adopted for an assessment of 'expectations' has already been addressed. Further need for clarification surrounds the complex relationships between satisfaction, attitude and quality (in particular, consumer-perceived service quality).

Earlier conceptualisations of patient satisfaction in the medical/health care literature generally did not distinguish between satisfaction and attitude. Hulka *et al.* (1970) for example, defined satisfaction as the patient's attitudes towards physicians and medical care. Roberts and Tugwell (1987) described both the 'Hulka' and 'Ware' patient satisfaction questionnaires as measuring attitudes. Fitzpatrick and Hopkins (1983) describe how one theme which emerges from the treatment by survey research of patients' evaluations of their health care, is that patients' views are attitudinal. In describing satisfaction as a positive attitude, Linder-Pelz (1982) emphasises that attitudes are affective and equates affect with evaluation; perceptions are equated with beliefs and described as cognitive, while cognitions are distinguished from attitudes. Ross *et al.* (1987) also support this view, emphasising that satisfaction is affective and equating expectations to beliefs, again describing these as cognitive.

Other patient satisfaction researchers (see for example, Pascoe, 1983; Singh, 1991) have highlighted Hunt's (1977) definition of satisfaction/dissatisfaction, in the consumer behaviour literature i.e. as an evaluation, a 'quasi-cognitive construct' rather than solely an emotion. Pascoe (1983) for example, describes patient satisfaction as involving a cognitive evaluation of health care and an emotional reaction to health care.

Further discussion of the relationship between satisfaction and attitude can be found in the consumer behaviour literature, where Oliver (1981) for example argues that:

> Attitude is the consumer's relatively enduring affective orientation ... while satisfaction is the emotional reaction following a disconfirmation experience which acts on the base attitude level and is consumption specific. Attitude is measured in terms more general to product or store and is less situationally oriented.
>
> (1981: 42)

He also states that satisfaction soon decays into one's overall attitude. Within a services management context, researchers have also argued that distinctions may vary according to whether, for example, continuous or discrete service transactions are under consideration (Vandamme and Leunis, 1993; Bolton and Drew, 1991a; 1991b).

A particular driver for a more recent focus on the need to delineate constructs, has been the attempts of researchers to define and measure 'service quality'. One early attempt (Parasuraman *et al.*, 1988) which describes the consumer's evaluation of service quality as similar to attitude, and therefore distinct from satisfaction, has provided a basis for considerable debate, often within a health care context (see for example Cronin and Taylor, 1992, 1994; Reidenbach and Sandifer-Smallwood, 1990; Woodside *et al.*, 1989.)

A number of suggestions can be made to distinguish service–quality evaluation from satisfaction, for example, the nature of the expectations measure; the timing of measurement; the inclusion of price and value in the evaluation process. In terms of the causal relationship however, an alternative view describes perceived service quality as a more detailed subset of criteria which consumers evaluate in their satisfaction of a service (see for example Oliver, 1993; Parasuraman *et al.*, 1994a; Mittal *et al.*, 1999) an additional perspective might be to suggest that satisfaction relates to experience of a service whereas service quality could be judged from other sources (Oliver, 1993).

Other researchers (Shemwell *et al.*, 1998) emphasise that service quality is a cognitive evaluation contrasting with the affective nature of satisfaction. Additionally, the degree of affect or cognition in service evaluation will differ according to the differing amount of credence, search and experience properties of the service under investigation. Thus for health services high in credence properties, the affective, human interaction element can be expected to dominate.

In view of the considerable number of SERVQUAL, and related, studies focusing on a health care context (see next section) discussion of patients' 'perceived service quality' has proliferated in both the management and health care literature. Traditional 'patient satisfaction' research, however, reflects an approach based on models of health care delivery similar in nature to those described in the management literature. The most prominent, suggested by Donabedian (1966), outlines three categories under which information can be classified i.e. structure, process and outcome. Process includes two core elements in the performance of practitioners i.e. technical performance, which depends on the knowledge and judgement used in arriving at the appropriate strategies of care and on skill in implementing those strategies; and interpersonal performance, which involves the communication of information essential to the level and success of technical performance (Donabedian, 1988).

The terminology here is at variance with the service quality literature where Grönroos (1984) for example, describes the 'technical quality dimension' as the outcome of the process, whereas the 'functional quality dimension' is the process itself. Alternatively, Edvardsson *et al.* (1989) define technical quality as the possession of the required skills (similar to Donabedian's definition) and Lehtinen and Lehtinen (1991) also suggest a two-dimensional structure – process quality and output quality, each to be measured by consumer evaluation. One further similarity is that Grönroos argues that the functional dimension has a major effect on the consumer's evaluation of service quality while Donabedian (1988) describes satisfaction as a process measure (particularly of the interpersonal process) and also as an outcome of the process. The efforts of both service quality and satisfaction researchers to identify the attributes of this process are described in the next section.

The dimensions of patient satisfaction: what should be measured?

The content of patient satisfaction measures reflects the researcher's interpretation of which factors/dimensions/traits/determinants underlie respondents' evaluations. As highlighted in the previous section, the substantial number of health-related service quality studies undertaken over recent years has produced equivocal findings. A number of distinctions were suggested in previous sections, in particular, a process vs. outcome distinction is made. The perceived inability of patients to evaluate outcomes is reflected in the focus on process-based satisfaction measures. Similarly service quality studies adopting the SERVQUAL model focus on five dimensions primarily concerned with process i.e. tangibles, responsiveness, reliability, assurance, empathy. A substantial number of studies (see for example Cronin and Taylor, 1992; Carman, 1990; Finn and Lamb, 1991; Babakus and Boller, 1992) have examined the validity of this model and have generally failed to identify an underlying five-dimensional structure. More recently, Mels *et al.* (1997) suggested that Grönroos' (1984) perspective is more relevant, and argue that service quality perceptions are largely determined by two factors which they term 'intrinsic' and 'extrinsic' service quality.

   One service setting which has proved particularly popular for studies of service quality dimensionality is that of health care (see, for example, Babakus and Mangold, 1989, 1992; Mangold and Babakus, 1991; Vandamme and Leunis, 1993; Reidenbach and Sandifer-Smallwood, 1990; Headley and Miller, 1993; White *et al.*, 1993; Peyrot *et al.*, 1993; Wallbridge and Delene, 1993; Soliman, 1992; Carman, 1990; Bowers *et al.*, 1994; Sower *et al.*, 2001). Although the majority of these studies have attempted to derive the factors posited by the SERVQUAL authors, these efforts have been unfruitful. Indeed, results have been so disparate as to suggest, at one extreme, six or more factors (Vandamme and Leunis, 1993; Carman, 1990) or at the other extreme to suggest that only one meaningful or major factor emerges (Babakus and Mangold, 1989; 1992; White *et al.*, 1993). Further support for a 'undimensional' measure of service quality is offered by researchers administering SERVQUAL in other service settings (see for example Cronin and Taylor, 1992; Peter *et al.*, 1993; Babakus and Boller, 1992).

In reconciling the disparity in both the number and nature of the factors derived in health care studies, one potential solution lies in recognising the differences between the nature of services, even within this particular sector. The multifaceted nature of hospital service delivery has been highlighted by a number of researchers (Carman, 1990; Shostack, 1987; Woodside *et al.*, 1989) and the series of encounters or acts, e.g. admission, nursing care, exhibit distinct similarities with factors derived from health care studies focusing on patient satisfaction with hospital services (Thompson, 1983). Evidently, the characteristics of these services differ in nature from those of the GP/physician.[1]

Evidence from the patient satisfaction literature supports the likelihood of few meaningful factors underlying consumer evaluations of GP services (Ware *et al.*, 1978; 1983; Pascoe, 1983; Hulka *et al.*, 1970; 1982; Zyzanski *et al.*, 1974; Hall and Dornan, 1988). These include primarily professional or technical competence, interpersonal qualities and convenience or accessibility of the service. As previously mentioned, attempts to measure patient expectations have also suggested what are essentially satisfaction determinants. One particular aspect of 'interpersonal' qualities highlighted in many studies is that of doctor/patient communication or 'collaboration' (Woolley *et al.*, 1978; Jun *et al.*, 1998, Barry *et al.*, 2001). Avis *et al.* (1997) have highlighted how experience of power, control and autonomy are essential in the professional–patient relationship, and patients' perceptions of these will influence subsequent evaluation. Additionally, the role of 'continuity of care' is emphasised (Woolley *et al.*, 1978; Smith, 2000; Ware *et al.*, 1983). The importance of 'networks' within health care services has been discussed in previous chapters. The patient's evaluation of the service will also reflect a perception of any problems, lack of communication or coordination etc. within that network, and this has been specifically examined by Baker *et al.* (1999) in the development of the patient career diary. This longitudinal approach combines quantitative and qualitative methods to measure attitudes towards care across the interface between primary and secondary care.

Measuring patient satisfaction: how should it be measured?

The determination of relevant criteria for measurement usually involves literature searches; expert interviews and qualitative research with a sample of the population of interest. In-depth interviews, focus group studies etc. may represent an alternative or complementary approach to data collection within a health care environment (see for example Rees Lewis [1994] for a review of health care related research methods) and can offer benefits of greater focus on the patient; depth of information etc. (Avis *et al.*, 1997; Crawford and Kessell, 1999).

Criticisms of patient satisfaction surveys include the relevance of a 'snapshot approach', which will typically result in positive evaluations which are of little use for decision-making. Williams' (1994) argues that patient satisfaction questionnaires do not access an independent phenomenon but in a sense actively construct it, by forcing users to express themselves in alien terms. Crawford and Kessell (1999) describe a tendency towards reductionism in self-administered questionnaires and some of the many methodological problems inherent in their design and administration are discussed in the later sections of this chapter. A number of researchers (Avis *et al.*, 1997; Baker *et al.*, 1999; Comley and De Meyer, 2001; Jackson *et al.*, 2001) have developed longitudinal research designs involving a variety of measurement approaches. Additionally, studies involving critical incidents technique (CIT) have been reported in the health care literature (Rees Lewis and Williamson, 1995). Within the management literature, a substantial number of studies have applied CIT in a variety of service contexts (see for example Bitner *et al.*, 1990; Solomon *et al.*, 1985) including satisfaction with general practitioner services (Gabbott and Hogg, 1996) and hospital services (John, 1996). Bitner *et al.* (1990) define a critical incident as 'One that contributes to or detracts from the general aim of the activity in a significant way'.

By requiring respondents to describe such incidents, researchers avoid the problems of pre-definition and reductionism described earlier. Responses can be categorised by content analysis, providing a combination of qualitative and quantitative data. The problems of content analysis, i.e. subjectivity and assessment of reliability and validity, are however potential limitations of this approach. A further consideration is the level of involvement of the respondent (although health care is usually perceived as a high involvement service experience) and therefore the ability to remember and describe critical incidents. Additionally, the collection, analysis and interpretation of such data has substantial resource implications and can be expected to involve relatively few respondents.

Questionnaire surveys however, are easily understood, result in relatively low-cost data collection and represent the main method for evaluating patient satisfaction. A wide variety of patient (and related) satisfaction measures have been developed and reported in the health care literature. A number of these are shown in Figure 7.2, classified according to scope and focus.

A variety of categorical criteria may be suggested for the satisfaction measures illustrated in Figure 7.2 and a number of authors have

FOCUS

Service provider
Macro-measures

Respondent
(e.g. carer, parent, elderly)

Wide
PSQ (US) GP service Ware *et al.*
1978, 1983
PSQ (UK), GP Service, Grogan *et al.*
1995,2000
PCSQ – pharmaceutical services
Gourley *et al.* 2001
Hulka Questionnaire (US) Hulka *et al.*
1970; Zyzanski *et al.* 1974

General health issues
Pain management/elderly
Kung *et al.* 2000
Parental satisfaction/paediatric care
Ygge and Arnetz, 2001

SCOPE
Specific encounter/visit
(Discrete)
Micro-measures
Narrow
Outpatients Rubin *et al.* 1933

Specific health issue

WOMBLSQ – birth/labour, Smith, 2001

CSQ* Larsen *et al.* 1979

CSQ* – Mental Health Larsen *et al.*
1979; Levois et al. 1981

QOC – Hospital Care Arnetz and
Arnetz, 1996

PSS – low back pain Cherkin *et al.* 1991

Hospital Care Hendriks *et al.* 2001

DMET – Diabetes Paddock *et al.* 2000

Hospital Care – Thompson 1983

MISS – Medical Interview Wolf *et al.* 1978

NSNS – Nursing Care Hospital
Walsh and Walsh, 1999

PMH/PSQ – MD – outpatient visit
Loblaw *et al.* 1999

CSQ^2 and SSQ Baker, 1990, 91

CSQ = Client Satisfaction Questionnaire; PSQ = Patient Satisfaction Questionnaire; PSS = Patient Satisfaction Scale; DMET = Diabetes Measurement and Evaluation Tool; PCSQ = Pharmaceutical Care Satisfaction Questionnaire; PMH/PSQ – MD = Princess Margaret Hospital Patient Satisfaction with Doctor Questionnaire; WOMBLSQ = Women's Views of Birth Labour Satisfaction Questionnaire; NSNS = Newcastle Satisfaction with Nursing Scale; CSQ^2 = Consultation Satisfaction Questionnaire; SSQ = Surgery Satisfaction Questionnaire; MISS = Medical Interview Satisfaction Scale

Figure 7.2 A classification of patient satisfaction questionnaires

presented useful analyses comparing and contrasting various scales (see for example Roberts and Tugwell, 1987; Hudak and Wright, 2000; Ware and Hays, 1988; Ross *et al.*, 1995; McNaughton, 1994). The distinction in terms of 'focus' here reflects the population of interest, where a service provider focus potentially requires a measurement instrument relevant to a wide population in terms of demographics, nature of treatment etc. Two often quoted US-based patient satisfaction measures, the 'Hulka Questionnaire' (Hulka *et al.*, 1970, 1982; Zyzanski *et al.*, 1974) and the 'Ware' 'Medical Outcomes' or 'Patient Satisfaction Questionnaire' (PSQ) (Ware *et al.*, 1978, 1983) have been developed and tested over a number of years. The former examines three dimensions – professional competence, personal qualities and cost/convenience – and the latter, access to care, financial aspects, availability of resources, continuity of care, interpersonal manner (e.g. explanation and consideration) and technical quality. The relevance to the UK context of questionnaires developed in the US has been questioned (Fitzpatrick, 1990). More recently a UK-based instrument to measure patient satisfaction with GP services has been developed and reported in the literature (Grogan *et al.*, 1995, 2000). This patient satisfaction questionnaire (PSQ) measures five dimensions – doctors, nurses, access, appointments and facilities. These three, together with the US-based CSQ which assesses satisfaction with pharmaceutical services, provide an overall consumer evaluation at a particular point in time, providing a 'macro' measure of care.

Alternatively, micro measures with a narrow supplier focus require respondents to assess an episode or encounter. Primary care-related measures include the US-based Medical Interview Satisfaction Scale (MISS) Wolf *et al.*, 1978; Consultation Satisfaction Questionnaire (CSQ^2) and Surgery Satisfaction Questionnaire (SSQ) (Baker, 1990, 91). Additionally, Loblaw *et al.* (1999) report the development of a scale to measure an outpatient visit at a UK hospital and Larsen *et al.* (1979) (also included as a respondent-focused measure due to its exclusivity for mental health care clients) one for a US-based mental health clinic.

A number of measures developed within a hospital-care context also reflect a specific episode of care (Thompson, 1983; Arnetz and Arntez, 1996; Hendriks *et al.*, 2001) however such episodes are likely to be complex, multifaceted and may be of considerable duration. It has therefore been noted that the distinction between satisfaction and attitude in the evaluation of hospital services may not be as apparent as it is for other services (Vandamme and Leunis, 1992). The potential for a service satisfaction questionnaire to include a wide range of encounters and facets is reflected in the questionnaire 'What the Patient Thinks' (Thompson, 1983) which is distributed as a 32-page document. Alternatively, Walsh and Walsh (1991), report the development of a scale to measure one facet of hospital care, i.e. nursing care, and McIver (1991) advised practitioners to use simple short questionnaires dealing with individual subject areas, for example, getting to the clinic; quality of information. Such questionnaires have been developed in the UK by the King's Fund.

The respondent focus described in Figure 7.2 includes those measures developed, either for a specific respondent group or health condition, where an individual measure may focus on both, for example, Kung *et al.* (2000) assesses satisfaction of elderly patients with oncology services. Respondent-focused questionnaires which are wide in scope reflect both the need to include other stakeholders in satisfaction evaluations and the particular requirements of various subject populations, as discussed earlier.

The nature of satisfaction measures in terms of focus and scope has a number of implications, for example:

- The ability to focus on outcomes (i.e. health outcomes) is more pronounced for those narrow in scope;
- The timing of questionnaire administration is of significant relevance, and a major discriminating factor of scope (as discussed later);
- Issues of generalisability across all subject populations are more complex with service provider focused measures;
- Relevant alternative (or supplementary) research methods differ between categories, for example, critical incidents technique (CIT) – discussed later – is relevant to a narrow scope/service provider focus and many researchers (Baker *et al.*, 1999; Godfrey and Wistow, 1995) have suggested a longitudinal and/or more holistic approach to measuring patient satisfaction with health care treatment for 'specific health issues'.

The SERVQUAL scale discussed in the next section represents a service provider focus, and has been used in studies both narrow and wide in scope. The many issues which have arisen from the application of this scale serve to provide a framework for discussion of considerations involved in developing and administering patient satisfaction measurement scales.

The SERVQUAL scale

In 1988, a self-administered questionnaire for measuring consumer-perceived service quality was published in the *Journal of Retailing*. Since then, a whole mini-industry has sprung up extending, defending, or criticising the SERVQUAL scale (Bowers, 1997). Described as a 'generic' scale for measuring consumer perceptions of service quality (Parasuraman *et al.*, 1988) SERVQUAL has been applied and tested across a wide range of service industries, including a considerable number of studies focusing on health care.

The SERVQUAL scale has in fact been revised a number of times due to the development activity of its authors and the criticisms advanced by researchers who have attempted to apply it. The original version (Parasuraman *et al.*, 1986, 1988) included 22 items, designed to measure the five dimensions described in the previous section i.e. reliability, responsiveness, empathy, assurance and tangibles; assessed by a seven-point Likert scale, anchored by end points labelled 'strongly agree' – 'strongly disagree', and presented in two formats – one for expectations and repeated for consumer perceptions. Expectations were defined as experience based norms (Woodruff *et al.*, 1983) for example, 'They should provide their services at the time they promise to do so'.

Half of the statements were presented in a negative format, an approach often suggested by scale designers in order to encourage the respondent to read the items carefully and prevent, for example, 'yea-saying' biases.

Once the respondent has completed both sections of the questionnaire, a gap score can be calculated which would represent the evaluation of service quality on an individual item, dimension, and on aggregate, for example:

	Strongly disagree						Strongly agree
The organisation should have modern-looking equipment	1	2	3	4	5	(6)	7
The organisation does have modern-looking equipment	1	2	3	(4)	5	6	7

Quality gap = 4 –6 = –2

Consequently, questions relating to overall perceptions of service quality could then be correlated with these scores, highlighting causes of poor quality perceptions. Similarly, questions relating to behavioural intentions, for example, 'intention to reattend' would provide both an understanding of service quality-related behaviour and assessments of concurrent validity. The many issues raised by this measure are detailed below.

Scale content

SERVQUAL was purported to be a generic measure of service quality, the 22 items were considered relevant to all services yet it was also stated that it provided a basic skeleton which could be adapted or supplemented for a particular organisation. It was later argued, however, that to do so would affect the integrity of the scale (Parasuraman *et al.*, 1991). Many researchers who have reported applications of the 'SERVQUAL scale' have in fact not included the items described. The need for an organisation to develop its own scale content based on qualitative research should therefore be emphasised.

Within the management (service quality) literature a number of scales have been developed relating to patients' perceptions of general practitioner services (see for example Brown and Swartz, 1989; White *et al.*, 1993) hospital services (Carman, 1990; Babakus and Mangold, 1992; Vandamme and Leunis, 1993) or specific service elements, for example family planning services (Smith, 2000). These have typically significantly changed the 22 item SERVQUAL scale in order to include relevant statements. One practical issue which arises is that of length of scale, where it is well documented that the number of items/length of questionnaire is a factor influencing response rates.

Nature of the expectations measure

A number of approaches to measuring expectations were discussed earlier and it was noted that patient satisfaction researchers, and others, have described a variety of expectations, some of which focus on determinants/factors and others on measures. The adoption here of experience-based norms, as a measure, creates a number of problems. First, they can be expected to encourage social desirability bias rather than the respondent's own 'true' evaluation, particularly since questionnaires typically include only vector attributes (i.e. attributes for which a respondent's ideal point is at an infinite level [Teas, 1993 a,b]) tend to generate extreme responses. These are particular problems in patient satisfaction research, as discussed later, and has a substantial impact on both data analysis and interpretation. For the SERVQUAL scale however, an additional problem arose because of the theoretical underpinnings of the model, i.e. where expected service equals perceived service, perceived quality is satisfactory, where the latter exceeds the former, quality is more than satisfactory and tends to ideal, and vice versa. Wall and Payne (1973) argued, with respect to job satisfaction, that a psychological constraint operates whereby respondents will rarely produce a positive gap score. Consequently, administration of this scale tends to produce negative scores, even when respondents rate the service as excellent (Smith, 1995).

Recognition of these problems resulted in a restatement of expectations in a revised SERVQUAL scale (Parasuraman *et al.*, 1991) as:

'Excellent companies/organisations will ....' thus inferring an ideal standard. This however resulted in little improvement, and failed to recognise the need to measure more realistic expectations (Smith, 1995). A further revised version (Parasuraman *et al.*, 1994b) included two measures of expectations i.e. desired and adequate, where the authors argued for a 'zone of tolerance' between the two measures, where consumers would be satisfied as suggested in both early consumer (Miller, 1979) and patient satisfaction (Pascoe, 1983) literature. These various developments raise questions as to what extent consumers can meaningfully rate their expectations. At one level, expectations may be unformed (Thompson and Sunol, 1995) at another what does a score of 'adequate expectations = 4; ideal = 6' actually mean?

Some authors have argued that expectations should not be measured (Cronin and Taylor, 1992) as this does little to improve the 'predictive validity' of scales, thus only perception measurement is necessary. Others (see for example Carman, 1990) feel that expectations statements need not be administered on every occasion. Clearly it is necessary to establish what is important to consumers/patients and this may be determined by qualitative research. Alternatively, some authors have substituted ratings of importance of items for expectations measures (Webster, 1989; Ennew *et al.*, 1993). The majority of patient satisfaction questionnaires highlighted in Figure 7.2 measure 'perceptions-related' constructs. A final issue concerning the measurement of expectations is when should these be assessed.

Timing of the measure

The service quality literature exhibits a difference of opinion with respect to when expectations statements should be administered, with some researchers administering both expectations and perceptions batteries at the same point in time while others measure expectations prior to an encounter and perceptions immediately afterwards. Clearly the timing of measurement has significant theoretical and practical implications since researchers (Latour and Peat, 1979; Oliver, 1980) emphasise the role of timing in differentiating satisfaction from attitude, while others (Andreason, 1977; Bolton and Drew, 1991a) describe the way in which consumers' evaluations change over time. Avis *et al.*, (1997) enquire whether anyone is in a position to express satisfaction immediately after a visit to an outpatient clinic, and emphasise the benefits of a longitudinal approach. The problem of timing is particularly relevant where patients are required to assess outcomes in addition to the traditional process measures, and it has been shown that reported satisfaction levels will change according to the timing of questioning (Jackson *et al.*, 2001).

Item interpretation

The complex nature of the health care context has been emphasised. A number of discrete episodes or encounters may be described. The entire service experience may involve contact with a number of nurses, doctors, administrative and other staff, and cross boundaries between primary and secondary care.

Consequently, a question requiring the respondent to assess 'the helpfulness of the staff' may be problematic. Even smaller groups of, for example, ward nurses may vary, thus a Likert scale measure may be incorrectly interpreted by decision makers. For example:

The nursing staff are helpful

strongly agree   strongly disagree

☐   ☐   ☐   ☑   ☐   ☐   ☐

Should this be interpreted as:

- Some nurses are helpful and some are not;
- All nurses are reasonably helpful but there is obviously room for improvement;
- I don't know, I haven't noticed;
- ....?

Second, what is considered helpful behaviour? What action should decision-makers and others take on the basis of the data? Winsted (1997) has highlighted that despite the considerable number of studies which have required respondents to evaluate service characteristics – such as helpfulness, courtesy etc. – few have attempted to establish how the respondent interprets such attributes. Indeed, the potential for groups of respondents to define such terms differently, both within and between cultural groups, is considerable. Again the need for context-specific data is emphasised. The example above also illustrates how the inclusion of a 'don't know' or non-response option may change the distribution of responses and thus achieve alternative results.

Use of negative statements

While negative statements are introduced into a measurement scale to avoid the incidence of 'yea-saying', these have been identified as the source of a number of problems. First, they can cause respondent error and confusion and therefore result in inaccurate data for decision-making. Second, such error can lead to incorrect inferences resulting from statistical analysis. It was noted for example (Babakus and Mangold, 1992) that the factor structure i.e. reliability, responsiveness, empathy, assurance and tangibles described by Parasuraman *et al.* (1988) may have been generated as a result of the inclusion of negative statements. This conclusion was reached due to the observation that two factors were comprised solely of the negative items. Other health-related studies (see for example, Brown and Swartz, 1989) also describe results which may be attributable to item phrasing.

Establishing reliability and validity

The paramount consideration when developing and administering any measurement scale concerns the reliability and validity of the measure. A variety of methods for establishing reliability may be adopted. Churchill's (1979) paradigm, the basis for the development of SERVQUAL, suggests Cronbach's coefficient alpha as the recommended measure of the internal reliability, or consistency of a set of items.

Typically, multi-attribute measures of service quality (SERVQUAL) and patient satisfaction questionnaires report alpha scores for the subscales or traits as confirmation of an underlying factor structure. It should also be noted, however, that high correlations between question-naire items may be nothing more than evidence of deficiencies within a measurement scale (Smith, 1999). Perceived duplication of items, response biases (see next section), inclusion of negative statements and respondent error generally can create plausible factor structures which have little to do with explaining underlying consumer or patient evalua-tions. Fitzpatrick (1990), for example, has emphasised how since patients tend to express high levels of satisfaction with most items, it is difficult to have confidence in correlations between items as a measure of the reliability of patient satisfaction measures. This problem persists with typical evaluations of validity which may adopt a variety of approaches.

The most basic forms of validity, i.e. face and/or content validity, focus on whether the instrument looks as if it is measuring what it is supposed to measure. Some authors use the terms interchangeably, while others suggest that the former requires non-expert reviewers such as members of the intended respondent population or professionals working in the industry and the latter requires researchers or other 'experts' in research design. Qualitative research, pilot and further development work contribute to establishing face and content validity.

Further assessment often includes establishing predictive and concurrent validity – described by Campbell (1960) as 'practical' validity – where he argues that the latter is usually simply an inexpensive and presumptive substitute for the former. Whereas predictive validity relates to the ability of the current measure to predict some future actions and is rarely assessed by satisfaction/service quality questionnaires, concurrent validity relates to the relationship between two current measures. Typically researchers include overall assessments of satisfaction with the service; measures of behavioural intention, such as intention to repeat visit, where it is assumed that the measurement scales are valid if they predict, through regression analysis, the scores on these other scales. It has been noted however that the ability of a scale to predict consumer responses to other variables (for example overall evaluation and behavioural intention) does not provide evidence of the integrity of the scale, for example, scales which omit items of key importance to consumers can perform as well statistically as one which includes such items (Smith, 1999). The often observed lack of convergence of intended and actual behaviour has already been discussed.

Both convergent and discriminant validity are required as evidence of trait validity (Campbell and Fiske, 1959; Bagozzi and Yi, 1991; Fishbein and Ajzen, 1975) where convergent validity is the degree to which attempts to measure the same concept using two or more measures yield the same results, and discriminant validity is established when the same method or instrument when used to measure different variables, achieves different results. Again correlations between scales are often provided as evidence of convergent validity, encountering the same problems as previously discussed. Additionally, since the introduction of SERVQUAL in 1988, several researchers (see for example, Vogels *et al.*, 1989; Carman, 1990; Babakus and Boller, 1992; Brown *et al.*, 1993; Peter *et al.*, 1993) have criticised attempts to analyse data derived from the computation of difference (gap) scores. These authors argue that such data should not be used because of problems which can occur relating to reliability, discriminant validity, spurious correlation generally and variance restriction.

Nomological validity involves an investigation of both the theoretical relationships between different constructs and the empirical relationship between measures of those different constructs. Evidently, the failure of measures to correlate with the theoretical assumptions underlying the research can infer errors in measurement or theory. Here the researcher returns to the beginning of the process i.e. the need to define patient satisfaction and the underlying assumptions on which the measurement scales were developed. It was noted earlier that the scales developed by patient satisfaction researchers appear to be measuring different constructs, for example, attitude. Finally, problems in establishing 'generalisability' to a variety of subject populations arise, where it is known that respondent groups may both evaluate satisfaction differently and offer a differing propensity to exhibit a specific response bias.

The impact of response biases

Assessments of reliability and validity typically require an examination of correlation coefficients. However, measurement scales generally, and patient satisfaction questionnaires in particular, are subject to biases which can invalidate research findings, leading to inaccurate conclusions and consequent actions. The propensity for service quality and consumer satisfaction scales to generate halo effects and other response biases such as acquiescence (yea-saying), opposition (nay-saying) extreme responses, neutral responses, the tendency to use only a few items, social desirability etc. is well documented (see for example, Peterson and Wilson, 1992; Danaher and Haddrell, 1996; Wirtz and Bateson, 1995). These are often the result of the adoption of Likert 'type' scales, which in particular tend to suffer from response sets (Javeline, 1999). Similarly, these problems are well documented in the patient satisfaction literature. (Ware *et al.*, 1978; Ross *et al.*, 1995; Levois *et al.*, 1981) and emphasised with respect for example to scale content. Ware *et al.* (1978) found that in the development of the Patient Satisfaction Questionnaire (PSQ), acquiescent response set (ARS) bias (a tendency to agree with statements of opinion regardless of content) was significantly correlated with single item satisfaction measures and with scales containing all favourably or all unfavourably worded items. Thompson (1983) in designing his hospital-based 'What the patient thinks' questionnaire adopted a process of response manipulation – 'procrustean transformation' in order to design options which would reduce the degree of skewness in the distribution of responses to each question. Additionally, Levois *et al.* (1981) suggest rank ordering of items as an alternative to traditional patient satisfaction scales.

It is also notable that these biases may differ in nature and extent across respondent groups, for example by income, age, education, socio-economic status. Ross *et al.* (1995) for example compared data from the same respondents across a number of patient satisfaction measures and found a very substantial acquiescent response bias which was particularly prevalent in older, less well-educated patients and in patients in poorer health.

While a number of differences in response biases have been detected within national groups, an area of growing interest within the service quality literature has been to collect cross cultural/national consumer-perceived service quality data due to the internationalisation of many service industries. There is already evidence to suggest that, at a minimum, extreme and neutral response styles differ cross-culturally. Indeed, the language used can result in variation in the level of extreme response (ERS) with a single respondent (Gibbons *et al.* 1999). Additionally, Chen *et al.* (1995) found that individuals from collectivist cultures tended to avoid extremes. Si and Cullen (1998) and Shiomi and Loo (1997) have shown that respondents from Asian countries (China, Japan and Hong Kong) are more likely to use the middle response categories than western respondents (USA, Germany, UK).

Clearly there are implications here for health service organisations operating within a multicultural environment. Cultural differences in requirements of the service may exist, but how can decision-makers assess whether such (or lack of) differences are merely an artefact of the measurement instrument used. A second area for concern derives from the focus within health care for learning from other national models and indeed for the development of international patient satisfaction questionnaires. Kersnik (2000), for example, describes 'an internationally standardised and validated instrument for patients evaluations of family practice care' (EUROPEP). Comparisons of cross-national patient satisfaction as indicators of service superiority should clearly highlight not only differences in ratings in cross-cultural expectations and the need to establish equivalence in the constructs under investigation, but also differences in cross-national response styles.

Evaluating health services through assessment of consumer (patient and carer) satisfaction therefore involves a considered analysis of a substantial number of issues. This final (and yet in another sense initial) stage in the service cycle should provide valuable information for ongoing service improvements and redesign. Failure to recognise the many potential problem areas involved, however, will result in flawed decision-making based on insubstantial and inaccurate data.

References

Andreason, A. R. (1977) 'A Taxonomy of Consumer Satisfaction/Dissatisfaction Measures,' *Journal of Consumer Affairs* 11: 11–24.

Arnetz, J. E. and Arnetz, B. B. (1996) 'The Development and Application of a Patient Satisfaction Measurement System for Hospital Wide Quality Improvement', *International Journal for Quality in Health Care* 8(6): 555–66.

Avis, M., Bond, M. and Arthur, A. (1995) 'Satisfying Solutions? A Review of Some Unresolved Issues in the Measurement of Patient Satisfaction', *Journal of Advanced Nursing* 22: 316–22.

Avis, M., Bond, M. and Arthur, A. (1997) 'Questioning Patient Satisfaction: An Empirical Investigation in Two Outpatient Clinics', *Social Science Medical* 44(1): 85–92.

Babakus, E. and Boller, G.W. (1992) 'An Empirical Assessment of the SERVQUAL Scale', *Journal of Business Research* 24: 253–68.

Babakus, E. and Mangold, W. G. (1989) 'Adapting the SERVQUAL Scale to a Healthcare Environment: An Empirical Assessment' in Bloom, P., Winer, R., Kassarjian, H., Scammon D., Weitz, B., Speckman, R., Mahajan, V. and Levy, M. (eds) *Enhancing Knowledge Development in Marketing*, American Marketing Association: Chicago.

Babakus, E. and Mangold, W. G. (1992) 'Adapting the SERVQUAL Scale to Hospital Services: An Empirical Investigation', *Health Services Research* 26(6): 767–86.

Bagozzi, R. P. and Yi, Y. (1991) 'Multitrait-Multimethod Matrices in Consumer Research', *Journal of Consumer Research* 17(4): 426–39.

Baker, R. (1990) 'Development of a Questionnaire to Assess Patients' Satisfaction with Consultations in General Practice', *British Journal of General Practice* 40: 487–90.

Baker, R. (1991) 'The Reliability and Criterion Validity of a Measure of Patients' Satisfaction with their General Practice', *Family Practice* 8: 171–7.

Baker, R., Preston, C., Cheater, F. *et al.* (1999) 'Measuring Patients' Attitudes to Care Across The Primary/Secondary Interface: The Development of the Patient Career Diary', *Quality in Health Care* 8: 154–60.

Barry, C. A., Stevenson, F. A., Britten, N., Barber, N. and Bradley, C. P. (2001) 'Giving Voice to the Lifeworld. More Humane, More Effective Medical Care? A Qualitative Study of Doctor-Patient Communication in General Practice', *Social Science and Medicine* 53(4): 487–505.

Bitner, M. J., Booms, B. H. and Tetreault, M. S. (1990) 'The Service Encounter: Diagnosing Favourable and Unfavourable Incidents', *Journal of Marketing* 54: 71–84.

Bolton, R. N. and Drew, J. H. (1991a) 'A Longitudinal Analysis of the Impact of Service Changes on Customer Attitudes', *Journal of Marketing* 55: 1–9.

Bolton, R. N. and Drew, J. H. (1991b) 'A Multistage Model of Customers' Assessments of Service Quality and Value', *Journal of Consumer Research* 17(4): 375–84.

Bowers, M. R., Swan, J. E. and Koehler, W. F. (1994) 'What Attributes Determine Quality and Satisfaction with Health Care Delivery?' *Health Care Management Review*, 19(4): 49–55.

Bowers, M. R. (1997) 'Book Review', *Journal of the Academy of Marketing Science* 25(3): 265–6.

Brown, S. W. and Swartz, T. A. (1989) 'A Gap Analysis of Professional Service Quality', *Journal of Marketing* 53(2): 92–8.

Brown, T. J., Churchill, G. A. Jr and Peter, J. P. (1993) 'Improving the Measurement of Service Quality', *Journal of Retailing* 69(1): 127–39.

Burton, K. E. and Wright, V. (1980) in Ross *et al.* (1987) *op cit.*

Campbell, D. T. and Fiske, D. W. (1959) 'Convergent and Discriminant Validation by the Multitrait-Multimethod Matrix', *Psychological Bulletin* 56: 81–105.

Campbell, D. T. (1960) 'Recommendations for APA Test Standards Regarding Construct, Trait and Discriminant Validity', *American Psychologist* 15: 546–53.

Carman, J. M. (1990) 'Consumer Perceptions of Service Quality: An Assessment of the SERVQUAL Dimensions', *Journal of Retailing* 66(1): 33–55.

Chen, C., Lee, S. and Stevenson, H. W. (1995) 'Response Style and Cross-Cultural Comparison of Rating Scales Among East Asian and North American Students', *Psychological Science* 6(3): 170–5.

Cherkin, D., Deyo, R.A. and Berg, A.O. (1991) 'Evaluation of a Physician Education Intervention to Improve Primary Care for Low-Back Pain: Impact of Patients', *Spine* 16: 1173–8.

Churchill, G. A. Jr (1979) 'A Paradigm for Developing Better Measure of Marketing Constructs', *Journal of Marketing Research* XVI: 64–73.

Clare, A.W. (1990) 'Some Conclusions' in Hopkins, A. and Costain, D. (eds) *Measuring the Outcomes of Medical Care*. The Royal College of Physicians of London: Kings Fund Centre for Health Services Development.

Comley, A. L. and De Meyer, E. (2001) 'Assessing Patient Satisfaction with Pain Management Through a Continuous Quality Improvement Effort', *Journal of Pain and Symptom Management* 21(1): 27–40.

Crawford, M. J. and Kessel A. S. (1999) 'Not Listening to Patients – The Use and Misuse of Patient Satisfaction Studies', *International Journal of Social Psychiatry* 45(1): 1–6.

Cronin, J. J. and Taylor, S. A. (1992) 'Measuring Service Quality: A Re-examination and Extension', *Journal of Marketing* 56: 55–68.

Cronin, J. J. and Taylor, S. A. (1994) 'SERVPERF Versus SERVQUAL: Reconciling Performance-Based and Perceptions-Minus-Expectations Measurement of Service Quality', *Journal of Marketing* 58: 125–31.

Danaher, P. J. and Haddrell, V. (1996) 'A Comparison of Question Scales Used for Measuring Customer Satisfaction', *International Journal of Service Industry Management* 7(4): 4–26.

Davies, A. R. and Ware, J. E. (1988) 'Involving Consumers in Quality of Care Assessment', *Health Affairs* 7: 33–48.

Department of Health (1997) *Modern and Dependable*, HMSO: London.

Department of Health (1989) *Working for Patients*, HMSO: London.

Donabedian, A. (1966) 'Evaluating the Quality of Medical Care', *Millbank Memorial Fund Quarterly* 44: 166–206.

Donabedian, A. (1988) 'The Quality of Care: How Can it be Assessed?' *Journal of the American Medical Association* 260 (12): 1743–8.

Edvardsson, B., Gustavsson, B. and Riddle, D. I. (1989) *'An Expanded Model of the Service Encounter with Emphasis on Cultural Context'*, CTF Service Research Centre, University of Karlstad, Research Report, 89: 4.

Ennew, C. T., Reed, G. U. and Binks, M. R. (1993) 'Importance-Performance Analysis and the Measurement of Service Quality', *European Journal of Marketing* 27(2): 59–70.

Finn, D. W. and Lamb, C. W. (1991) 'An Evaluation of the SERVQUAL Scales in a Retailing Setting', *Advances in Consumer Research* 18: 483–90.

Fishbein, M. and Ajzen, I. (1975) *Belief, Attitude, Intention and Behaviour: An Introduction to Theory and Research*, Addison-Wesley Publishing Company: Reading, MA and London.

Fitzpatrick, R. and Hopkins, A. (1983) 'Problems in the Conceptual Framework of Patient Satisfaction Research: An Empirical Exploration', *Sociology of Health and Illness* 5(3): 297–311.

Fitzpatrick, R. (1990) 'Measurement of Patient Satisfaction' in Hopkins, A. and Costain, D. (eds) *Measuring the Outcomes of Medical Care*, The Royal College of Physicians of London: Kings Fund Centre for Health Services Development.

Fornell, C. (1992) 'A National Customer Satisfaction Barometer: The Swedish Experience', *Journal of Marketing* 56: 6–21.

Gabbott, M. and Hogg, G. (1995) 'Grounds for Discrimination: Establishing Criteria for Evaluating Health Services', *The Service Industries Journal* 15(1): 90–101.

Gabbott, M. and Hogg, G. (1996) 'The Glory of Stories: Using Critical Incidents to Understand Service Evaluation in the Primary Healthcare Context', *Journal of Marketing Management* 12(6): 493–503.

Gibbons, J. L., Zellner, J. A. and Rudek, D. J. (1999) 'Effects of Language and Meaningfulness on the Use of Extreme Response Styles by Spanish-English Bilinguals', *Cross-Cultural Research* 33(4): 369–81.

Godfrey, M. and Wistow, G. (1997) 'The User Perspective on Managing for Health Outcomes: the Case of Mental Health', *Health and Social Care in the Community* 5(5): 325–32.

Gourlay, G. K., Gourlay, D. R., Rigolosi, E., Reed, P., Solomon, D. K. and Washington, E. (2001) 'Development and Validation of the Pharmaceutical Care Satisfaction Questionnaire', *The American Journal of Managed Care* 7(5): 461–6.

Gremler, D. D. and Brown, S. W. (1999) 'The Loyalty Ripple Effect – Appreciating the Full-Value of Customers', *International Journal of Service Industry Management* 10(3): 271–91.

Grogan, S., Conner, M. and Willits, Norman P. (1995) 'Development of a Questionnaire to Measure Patients' Satisfaction with General Practitioners' Services', *British Journal of General Practice* 45: 525–9.

Grogan, S., Conner, M., Willits, Norman P., Willits, D. and Porter, I. (2000) 'Validation of a Questionnaire Measuring Patient Satisfaction with General Practitioner Services', *Quality in Health Care* 9: 210–15.

Grönroos, C. (1984) 'A Service Quality Model and its Marketing Implications', *European Journal of Marketing* 18(4) 36–44.

Hall, J. and Dornan, M. (1988) 'What Patients Like About Their Medical Care and How Often They are Asked', *Social Science Medical* 21: 935–9.

Headley, D. E. and Miller S. J. (1993) 'Measuring Service Quality and its Relationship to Future Consumer Behaviour', *Journal of Health Care Marketing* 12(4): 32–41.

Hendriks, A. A. J., Vrielink, M. R., Smets, E., van Es, S. Q. and De Haes, J. C. (2001) 'Improving the Assessment of (In) Patients' Satisfaction with Hospital Care', *Medical Care* 39(3): 270–83.

Hopkins, A. (1990) *Measuring the Quality of Medical Care*, Royal College of Physicians of London: Kings Fund Centre for Health Services Development.

Hudak, P. L. and Wright, J. G. (2000) 'The Characteristics of Patient Satisfaction Measures', *Spine* 25(24): 3167–77.

Hulka, B. S. and Zysanski, S. J. (1982) 'Validation of a Patient Satisfaction Scale: Theory, Methods and Practice', *Medical Care* XX(6): 649–53.

Hulka, B. S., Zyzanski, S. J., Cassel, J. C. and Thompson, W. J. (1970) 'Scale for the Measurement of Attitudes Towards Physicians and Primary Health Care', *Medical Care* 8: 429.

Hunt, K. (1977) 'CS/D: Overview and Future Research Directions' in Hunt, H. K. (eds) *Conceptualisation and Measurement of Consumer Satisfaction and Dissatisfaction*, Marketing Science Institute: Cambridge.

Jackson, J. L., Chamberlin, J. and Kroenke, K. (2001) 'Predictors of Patient Satisfaction', *Social Science and Medicine* 52(4): 609–20.

Javeline, D. (1999) 'Response Effects in Polite Cultures: A Test of Acquiescence in Kazakhstan', *Public Opinion Quarterly* 63: 1–28.

John, J. (1996) 'A Dramaturgical View of the Health Care Service Encounter', *European Journal of Marketing* 30(9): 60–74.

Jones, L., MacLean, U. and Leneman, L. (1987) *Consumer Feedback for the NHS: A Literature Review*, King Edward's Hospital Fund for London: London.

Jun, M., Peterson, R. T., Zsidisin, G. A. (1998) 'The Identification and Measurement of Quality Dimensions in Health Care: Focus Group Interview Results', *Health Care Management Review* 23(4): 81–96.

Kersnik, J. (2000) 'An Evaluation of Patient Satisfaction with Family Practice Care in Slovenia', *International Journal for Quality in Health Care* 12(2): 143–7.

Kung, F., Gibson, S. J. and Helme, R. D. (2000) 'The Development of a Pain Management Strategies Survey Questionnaire – Preliminary Findings', *The Pain Clinic* 12(4): 299–315.

Larsen, D. L., Attkisson, C. C., Hargreaves, W. A. and Nguyen, T. D. (1979) 'Assessment of Client/Patient Satisfaction in Human Service Programs: Development of a General Scale', *Evaluation and Programme Planning* 2: 197–207.

Latour, S. A. and Peat, N. C. (1979) 'Conceptual and Methodological Issues in Consumer Satisfaction Research', *Advances in Consumer Research* 6: 431–7.

Lehtinen, U. and Lehtinen, J. R. (1991) 'Two approaches to Service Quality Dimensions', *The Service Industries Journal* 11(3): 287–303.

Levois, M., Nguyen, T., Attkisson, C. (1981) 'Artifact in Client Satisfaction Assessment: Experience in Community Mental Health Settings', *Evaluation and Program Planning* 4: 139–50.

Lewis, C. C., Scott, D. E., Pantell, R. H. and Wolf, M. H. (1986) 'Parent Satisfaction with Children's Medical Care. Development, Fieldtest and Validation of a Questionnaire', *Medical Care* 24: 209–15.

Linder-Pelz, S. (1982) 'Social Psychological Determinants of Patient Satisfaction: A Test of Five Hypotheses', *Social Science and Medicine* 16: 583–9.

Linn, L. S. and Greenfield, S. (1984) 'Patient Suffering and Patient Satisfaction', *Medical Care* 22: 804–12.

Loblaw, D. A., Bezjak, A., Bunston, T. (1999) 'Development and Testing of a Visit-Specific Patient Satisfaction Questionnaire: The Princess Margaret Hospital Satisfaction with Doctor Questionnaire', *Journal of Clinical Oncology* 17: 1931–8.

Locker, D. and Dunt, D. (1978) 'Theoretical and Methodological Issues in Sociological Studies of Consumer Satisfaction with Medical Care', *Social Science and Medicine* 12: 283–92.

McIver, S. (1991) *An Introduction to Obtaining the Views of Users of Health Services.* Consumer Feedback Resource, King's Fund Centre, Quality Improvement Programme: King's Fund Centre for Health Services Development: London.

McIver, S. and Carr-Hill, R. (1989) *The NHS and its Customers: I. A Survey of the Current Practice of Customer Relations'* Centre for Health Economics, University of York.

McNaughton, D. (1994) 'Measuring Parent Satisfaction with Early Childhood Intervention Programs: Current Practice, Problems, and Future Perspectives', *Topics in Early Childhood Special Education* 14(1): 26–48.

Mels, G., Boshoff, C. and Nel, D. (1997) 'The Dimensions of Service Quality: The Original European Perspective Revisited', *The Services Industries Journal* 17(1): 173–89.

Miller, J. A. (1979) 'Studying Satisfaction, Modifying Models, Eliciting Expectations, Posing Problems, and Making Meaningful Measurements', in Hunt, H. K. (ed.) *Conceptualisation and Measurement of Consumer Satisfaction and Dissatisfaction,* Cambridge, MA: Marketing Science Institute.

Mittal, V., Kumar, P. and Tsiros, M. (1999) 'Attribute-level Performance, Satisfaction and Behavioural Intentions Over Time: A Consumption-System Approach', *Journal of Marketing* 63(2): 88–101.

NHS Management Inquiry (1983) *The Griffiths Report*, London: DHSS.

Noyes, R., Levy, M., Chase, C. and Udrey, R. (1974) in Ross *et al.* (1987) *op cit.*

Oliver, R. L. (1980) 'A Cognitive Model of the Antecedents and Consequences of Satisfaction Decisions', *Journal of Marketing Research* XVII: 460–9.

Oliver, R. L. (1981) 'Measurement and Evaluation of Satisfaction Processes in Retail Settings', *Journal of Retailing* 57(3): 25–48.

Oliver, R. L. (1993) 'A Conceptual Model of Service Quality and Service Satisfaction: Compatible Goals, Different Concepts', in Swartz, T. A., Bowen, D. E. and Brown S. W. (eds) *Advances in Services Marketing and Management*, Vol. 2, JAI Press: Greenwich CT.

Paddock, L. E., Veloski, J., Chatterton, M. L. *et al.* (2000) 'Development and Validation of a Questionnaire to Evaluate Patient Satisfaction With Diabetes Disease Management', *Diabetes Care* 23: 951–6.

Parasuraman, A., Zeithaml, V. A. and Berry, L. L. (1985) 'A Conceptual Model of Service Quality and its Implications for Future Research', *Journal of Marketing* 49: 41–50.

Parasuraman, A., Zeithaml, V. A. and Berry, L. L. (1986) *SERVQUAL: A Multiple-Item Scale for Measuring Customer Perceptions of Service Quality*, Report No. 86–108, Marketing Science Institute, Cambridge, M.A.

Parasuraman, A., Zeithaml, V. A. and Berry, L. L. (1988) 'SERVQUAL: A Multiple-Item Scale for Measuring Consumer Perceptions of Service Quality', *Journal of Retailing* 64(1): 14–40.

Parasuraman, A., Berry, L. L. and Zeithaml, V. A. (1991) 'Refinement and Reassessment of the SERVQUAL Scale', *Journal of Retailing* 67(4): 420–50.

Parasuraman, A., Zeithaml, V. A. and Berry, L. L. (1994a) 'Reassessment of Expectations as a Comparison Standard in Measuring Service Quality: Implications for Further Research', *Journal of Marketing* 58: 111–24.

Parasuraman, A., Zeithaml, V. A. and Berry, L. L. (1994b) 'Alternative Scales for Measuring Service Quality: A Comparitive Assessment Based on Psychometric and Diagnostic Criteria', *Journal of Retailing* 70(3): 201–30.

Pascoe, G. (1983) 'Patient Satisfaction in Primary Health Care: A Literature Review and Analysis', *Evaluation and Program Planning* 6: 185–210.

Peter, J. P., Gilbert, A. C. Jr. and Brown, T. J. (1993) 'Caution in the Use of Difference Scores in Consumer Research', *Journal of Consumer Research* 19: 655–62.

Peterson, R. A. and Wilson, W. R. (1992) 'Measuring Customer Satisfaction: Fact and Artifact', *Journal of the Academy of Marketing Science* 20: 61–71.

Peyrot, H., Cooper, P. D. and Schnapf, D. (1993) 'Consumer Satisfaction and Perceived Quality of Outpatient Health Services', *Journal of Health Care Marketing* 13: 24–33.

Rashid, A., Forman, W., Jagger, C. and Mann, R. (1989) 'Consultations in General Practice: A Comparison of Patients' and Doctors' Satisfaction', *BMJ* 299: 1015–6.

Rees Lewis, J. (1994) 'Patient Views on Quality Care in General Practice: Literature Review', *Social Science and Medicine* 39(5): 655–70.

Rees Lewis, J. and Williamson, V. (1995) 'Examining Patient Perceptions of Quality Care in General Practice: Comparison of Quantitative and Qualitative Methods', *British Journal of General Practice* 45: 249–53.

Reidenbach, R. E. and Sandifer-Smallwood, B. (1990) 'Exploring Perceptions of Hospital Operations by a Modified SERVQUAL Approach', *Journal of Health Care Marketing* 10(4): 47–55.

Roberts, J. G. and Tugwell, P. (1987) 'Comparison of Questionnaires Determining Patient Satisfaction with Medical Care', *Health Services Research* 22: 637–54.

Rogers, M., Liang, M. H., Poss, R. and Cullen, K. (1982) in Ross *et al.* (1987) *op. cit.*

Ross, C. E., Blair, W. and Duff, R. S. (1981) in Ross *et al.* (1987) *op. cit.*

Ross, C. K., Frommelt, G., Hazelwood, L. and Chang, R. W. (1987) 'The Role of Expectations in Patient Satisfaction with Medical Care', *Journal of Health Care Marketing* 7(4): 16–26.

Ross, C. K., Steward, C. A. and Sinacore, J. M. (1995) 'A Comparative Study of Seven Measures of Patient Satisfaction', *Medical Care* 33(4): 392–406.

Rubin, H. R., Gandek, B., Rogers, W. H., Kosinski, M., McHorney, C. A. and Ware, J. E. (1993) 'Patients Ratings of Outpatient Visits in Different Practice Settings. Results of the Medical Outcomes Study', *Journal of the American Medical Association* 270: 835–40.

Shemwell, D. J., Yavas, U., Bilgin, Z. (1998) 'Customer-Service Provider Relationships: An Empirical Test of a Model of Service Quality, Satisfaction and Relationship-Oriented Outcomes', *International Journal of Service Industry Management* 19(2): 155–68.

Shostack, G. L. (1987) 'Service Positioning Through Structural Change', *Journal of Marketing* 51: 34–43.

Shiomi, K. and Loo, R. (1999) 'Cross-Cultural Response Styles on the Kirton Adaption-Innovation Inventory', *Social Behaviour and Personality* 27(4): 413–20.

Si, S. X. and Cullen, J. B. (1998) 'Response Categories and Potential Cultural Bias: Effects of an Explicit Middle Point in Cross-Cultural Surveys', *The International Journal of Organisational Analysis* 6(3): 218–30.

Singh, J. (1991) 'Understanding the Structure of Consumers' Satisfaction Evaluations of Service Delivery', *Journal of the Academy of Marketing Science* 19(3): 223–44.

Sitzia, J. and Wood, N. (1997) 'Patient Satisfaction: A Review of Issues and Concepts', *Social Science and Medicine* 45(12): 1829–43.

Smith, A. M. (1993) 'Elderly Consumers' Evaluation of Service Quality', *Marketing Intelligence and Planning* 11(4): 13–19.

Smith, A. M. (1995) 'Measuring Service Quality: Is SERVQUAL Now Redundant?' *Journal of Marketing Management* 11(1–3): 257–76.

Smith, A. M. (1999) 'Some Problems When Adopting Churchill's Paradigm for the Development of Service Quality Measurement Scales', *Journal of Business Research* 46(2): 109–20.

Smith, A. M. (2000) 'The Impact of Scale Characteristics on the Dimensionality of the Service Quality Construct', *The Service Industries Journal* 20(3): 167–90.

Smith, C. H. and Armstrong, D. (1989) 'Comparison of Criteria Derived by Government and Patients for Evaluating General Practitioner Services', *BMJ* 299: 494–6.

Smith, L. F. P. (2001) 'Development of a Multidimensional Labour Satisfaction Questionnaire: Dimensions, Validity and Internal Reliability', *Quality in Health Care* 10: 17–22.

Soliman, A. A. (1992) 'Assessing the Quality of Health Care: A Consumerist Approach', *Health Marketing Quarterly* 10(1/2): 121–41.

Solomon, M. R., Suprenant, C., Czepiel, J. A. and Gutman, E. G. (1985) 'A Role Theory Perspective on Dyadic Interactions: The Service Encounter', *Journal of Marketing* 49: 99–111.

Sower, V., Duffy, J., Kilbourne, W., Kohers, G. and Jones, P. (2001) 'The Dimensions of Service Quality for Hospitals: Development and Use of the KOCAH Scale', *Health Care Management Review* 26(2): 47–59.

Taylor, B. (1996) 'Parents as Partners in Care', *Paediatric Nursing* 8: 24–7.

Teas, R. K. (1993a) 'Consumer Expectations and the Measurement of Perceived Service Quality', *Journal of Professional Services Marketing* 8(2): 33–54.

Teas, R. K. (1993b) 'Expectations, Performance Evaluation and Consumers' Perception of Quality', *Journal of Marketing* 57: 18–34.

Thompson, A. G. H. (1983) 'The Measurement of Patients' Perceptions of the Quality of Hospital Care'. Ph.D. Thesis, Manchester School of Management, UMIST, October.

Thompson, A. G. and Sunol, R. (1995) 'Expectations as Determinants of Patient Satisfaction: Concepts, Theory, Evidence', *International Journal of Quality in Health Care* 7: 127–41.

Vandamme, R. and Leunis, J. (1993) 'Development of a Multiple-Item Scale for Measuring Hospital Service Quality', *International Journal of Service Industry Management* 4(3): 30–49.

Vogels, R., Lemmink, J. and Kasper, H. (1989) 'Some Methodological Remarks on the SERVQUAL Model' in Avlonitis, G.J., Papavasitiou, N.K. and Kouiemenos, A.G. (eds) *Marketing Thought and Practice in the 1990s*, European Marketing Academy Conference, Greece.

Walbridge, S. W. and Delene, L. W. (1993) 'Measuring Physician Attitudes of Service Quality', *Journal of Health Care Marketing* 13: 6–15.

Wall, T. D. and Payne, R. (1973) 'Are Deficiency Scores Deficient?' *Journal of Applied Psychology* 58: 322–6.

Walsh, M. and Walsh, A. (1999) 'Measuring Patient Satisfaction with Nursing Care: Experience of Using the Newcastle Satisfaction with Nursing Scale', *Journal of Advanced Nursing* 29(2): 307–15.

Ware, J. E. Jr., Davies-Avery, A. and Stewart, A. L. (1978) 'The Measurement and Meaning of Patient Satisfaction: A Review of the Recent Literature', *Health and Medical Care Services Review* 1: 1–15.

Ware, J. E., Snyder, M. K., Wright, W. R. and Davies, A. R. (1983) 'Defining and Measuring Patient Satisfaction with Medical Care', *Evaluation and Program Planning* 6: 247–63.

Ware, J. E. and Hays, R. D. (1988) 'Methods for Measuring Patient Satisfaction with Specific Medical Encounters', *Medical Care* 26: 393–402.

Webster, C. (1989) 'Can Consumers Be Segmented on the Basis of their Service Quality Expectations?' *The Journal of Services Marketing* 3(2): 35–53.

White, B., Robertson, I. and Lewis, B. (1993) *A Survey of Patient Satisfaction with General Practitioner Services*, Manchester School of Management, UMIST, Unpublished.

Williams, B. (1994) 'Patient Satisfaction: A Valid Concept?' *Social Science of Medicine* 38: 509–16.

Winsted, K. F. (1997) 'The Service Experience in Two Cultures: A Behavioural Perceptive', *Journal of Retailing* 73(3): 337–60.

Wirtz, J. and Bateson, J. E. G. (1995) 'An Experimental Investigation of Halo Effects in Satisfaction Measures of Service Attributes', *International Journal of Service Industry Management* 6(3): 84–102.

Wolf, M., Putnam, S., James, J. and Stiles, W. (1978) 'The Medical Interview Satisfaction Scale: Development of a Scale to Measure Patient Perceptions of Physician Behaviour', *Journal of Behavioural Medicine* 1: 391–401.

Woodruff, R. B., Cadotte, E. R. and Jenkins, R. L. (1983) 'Modelling Consumer Satisfaction Processes Using Experience-Based Norms', *Journal of Marketing Research* XX: 296–304.

Woodside, A. G., Frey, L. L. and Daly, R. T. (1989) 'Linking Service Quality, Customer Satisfaction, and Behavioural Intention', *Journal of Health Care Marketing* 9: 5–17.

Woolley, F., Kane, R., Hughes, C. and Wright, D. (1978) 'The Effects of Doctor-Patient Communication on Satisfaction and Outcome of Care', *Social Science and Medicine* 12: 123–8.

Ygge, B. M. and Arnetz, J. E. (2001) 'Quality of Paediatric Care: Application and Validation of an Instrument for Measuring Patient Satisfaction with Hospital Care', *International Journal for Quality in Health Care* 13(1): 33–43.

Zahorik, A. J. and Rust, R. T. (1992) 'Modelling the Impact of Service Quality on Profitability: A Review' in Swartz, T. A., Bowen, D. E. and Brown, S. W. *Advances in Services Marketing and Management*, Vol. 1, J.A.I Press: Greenwich CT.

Zyzanski, S. J., Hulka, B. S. and Cassel, J. D. (1974) 'Scale for the Measurement of Satisfaction with Medical Care: Modifications in Content, Format and Scoring', *Medical Care* XII(7): 611–20.

Note

[1] Other explanations lie in the nature of the data and consequent impact on statistical analysis (Smith, 2000).

8 Conclusion
Meeting performance expectations

Introduction

Health care managers and professionals are increasingly confronted by the need to deliver high quality, cost-effective health care that meets, and is influenced by, various stakeholder expectations, in particular those identified in Figure 8.1 – policy makers, patients and professionals. As earlier chapters have discussed, policy makers' concerns relate mainly to aspects such as organisational structures, performance criteria and societal values. Patients, meanwhile, seek to influence policy makers and health care providers concerning their needs and expectations, and are often driven by increasingly available information about diseases, conditions and treatments. Professionals on the other hand, seek to maintain a self-regulated profession with a reputation for quality as well as academic and technical advances that engage their minds and spirits and improve the delivery of health care. Many others though, such as non-clinical staff, carers, and voluntary service organisations also have expectations of, and a direct involvement in, co-producing health care. Improving service quality and meeting stakeholder expectations needs to be done, however, with increasingly constrained resources in both public and privately funded health care systems and requires careful management of the interactions and relationships within and between organisations.

The preceding chapters have addressed these issues drawing extensively on insights from strategic management and strategic marketing literature in order that a better understanding of these complex processes and relationships might be gained, and that this understanding might thereby lead to enhanced delivery of health care services. This concluding chapter provides a synthesis of these central managerial issues, with the underlying logic of the discussion being based on the service cycle, introduced in the Preface. The service cycle model places the patient at the centre of health care, embedded within the social and structural relationships between professionals, policy makers and organisations. These elements underlie the cyclical processes of service design, service organisation, service consumption and service evaluation the output, or product, of which is the service delivery upon which much public policy and scrutiny focuses, and for which measurable levels of performance are increasingly required. The model is used here to develop a strategic, patient-centred managerial and professional agenda within the context of a dynamic health care environment.

The service cycle: integrating service processes

Central to the concept of the service cycle (see Figure 8.1) are the connections that exist between the processes of service design, service structure, service consumption and service evaluation. Although examined independently in the preceding chapters, in understanding the nature of service delivery in a complex professional service such as health care it is the interrelationship between these constituent processes which is critical. Service delivery in this context must be viewed as the overall product or outcome of the service cycle, rather than as one of the constituent components of the service cycle. Specifically the delivery of health care services involves an interconnected cyclical flow of processes, with changes in any one of the constituent processes having significant consequences for other parts of the service cycle. For example service design and service structure are closely interlinked, with the design of service provision being dependent on the prevailing macro-level structuring of service organisations in terms of governance arrangements. Similarly, changes in the macro, that is policy level structuring of services by impacting on consumer access to, and utilisation of, service provision will affect patterns of consumer behaviour within the extended service encounter and the subsequent evaluation of service provision. The challenge confronting health care professionals and managers is that the constituent processes within the service cycle, irrespective of prevailing governance arrangements, typically cut across formal organisational and professional boundaries, raising problems in assessing at a system-wide level the consequential impact of change on service delivery and evaluation.

In seeking to secure a systemic perspective on the delivery of health care services it is helpful to utilise the idea of the value chain alongside the service cycle. Derived from the mainstream marketing literature, the concept of the value chain is concerned with identifying ways in which organisations enhance the delivery of customer value. Within the value chain framework every organisation can best be viewed as a collection of

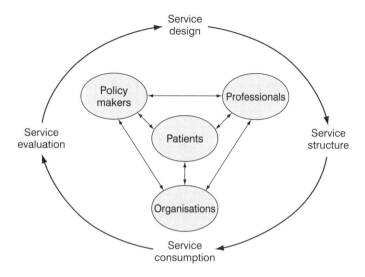

Figure 8.1 **The service cycle for health care**

activities that are performed to design, produce and support its product or service. At the core of the management task is the constant examination of costs and performance in each value creating activity, and the search for ways to enhance the delivery of customer value. Critically the success of an organisation depends not simply on the performance of individual units but how the individual units are coordinated.

In the context of the delivery of health care, from the setting of the overall policy framework through to the post-consumption evaluation of service provision, each element of the service cycle is concerned with adding value. Value is created through delivering the required service in the format sought by the ultimate users of the service, who as already highlighted, themselves constitute an integral part of both the delivery and value adding process within health care. Adopting a value chain based approach, the critical assessment of service value occurs at the point of consumer evaluation. Reflecting the inherent complexity of health care, it is critical to recognise that consumer assessment of service value is predominantly based on the process of service delivery rather than the service outcome. In an organisational environment characterised by increasing patient empowerment, if consumers perceive service value to be poor, policy makers, professionals and managers are collectively confronted with a need to reconfigure service provision from initial policy formulation through to the management of the service encounter. As highlighted by the service cycle, the process of service reconfiguration ought to be continuous, with managers and professionals constantly engaged in service innovation and development. In successfully delivering such ongoing service reconfiguration understanding the dynamics of the constituent processes of service design, that is, service structuring, service consumption and service evaluation is critical. Only through such detailed understanding can value, and hence satisfaction, be delivered to the users and communities being served.

Underpinning these interconnected processes and hence the delivery of value, is the complex network of relationships between policy makers, professionals, organisations and patients. The interaction of these parties is central both to the internal dynamics of the constituent processes underpinning the provision of services and to that of the overall service cycle. Although the relationship between professionals and the organisations within which they operate has been extensively addressed in the established health management literature, within modern health care systems it is increasingly questionable whether this is the critical relationship impacting on the delivery of services. Rather than focusing on this aspect, it is more helpful to concentrate on the patient as the focal point from which all other policies and actions should be determined. This reflects a move from a production orientation, to a customer/consumer orientation. In other words, from the perspective of managing the overall process of service delivery, the nodal point in the underpinning set of relationships is the patient, i.e. the health care consumer. The network of relationships between patients and health care professionals, organisations and policy makers, is then critical in shaping the nature of the overall process of service delivery in modern health care systems. In particular it is the changing relationship between the users of health care services and those individuals and organisations directly responsible for service provision which lies at the core of the managerial and organisational challenges confronting modern health care systems.

Reflecting the impact of a public policy aimed at promoting patient empowerment as well as broader socio-economic and technological change, the evolving relationship between patients and health care professionals lies at the core of shifts in the prevailing pattern of health care service provision. There has been a generic shift from organisationally designed and professionally dominated paternalistic models of service delivery to increasingly egalitarian participative models. For professionals at the operational level this shift has involved a fundamental reappraisal of the information and power balance within the patient–professional relationship. For organisations at the strategic level this has involved embracing patients as active participants, as opposed to passive recipients, in the organisation and management of services. These shifting relationships between patients, professionals, organisations and policy makers have to a significant degree informed, and are likely to continue to influence, the shape and format of service delivery in health care through impacting on the processes of service design, service structuring, service consumption and service evaluation. Against this backdrop, the adaptation and application of strategic management and marketing concepts are increasingly critical to the ability of health care organisations to effectively confront the challenges of delivering health care in the twenty-first century.

In exploring the application of such strategic marketing and management concepts to the challenges confronting health care organisations in the twenty-first century, it is valuable to extract the core managerial issues emerging from the themes which have formed the central focus of the book. Through drawing out these issues within the integrative framework of the service cycle, it is possible to articulate a strategic patient-centred managerial and professional agenda which offers a framework within which to manage the increasingly dynamic health care environment.

Service design: integrating multiple perspectives

At the core of successive reforms of the NHS has been the objective of reorienting patterns of service provision, with services being designed around the needs of patients rather than the convenience of the service professionals. As a consequence the way in which services are designed has attracted growing attention from health care policy makers, managers and professionals. This increasing concern with the design of services has been reinforced by the growing emphasis placed on performance measurement, both clinical and organisational, within health care organisations as part of the emerging clinical governance agenda. Having once been an incidental activity, as a result of such drivers, service design is increasingly becoming a core activity for those involved in the delivery of health care services.

For health care managers and professionals this growing emphasis on the importance of service design poses significant challenges, because the service design process is resource intensive. At the most basic level effective service design, whether the design of new services or the redesign of existing services, requires significant investment in terms of time, money and staff. Good service design cannot be done 'on the cheap' – rather it is a resource-intensive activity. Beyond the resource implications, effective service design requires the fostering of an organisational culture that encourages and rewards innovation and learning. It is arguable in this regard that the risk averse culture characteristic of many public sector organisations militates against good service design. The challenge for health care policy makers and managers is to ensure not only that the requisite resources are available but also that front-line professionals operate within an organisational environment within which innovation is encouraged.

Equally it is necessary to acknowledge that within health care the service design process occurs in a highly complex environment, in that there are a multiplicity of actors who have a legitimate interest in the design of any service. Ensuring effective input from all such stakeholders is critical to the success of the design process, and failure to embrace the perspectives of any particular stakeholders will impact negatively on satisfaction with the resultant service provision. A critical managerial task is to effectively combine the diverse, and sometimes conflicting, perspectives and requirements of different stakeholders. Indeed evidence suggests that organisational capacity to integrate the range of tangible and intangible resources possessed by different groups of stakeholders will determine the degree to which any service design initiative will be effective. In this regard, detailed understanding of internal organisational factors impacting on service design, for example interprofessional relationships, has to be set within the broader organisational context of the NHS and the society within which the services are subsequently consumed and evaluated. Service design cannot be viewed as a closed internal organisational process; rather it is best understood as an open process embracing a broad network of actors. The service design process is concerned as much with the management of this network of stakeholders as with internal organisational processes.

In respect of the internal organisation of the service design process, three dimensions are critical – these are the service concept, the service system, and the service process dimensions. Collectively they address the primary and secondary services that need to be offered in order to meet patients' needs; the resources required to support the delivery of the service (e.g. human resources and physical requirements); and the service processes that underpin delivery, such as relationships between departments and between the service provider and its customers and suppliers. Integral to these three dimensions is the need to take account of the potential variability that can occur in terms of functional quality as well as the requirement to reduce variability in technical quality. Methods such as blueprinting, for example, can assist health care providers in designing services that offer consistency through greater standardisation in terms of functional quality while strategic policy initiatives focus on ensuring consistency in technical quality through the creation of national assessment panels and national guidelines. Within the context of a complex professional service such as health care however, a particular challenge in service design lies in securing an appropriate balance between standardising basic service processes, to ensure efficient patient throughput and ensuring flexibility in more complex service processes to meet the requirements of particular patients. This tension between standardised and customised service provision is a critical issue facing modern professional service organisations in that the organisational structure, culture and staffing requirements of each are radically different.

In addressing such service challenges, the process by which organisations reach design decisions lies on a spectrum between highly structured, planned approaches and ad hoc emergent approaches. The service design process in this regard may be viewed as mirroring the broader process of strategy formulation. The adoption of a planned approach to service design ensures clarity of purpose, aiding transparency and thus public accountability. Where service design involves the utilisation of scarce public funds, such concerns are of paramount importance. Similarly, highly structured and formal approaches to service design facilitate effective communication of the overall service strategy to the broad network of stakeholders who have an interest in the design and delivery of the service. However, such approaches place significant constraints on the service design process; in particular, they elongate the design timescale. Equally such an approach limits the ability of the lead organisations(s) to respond to changing needs as well as environmental changes. For managers within health care organisations the challenge is to engineer the flexibility inherent in the more emergent approaches to service design into what is of necessity a highly planned and tightly structured process of service design.

Service structure: managing inter-organisational relationships

The underlying service requirements confronting modern health care organisations are complex and multidimensional. Patient needs typically extend beyond the scope and boundaries of any single organisation within the NHS, with the delivery of the required services being dependent on input from multiple organisations and professionals. The delivery of modern health care is therefore a multi-organisational, multiprofessional endeavour. Value from the perspective of the patient, the service user, is derived from the activities of all the organisations contributing to the design and delivery of that particular service. The management of the relationships between health care organisations and the constituent professionals is thus central to the delivery of effective health care services. Equally the management of the relationships between health care organisations is critical to the efficiency of service delivery, i.e. the maximisation of patient throughput and hence productivity at the system-wide level. As a consequence of the ongoing demand for improved effectiveness and efficiency, the structuring of inter-organisational linkages is central to the modern health policy debate.

At the core of this debate has been the ongoing tension between hierarchies, markets and networks as alternative mechanisms for governing the relationships between organisations involved in the delivery of health care services. The contest between these alternative governance mechanisms is not unique to health care; rather this tension constitutes a central aspect of the modern managerial agenda as organisations constantly strive to enhance the efficiency and effectiveness of their operations. To a significant degree this broader debate has revolved around issues of the relative efficiency of such alternative mechanisms with transaction costs, that is, the relative costs incurred in coordinating activities, being central to that debate. For the new Right steeped in neo-classical economic thinking, markets were inherently more efficient than hierarchies, and this thinking was a catalyst for the creation of an (internal) NHS market. It became readily apparent, however, that neo-classical perspectives on markets bore little relation or relevance to the operation of health care markets. The NHS market structure was characterised by limited numbers of buyers and sellers, high entry and exit barriers, and informational asymmetries which mitigated against its operation as an efficient mechanism. In addition, core service characteristics of service complexity, intangibility, and heterogeneity impacted further on patterns of market behaviour and hence efficiency. Together, these structural and service characteristics resulted in high levels of transaction costs and the existence of strong socio-professional networks. As a result, the Government's experiment with market mechanisms did not produce the intended effects. Relationships between purchasers and providers emerged as relational networks rather than arm's-length contracts.

The new Left, who perceived markets in many settings, such as health care, to be inherently inefficient, sought to capitalise on these network-type relations in their post-market NHS reforms. Thus network development may be viewed as much an outcome of the underlying relational nature of health care markets as of deliberate government policy. Networks were seen to offer a viable alternative to the failures of markets and hierarchies for a number of reasons. They are generally characterised by high degrees of stability, extensive collaboration and mutual interdependence, where the management of inter-organisational linkages is not concerned with constant switching in search of short-term advantage, but with initiating and maintaining long-term relationships. Networks are also believed to contribute to competitive advantage, offer greater scope for learning and innovation, and are characterised by information exchange, knowledge sharing and creativity, whilst avoiding the respective inefficiencies of either hierarchies or markets. Under these arrangements, value is produced through collaborative not conflictual relationships, where parties pursue a mutual advantage, in this case with the ultimate effect of improving health care quality and efficiency.

Collaborative structural arrangements were perceived to offer a means of reducing the costs inherent in formal market transactions while at the same time facilitating the integration of service provision across organisational boundaries. That is, such arrangements were a more efficient and effective means of structuring service delivery than were hierarchies or markets. In critically examining alternative structures under which health care services may be delivered, however, it is also important to recognise that networks cannot automatically be viewed as inherently efficient structural arrangements. In this regard it is necessary to question some of the underlying assumptions regarding the value of networks as a basis for structuring health care delivery.

The hidden 'transaction' costs inherent in the management of service delivery require specific acknowledgement. Three particular sources of transaction costs are critical. First, the costs of developing the inter-organisational trust which underpins network organisations as a 'glue' to bind the parties together. Second, the costs of maintaining potentially unstable coalition-type structures in terms of establishing appropriate managerial and communication processes and frameworks. Third, the costs of curbing collusion which could result in suboptimal service delivery. All three have significant managerial cost implications in terms of the investment of time, learning, expertise, finance and the possible development of inter-organisational dependencies where parties effectively become 'locked' into relationships with one another. As such the formation and maintenance of networks cannot automatically be seen as necessarily less costly, and hence more efficient, than alternative governance arrangements. The presence of such costs within network systems gives rise to questions about the uniform applicability of networks as a means of structuring service delivery. While they may constitute the most appropriate approach under certain conditions, networks are unlikely to provide uniformly appropriate frameworks.

That the governance of health systems has become a central issue – over the last two decades in particular – presents a number of challenges for policy makers, managers and professionals. For those directly involved in managing the service, there is the difficulty of ensuring consistency in service delivery, when the political environment is fluid, and when the NHS experiences both continuous and discontinuous structural and cultural change. Seeking and maintaining strategic direction and consonance of objectives and goals over time is particularly problematic when the organisational environment is in a state of constant flux. Moreover, the cultural changes brought on by moves from competitive to collaborative structures, or other blends of private and public sector thinking, should not be underestimated. They will require considerable time to become embedded within practice, particularly as they are unlikely to be universally acceptable across the organisation and thus will incite a degree of political upheaval. Maintaining a focus on patient needs within such fluid, uncertain, and transformational periods is a central challenge. Managers and professionals need simultaneously to alter reporting structures, accountability frameworks and operational policies while attempting to offer a seamless, continuous service to the patient which is not jeopardised by uncertainties in intra- and inter-organisational working practices. The current climate of evidence-based policy and practice suggests that policy makers and managers need to acknowledge the respective merits and demerits of these alternative approaches, and to ensure that particular structural approaches are utilised not on the basis of ideology but on the basis of demonstrable suitability. Because organisational change takes a significant period of time to deliver the intended outcomes, and is highly complex to measure and evaluate, it is particularly problematic to identify those policies that have, and have not, been successful.

Achieving effective service delivery, or indeed service design, is ultimately dependent on the operational dynamics of the individual inter-organisational linkages, regardless of whether market or network based governance arrangements are in place. Understanding the dynamics of such relationships is key to effective relationship management. The specific dynamics of inter-organisational relationships are a product of the complex interplay between the nature of the respective organisations, the nature of the formal and informal interaction processes, and the atmosphere within which such relationships occur. Although it is necessary to avoid an over-socialised view of inter-organisational relationships, within health care it is evident that the connection between informal socio-professional ties and formal inter-organisational links is of major importance in shaping not only the day to day operation of the relationship, but also the long-term development of that relationship. Given that inter-organisational relationships are the product of such a complex interplay of influences, relationships do not subscribe to a single common format. Rather they exhibit a high degree of diversity, existing along a spectrum from arm's-length to de facto integration.

Such multiple relationship formats possess very distinct characteristics, with each in turn posing a distinct set of managerial challenges. The fostering and maintenance of a complex network of inter-organisational relationships is one of the critical tasks confronting health care managers. In particular, the boundary-spanning functions of both managers and professionals is increasingly core to the efficient and effective delivery of health care services to patients.

Service consumption: from patients to consumers

Central to any modern health care system is an understanding of the patient as consumer of the service. Although the health service has been slow to accept the principles of modern consumerism, the system is increasingly predicated on the idea of an active consumer, taking responsibility for their own well-being. The marketing concept does just this and places the customer at the centre of the exchange relationship. As a result it is assumed that market forces, where the consumer drives demand, will provide the mechanism for improvement of the whole service. The effectiveness of this type of initiative is ultimately dependent on the willingness of consumers to exercise the rights and accept the responsibilities given to them. The challenge for service providers is to understand the how patients act as consumers and what motivates their consumption behaviour.

This illustrates a fundamental issue in the discussion of the role of the consumer in health care. Unlike most services this is not a two-way transaction; instead it is a triangular relationship, with 'users' being distinct from 'purchaser'. Power in any market is driven by resources and therefore inevitably the main drivers of the market will be the 'purchasers' or agents rather than the users. One of the problems with understanding the role of the consumer in this context is the underlying hostility to the term. Professionals have traditionally separated themselves from the everyday commercial mêlée of trade and espoused values such as public service, service on the basis of need rather than ability to pay and citizenship. During the reforms of the 1980s many professions were forced to recognise commercial necessities and to open themselves to the market. For example, with the deregulation of professions lawyers found themselves operating in increasingly competitive environments and were forced to confront the reality of marketing. Few professions were happy with this; many felt that the emphasis on the market was alien to their intellectual traditions and therefore inappropriate. While consumers embraced this in many contexts, the nature of health care meant that the role of the consumer requires a more in-depth understanding.

Consumer behaviour theory provides the basis for this understanding, offering insights into consumer decision-making in other service contexts that provides a basis for the discussion of consumer behaviour in health care. The first problem in this discussion is in conceptualising consumer behaviour in a service which is not transaction bound. While policy makers may see clear advantages in the operation of market forces to improve service provision they are by no means apparent to the consumer; indeed the very nature of health care services suggests that it is a high risk, high involvement decision that is better avoided if at all possible. As a result discussion of consumer behaviour is unlikely to be focused on the choice decision, as it would be for other services, but on the conduct of the service encounter.

Service encounters are primarily an interpersonal interaction and as such are governed by the normal rules of social interaction. A key component of the service encounter has been the provision of information by the service supplier, that is the individual service professional, to the consumer. Such service professionals, for example in health care, enjoy both access to information and the cognitive tools to utilise that information which the consumer has been considered not to possess. In such service encounters the consumer relies on credence factors – notably professionalism, trust and the relationship between consumer and provider – to evaluate the quality of service provision. Thus the 'soft' interpersonal elements of the service encounter are the critical factors. The problem for managers is that these elements are subjective, unpredictable and rely to a large extent on impression management rather then measurable criteria. In the absence of the market mechanism the possibility of patient discontent erupting into consumer action is increasingly present and, given the political nature of public health care provision, this tends to be focused on the governing party. Consumers may not drive the health care 'market' but they do drive the political agenda for health provision.

The service encounter is the heart of any professional service. Yet this is an encounter that has characteristically been based on an information, and thus a power, imbalance between knowledgeable professional and supplicant patient. The traditional view of a beneficent doctor dispensing care to a grateful patient was swept away in the tide of consumerism in the late twentieth century. With watchwords of empowerment, quality and satisfaction an increasingly educated, active consumer, empowered by technological changes, became ready to challenge the traditional status of the professional. The growth of the Internet and the access to unprecedented amounts of – largely unregulated – information is addressing the asymmetries inherent in the relationship, whilst mass media remind consumers of their rights and determine their expectations of service providers. The service cycle for health care described above places the patient at the centre: successful delivery of this cycle is dependent on understanding how the consumer determines value and importantly, how the voice of the consumer can be incorporated into the process.

Service evaluation: assessing consumer satisfaction

As a consequence over the past two decades there has been an ongoing emphasis on measuring patient, and other users', satisfaction with the delivery of health care services. Reflecting both an explicit policy commitment to patient empowerment and changing patterns of patient behaviour in respect of professional services such as health care, there is increasing pressure on health care managers and professionals to deliver services which meet the overall quality expectations of patients and not simply the quality specifications determined by the service profession-als. Managers and other professionals need to ensure that the views of service users are taken into account in the design of service provision. At the core of the re-engineering agenda within the NHS is a commitment to the delivery of patient-centred care. The realisation of this agenda is ultimately dependent on securing an accurate and representative under-standing of the views of services users as to their expectations of service provision. While the need to collect information from patients is recog-nised by the majority of health care managers and professionals, the problems experienced in securing such information are considerable, and mirror those of other professional service settings. In particular such professional services are high in credence properties where service users may be unable to evaluate technical process dimensions or outcomes.

The health care and marketing literatures collectively provide a substantial body of research and debate concerning the conceptualisa-tion of service user satisfaction in complex professional service settings such as health care. Linked to this and, given the underlying characteris-tics of such services, there is in both fields a growing literature address-ing the measurement of consumer satisfaction in such contexts. From this literature a number of key managerial questions have emerged, among which are; what is patient satisfaction, what can and should be measured, what measurement problems should be anticipated? These issues are central to any robust assessment of consumer satisfaction within health care. Specifically any initiative to assess patient satisfac-tion requires a clear definition of what constitutes this construct and its relationship with other constructs, such as attitude and perceived quality. Failure to effectively delineate the relevant constructs and their interrelationship within a nomological framework precludes valid cross study comparisons, establishment of the reliability and validity of the measurement scales employed, and the ability to predict associated behaviours.

Patient satisfaction studies implicitly often concentrate on discrepancies between expectations and perceptions of service quality. This approach, which is explicitly typified in the SERVQUAL instrument, one which has been widely used across a range of service organisations, raises questions concerning the conceptualisation and measurement of expectations. It is argued that expectations are often unformed and include outcomes unanticipated by patients: thus the process of defining and measuring expectations becomes particularly complex and problematic.

Such complexities present two central challenges for health care providers. First, those involved in measuring satisfaction, and in designing services that will offer value and quality, need to establish effective measures of patient satisfaction. Second, it is essential that those involved in collecting, interpreting and utilising patient satisfaction data understand the limitations of existing published questionnaires and the problems associated with developing measurement scales. Particular concerns in using existing instruments (such as SERVQUAL) relate to the fact that assessments of reliability and validity depend on an examination of correlation coefficients, yet consumer satisfaction scales in general, and patient satisfaction measures in particular, tend to generate effects such as response biases which render assessments potentially meaningless.

Qualitative research, which offers deeper insights into patients' underlying constructs, has been recognised as improving understanding of both expectations and satisfaction. While it is undoubtedly costly, time-consuming and does not yield the scale of response often desired by decision-makers, its value both as a method in its own right and as a complement to quantitative research should not be underestimated. Indeed, health care providers ought to consider combining such methods (including adopting longitudinal approaches, critical incident techniques and others discussed earlier), when investigating the factors and processes that determine consumer evaluations, since this will undoubtedly contribute to a more meaningful evaluation of consumer satisfaction. Only through the use of such methodologies will managers and professionals have the performance data necessary to enhance the design of health care services and meet the expectations of patients.

Strategic relationship management: towards successful service delivery

The chapters in this book have collectively presented a range of relationships between individuals, groups and organisations within which the delivery of health care needs to be understood. Individually, policy makers, professionals, patients and others involved in health care delivery, have known that the success or failure of any health care intervention is determined to some extent by the relationship between the various inputs (patients, staff, systems, structures and of course therapeutic approach) into the health care value chain. The growing emphasis on performance of health systems, however, has lead to a much greater need for a collective approach to understanding and managing the relationships between the various elements of the health service system. As highlighted in the service cycle, the management of health care services is ultimately concerned with the management of a number of key relationships. In this regard, the complex network of inter-organisational relationships involved in the design and delivery of health care services and the rapidly changing relationship between patients and professionals are crucial to the efficient and effective delivery of modern health care.

In confronting the challenges inherent in managing such relationships there is a requirement for a fundamental reconfiguration of the managerial agenda within health care. Arguably the conventional managerial focus within health care on the management of a specific set of activities within a discrete organisational setting is unsuited to dealing with the increasingly interconnected nature of modern health care services. Against this backdrop the focus of the managerial agenda requires a shift to that of managing the multifaceted boundaries between organisations, professionals and patients. The blurring of such boundaries, together with the increasing complexity of the resultant relationships, places a premium on the ability of managers to span such boundaries effectively. To view such boundary-spanning relationship management as an operational function is to negate its centrality to the overall process of health care delivery. In delivering efficient and effective health care the management of these multidimensional relationships needs to be regarded as a matter of strategic importance. Ultimately the management of such relationships must be placed at the very core of health care strategy if the increasing expectations of health care consumers are to be met.

For health care organisations, this means that each needs a clearly articulated network strategy which sets out which organisations are the key collaborators; recognises areas of mutual advantage, potential conflicts, opportunities for learning and knowledge creation; and which identifies cultural (in)compatibilities and formal and informal mechanisms of interaction. It is essential that policy makers and health care organisations recognise the significant investment of time that is required to initiate and sustain changes to intra- and inter-organisational relationships. It is also crucial that policy makers and health care providers understand the time frame within which desired changes to health systems can realistically be expected to take place, as well as the complications associated with measuring performance.

Strategic perspectives of the role of the patient as a consumer and central node within health networks also need to be developed. While most health care organisations would recognise a range of stakeholder interests and would quickly regard patients as a priority, the UK health system has historically been influenced and directed more by Government and the medical profession than by any other stakeholder group. As current policy documents recognise, engaging patients more meaningfully in all stages from design to evaluation represents a central component in the successful performance of the service cycle for health care.

Index